To Linda —

May this comfort, inspire and deepen your walk with God.

Love,
Mimi

LORD I'M LISTENING...,

BUT SOMETIMES I SQUAWK

LORD I'M LISTENING..,

BUT SOMETIMES I SQUAWK

Frances Johnston Nash

Library of Congress Control Number
2006933100

ISBN: 0-9748086-4-4

Cover art and illustrations by Frances Johnston Nash

Amelia Island Publishing, Inc.
Amelia Island, Florida

Printed in the United States of America

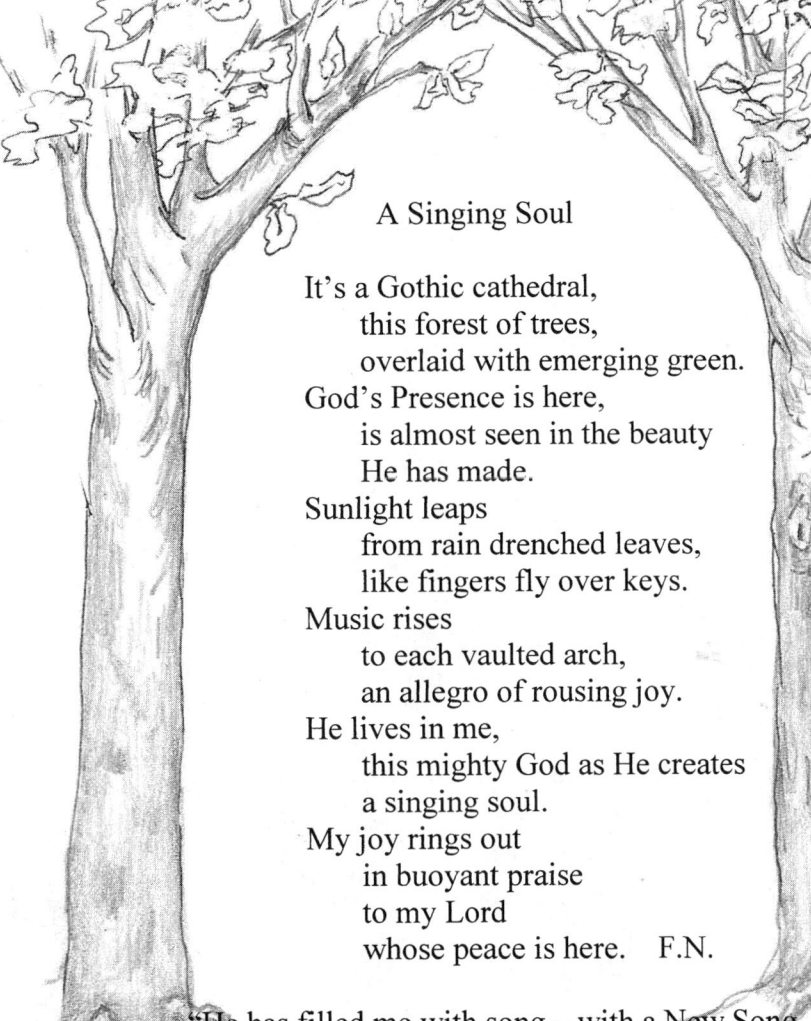

A Singing Soul

It's a Gothic cathedral,
    this forest of trees,
    overlaid with emerging green.
God's Presence is here,
    is almost seen in the beauty
    He has made.
Sunlight leaps
    from rain drenched leaves,
    like fingers fly over keys.
Music rises
    to each vaulted arch,
    an allegro of rousing joy.
He lives in me,
    this mighty God as He creates
    a singing soul.
My joy rings out
    in buoyant praise
    to my Lord
    whose peace is here.   F.N.

"He has filled me with song – with a New Song. It is praise to our God." (Psalm 40:3)

Lord, it's true! To see a preview of Your glory in nature or to recognize Your living Presence in another of Your children invariably starts a song singing itself out in me.

DEDICATION

TO OUR FAMILY

My husband, E. William Nash, Jr.

My children,
E. William Nash, III, Laurie Dent Nash,
Katherine Nash Roberts, Don Darrell Roberts

My grandchildren,
E. William Nash, IV, Laura Frances Nash
Donald Johnston Roberts, Parker Nash Roberts,
David William Nash

ACKNOWLEDGEMENTS

God's Bountiful Process

First of all, Lord, I thank You for Your Bountiful Process in bringing me this challenge and bringing me those who showed me how to make this book.

Thanks to my sister Kay Petty, my daughter Kakie Roberts, Lou Beck and Bonnie Hanson for their encouragement. Ted Schroder, friend, pastor and author read the manuscript and directed me to publish.

Without the support of my husband, Emanuel William Nash, Jr., I would have missed decades of early morning prayer, Bible study, journaling and meditation. Bill brings me coffee before my eyes are open. He fixes breakfast while I sip and write.

Huge appreciation goes to our neighbor, friend and computer expert, Dick Buck, who for the past years has patiently guided me in the do's and don'ts of using this pesky word processor. He also scanned my sketches into position. The book would have no pictures without Dick's unerring eye and merciful generosity of his time.

Christine Gill, our cousin came across from West Yorkshire, England, and stayed with us two weeks to record the folders on her computer.

Many thanks to my editor, and now dear friend, Betty Bedell, who cut extraneous thoughts, polished phrases, helped distill ideas. When I grew too weary for the next step, she boosted my lagging spirits. Betty, you are truly a patient and skilled woman.

John Ropp, artist and friend of many years, used my small bird painting and wove it into the book jacket. Thank you, John.

My husband, Bill, advised on clarity and Lou Beck proofed the pages.

There are others whom I must also acknowledge who helped me know, trust and love God more through their books. During my fifty-five or sixty years of journaling, I have put many of their words, phrases and thoughts into my journals to keep from losing them. Never dreaming I would write a book to share with others, I failed to add the source of my information.

After all these years there is no way I can separate some of their words from my own. Many of the books are no longer in my library. I've worked hard trying to separate them. I hope, pray and trust I am not plagiarizing in this book.

The names of some writers I have cherished are Andrew Murray, Oswald Chambers, George Muller, Nathan Stone, Amy Carmichael, George MacDonald, Richard Wumbrandt, David Watson, William Barclay, Catherine Marshall, Earl Palmer, Eugene Peterson, Manfred Gutzke, Donald Barnhouse, C. S. Lewis, Helmut Thielicke, Paul Tournier and John Stott.

May God bless all of you dear people, keep and prosper you and your work in His service.

PREFACE

The Quiet Work of God,
The Hero of Heaven and Earth

I chose the painting on the cover of the book because I have been like both birds. One bird is listening. The other is squawking and grumbling over something or other.

I see this book as the quiet and quieting work of God in my life. In His loving mercy He enabled me to hear Him above the loud babblings of my inner demands and our worldly society. He is my daily Bread, my nourishment, new every morning and fresh every evening.

These pages tell of experiences of my life which I recorded in my journal as they occurred or as I read something which fed my soul. Woven through the ups and downs of faith and doubt, joy and pain, sickness and health, is the growing knowledge of the Lord's unshakable faithfulness to this squawker.

It is written largely as prayer. I pray more easily with pen and paper than with words or thoughts. In some pages I talk to Him. In some He talks to me. Some are in the mode of poetry, others are questions and answers. I question, He answers. Sometimes He questions me and demands an answer. I have paraphrased some Psalms and Scripture. Some true stories from the family are included. There are truths taken from Bible studies Bill and I have given as a teaching team or studies we have attended. A few reach far back in time while others are as new as this morning.

The project began with notes and questions I kept during a Bible Survey course at Wheaton College in Illinois. It was at Wheaton that I met the two most important people of my life, Jesus Christ as Savior and E. William Nash, Jr. as husband. I soon began writing of my new life with the Lord. This continued year after year until it became an eagerly anticipated early morning time of prayer, Bible study and praise.

After our last move to Jacksonville, I heard discussions at church about what to do or "give up" for Lent, like saving coke cans or not eating chocolate. I thought, *Does God want me to give up inconsequential things, or give out praise to Him? I'll put my praise in a small booklet and give it to my friends.*

Next my daughter asked me to recommend a devotional for her. It seemed the Lord was saying to me, *"You write it."* Like Moses, I patiently explained to the Lord why this was impossible. But He held His request before me like a lamp I couldn't turn off. It became a book I called *The Kakie Book.* It was clumsy, choppy and handwritten, but friends encouraged me to do more.

Then two cancer operations and three hip replacements put a crimp in my mobility. So the third writing project was a happy, nourishing one for me. Paraphrasing the Psalms, during the five years of surgery/recuperation was heaven-sent therapy which transformed my attitude. "Poor me" disappeared totally and recuperation became opportunity rather than boring necessity. The Psalms used in this book are Psalms I paraphrased during that period.

This current book, which I thought of as my legacy to my children and grandchildren, I'm now thinking of as a book others might read too. It is a summary, written in the season of age, concerning the Hero of heaven and earth, and His work in my life. He has brought me forgiveness, purpose, thanksgiving, anticipation and a deep sense of joy.

March	April
1 Lion and Lamb	1 April's Dawn
2 Don't Fret, Trust, Ps. 37	2 The Pivotal Point
3 The Covenant of Faith	3 Lord, *Was* it a Good Day?
4 David's Pain, Ps. 22	4 Why did Jesus Have to Die?
5 Making of a Soldier	5 Our Risen Lord
6 Fitted for Battle	6 The Hunt
7 Provision for Protection	7 The Hush of Your Presence
8 The Wedding Dress	8 Lessons From a Squirrel
9 In Blue Tissue Paper	9 The True Vine
10 You Must Remember Ps 103	10 You Are the Supplier
11 Praiseworthy Benefits	11 Why Should I Fear? Ps. 56
12 Lord of the Morning	12 Ol' Man River
13 Of Dust and Glory	13 Jesus is our Bridge
14 Temporary Endings	14 Praise Brings Joy, Ps. 92
15 A Garment of Shining Light	15 Hard Evidence
16 Lord of the Living	16 Faith is a Gift
17 New Life Pictures	17 What? Where? Why? How?
18 Water of Life Poured Out	18 The Covenant of Love
19 A Donkey Ride	19 Only the Spirit
20 Eternity in the Balance	20 Many Crowns
21 Our Praying Lord	21 The Song Tells the Story
22 Without Defence	22 The King's Banquet
23 On Your Shoulders	23 They're Coming In
24 Simon	24 The Open Door
25 Sounds of Weeping	25 The Divine Laundryman
26 The Place of the Skull	26 An Acceptable Covering
27 Pierced	27 You Are Invited
28 Planned From Eternity	28 I Accept
29 It Is Finished!	29 The Polluted Man, Ps. 14
30 Torn Body, Torn Curtain	30 Gumption and Grace
31 A Sealed Tomb	

July

1 Trees by The River, Ps. 1
2 Jehovah-nissi
3 Our Lord, Our Banner Ps 60
4 Sweet Land of Liberty
5 Our Instructing Lord
6 This Sleeping Nation
7 Jehovah-jireh
8 There is a Difference
9 God's Pattern for Love
10 Summer Time
11 Another Goodbye
12 A Task in Common
13 Give and Take
14 Every Christian Can
15 Look Above the Storm,
   Ps 29
16 Our Enabling Lord
17 New Covenant in Jeremiah
18 To Know God
19 He Lets Us Know Him
20 Truth in a Mixed Up World
21 Faith and Fear at Work,
   Ps. 27
22 Temptation \ Inspiration
23 Once Upon a Day
24 Eat the Words
25 It is Reliable
26 Hold Tight to the Word
27 Power to Change
28 "You Don't Know Scripture"
29 A Beautiful Thing
30 Resentment: a Prison
31 Our Transforming Lord

August

1 Good Morning, Lord
2 Every Eye Shall See
3 Jehovah-rohi
4 God's X-ray, Ps.139
5 Jehovah-tsidkenu, I
6 Jehovah-tsidkenu, II
7 Needed: A New Attitude
8 Definition of a Fool
9 Look to the Shepard, Ps.23
10 Stunned by His Mercy
11 From Blessing to Blessing
12 I Cannot Tell...
13 That They Might Know
14 Balance in Prayer
15 Prayer for Dear Ones
16 For the Church Universal
17 Let the Little Children
18 For Protection
19 For Relationships
20 Faith of an Old Man, Ps 71
21 An Old Man Remembers
22 The Psalmist Sings, Ps. 96
23 Both Saviour and Judge
24 How Very Like You Lord
25 Longing for the Temple,
   Ps. 84
26 Lord, Teach Me to Wait
27 What do you Seek?
28 Lord, Keep Me Salty
29 Read the Small Print
30 Dark Clouds
31 Calamity

January 1

Old Things, New Things

Lord, this New Year is fresh, unspoiled by mistakes. But I take my same old self into its new beginning. Without You, I can splotch it up in a hurry. With You a more important *same* enters the year with me. You're always "the same, yesterday, today and forever." You are never stale, never usual, never boring. You are Yourself every morning and every night, the Alpha and Omega, the Beginning and Ending of everything.

My hope changes some each year. It's becoming more important to me to "see You more clearly, love You more dearly and follow You more nearly day by day." I want to be careful to let go of the anxieties of the past as I stretch toward my goal. I want to emphasize that neither last year nor other years were the "good old days." This will be a good year in its own unique way.

St. Paul writes, "I haven't reached my goal yet, but here's my program. I don't fret over what's past. I stretch toward God's call in Christ Jesus." (Philippians 3:13-14)

Lord, help me resist discontentment, complaints, resentment, moodiness and unforgiveness. You forgive and don't call my sins to Your mind. I want to do that with others. Work that grace in me. Breathe into my same, very human self the freshness of strengthened trust. I want to please You by being full of faith. You are able to do new things in old lives. I believe You, Lord. Help my unbelief.

January 2

Looking Both Ways

Rome named her months of the year after her gods, to gain the god's good will. This ancient Roman fingerprint remains on our calendar today. January was named for their god, Janus. Janus, the god of doors, had two faces, one looking back at the past and the other looking forward to the future.

That's what we should do, isn't it Lord? You remind us of what You have done and will do in the future. Even though the past is past, it is not through with us, nor are we through with it.

Each New Year comes with hopeful plans but not with a guarantee of fulfillment. Instead it comes with Your promise, Lord Jesus, "I will neither leave nor forsake you, and I am always with you, until this world ends." (Hebrews 13 and Matthew 28) In looking back at Your past faithfulness and Your promises for the future, we may take hope, with assurance, for the coming year.

Lord, whatever else we may take with us into this coming year, grant that we may take trust in Your abiding presence. Give us a mind awake to You, a life open to Your guidance. This takes prayer and study on our part. It takes exercising faith that has been forged in the past. It takes reaching faith for the future. Reaching faith is a stretching exercise of the spirit. Stretching unused muscles can hurt, but Lord, You, our skilled Therapist, will persevere in stretching willing hearts and minds.

There's another God-promise to take into the future: "All things, good or bad, work interactively for good, in the lives of those *who love God, and are called to His purposes.*" (Romans 8:28) You Lord, can use whatever comes to us for our good as it is yielded to You.

You have proven the truth of Your promises and Your past faithfulness breeds confidence in us that You never change; You are as reliable today and tomorrow as You were in all our yesterdays.

January 3

God's Opinion of Us?

Lord, help Believers everywhere to know Your opinion of us. It's often true that our views of ourselves are over inflated, but isn't it also true that there are times when we fail to see ourselves and others as special treasures in Your eyes?

One night about 3,000 years ago, King David was pacing back and forth on his rooftop patio, looking out over Jerusalem and into the night. He wrote, "When I see the blazing stars and brilliant moon You have made and hung in the night sky, I cannot help but wonder why You notice the family of mankind. Of what possible value are we to You that You make Yourself known to us?" (Psalm 8: 3-4)

David was filled with awe that the Creator of the night lights of the heavens honors us with His attention and love. He welcomes us as His children into His family. He allows us to grow in the family likeness. He wants to permeate our spirits, minds and bodies with His Spirit, to give us all we need for life -- for abundant life.

God's opinion of us? He died and rose from death for us. We are strongly and mercifully loved by the Mighty God, God the Father, God the Son and God the Holy Spirit, one God, three Persons. He will not, cannot, forget us or withdraw His love from us. He manifests His character in and through us so we may declare Him to others.

After David's awe at God's handiwork had pulled the words of this Psalm from his depths -- after he asked the Lord why He bothers with sinful humanity and why He loves us so greatly, he seems to have simply run out of words, for he could only exclaim, "O Lord, our Lord, how *excellent* is Your Name in all the earth!"

January 4

Lord of the Perfect Name, Psalm 8

Jehovah-God! That Name above all names!
It echoes through the halls of Creation
    and overfills the heavens.
Babies and toddlers lisp Your Name,
    bringing their prayers to You.
Surely Lord, their trusting praise should squelch
    pagan mockery.

That night sky above me, Lord ... Huge! Enormous!
    Overdoming Your earth.
Even its blackness is aflame with Your glory.
Crowded stars. Brilliant moon. All burning.
Shining. Praising. Magnifying Your power.

It all causes me to wonder, Lord, why You bother
    with us earthlings.
We are minuscule specks in this throbbing cosmos.
And yet, You made us, just a bit lower than angels.
You honor us with Your love. You crown us with
Your mercy. You visit us with forgiveness
    and put Creation under our rule.

In Eden's morning we came so close to Your perfect plan.
    And yet ...
O Lord, our Lord! Your perfect Name thunders.
It whispers. It permeates the cosmos, for it is the
    Name above every name!

January 5

A Healthy Breakfast

Today is a busy day, Lord. Let Your quieting Presence stay with me as I move through it. Fifty guests are coming for dinner, the house and tables need attention. My old habit of feeling flustered is lurking near. Lord, be in my attitudes so peace is not an act for others to see but Your actual gift of inner quietness.

Psalm 18 has been a hearty, nourishing spiritual breakfast. David claims You as his Rock (solidarity), his Deliverer (from his enemies), his Fortress (a strong, safe place), his God (ruler over circumstances and timing), his protecting Shield, his Strength (power, endurance), and high Tower (or lookout).

Be these to me, O Lord, as I seek to stay open to You and to work efficiently, with quiet anticipation. Guard my mind and spirit, Father, for I want this party to be fun, magnifying Your Name.

Verse 29 and 32 are special. "With Your help I can overcome a troop (of many details), and scramble over a wall (of many tasks). It is God who gives me strength and clears the way for me. He makes my feet as quick as a sure footed deer."

Lord, I realize David was fighting a battle against swords, hatchets and arrows, while my battle today is for inner peace. But inner peace is Your gift to people who love You and accept Your gift. In order to receive the gift we must claim it and put it to work. Large dinner parties are not a peaceful situation for me. Time and worry are my enemies here. Thank You for letting David remind me that You take pleasure in meeting all kinds of needs. All You need from me is a seeking, willing and trusting heart.

Bless You, Lord.   My soul delights in You.   What an education commences when one is willing and eager for You to be Lord of her life! Keep teaching me, Lord, for You and I both know I have much to learn -- and to unlearn.

January 6

The Morning After

"Let's sing praises to the Lord, for He takes pleasure in His people." (Psalm 149:3)

Lord, it was a lovely party! Everyone seemed to enjoy it. Food was good, everything hot at the same time. The house sparkled and the fire was perfect. Love was there in Your Presence. With Your help I "jumped over the wall of anxiety and ran through the troops" of Prudential executives.

But today I'm too tired to reach out to You. But I reach anyway, and find thanks rising within me. Thanks become praise and weariness is melting away. New strength and joy are claiming me.

The beautiful wonders of morning reach deeply into my soul and call me to worship. The bay window overlooking the woods shows early mist curling into hollows of the hills like contented kittens. Each object is washed in the rosy light of early day. Winter trees, bony and bare, stand watch. They seem to be waiting patiently for their spring resurrection.

There is strong renewal in praising You, Almighty God. Is it because in looking at You rather than at our wobbly weariness we are directed to the Strong One? Perhaps the Old Testament prophet, Zephaniah, had the answer when he wrote, "The Lord your God in your midst is mighty. He will save. He will celebrate over you with His love and rejoice over you with joy: He will rest in His love. He will rejoice over you with singing." (Zephaniah 23:17)

What a powerful verse, Lord! Your love is with us, surrounding and lifting us, giving energy and strength. Perhaps Lord, You are pleased, because visiting with You this morning was more important to me than crawling back between the covers for more rest. You shared Your joy with me. It delights and stuns me to realize that WE may bring YOU joy.

January Sketches

Cold and snowy, glittering white,
  or darkly gray with bitter bite.
Days grow short; nights linger longer,
  mercury drops in the thermometer.
Waterford etchings on window pane,
  wind whistles its shrill refrain.
Shadows crouching beneath each tree
  till fading light sets them free.

Sparrows fluffed against the coldness,
  wait and watch with cheeky boldness.
Crimson faces, fingers blue, noses running –
  could be flu?
Coats buttoned snug, chins pulled low,
  snow piled high on each chapeau.

Home's blazing hearths, radiating heat,
  steaming chocolate a fragrant treat.
Sparks fly up on velvet smoke calling up dreams
  memories evoke.

Snug with warmth I watch content the frigid
  storm with wonderment.
My shivering body at last grows warm
  and I can appreciate Winter's Charm.

F.N.

January 8

Letting Peace be the Umpire

Paul writes: "Let the peace of Christ rule (or be the umpire) in your hearts, for as members of Christ's body, you are called to peace." (Colossians 3:15) *Let* seems a strange word to use here. Webster defines let as "to allow, permit, to neither forbid nor prevent." Who would want to prevent peace in their life? Peacelessness is being stressed, anxious, sleepless, tense, worried.

Both David and Peter tell us to "...seek peace and pursue it." (Psalm 34:14, I Peter 3:11). It's not unlike a serious game of hide and seek. Inner peace hides sometimes. We are to seek it, and when we find a way to it, we are to run after it, catch and hold it.

It's not simply life's conflicts that keep us from Your peace, Lord. When Your peace deserts us it's often we ourselves who prevent its return, even as we ask You to restore it. Isn't it because we, like Peter on the sea, take our eyes off You and stare only at the frightening waves? Peter's fear became the umpire in his mind rather than the Prince of Peace. (Matthew 14:29-30)

Peace of mind is more than absence of trouble. Everyone has trouble. Job writes, "Man is born to trouble as sparks fly up from fire." (Job 5:7) Peace of mind is the steady conviction that You reign, Lord, and Your plans will work out for eventual good. If we believe that, if we truly rest in that belief, instead of becoming bitter, angry or disbelieving, the fear begins to leak out of our minds and quiet assurance seeps in. David wrote of this in Psalm 34, "I sought the Lord and He heard me and delivered me from all my fears." God took away his fear of the difficulties, not necessarily the troubles which caused them. The key here is seeking Your help, Lord.

By looking only at scary circumstances or reports we build a wall around our fear, closing ourselves in with it and cutting off our access to Your gift of peace of heart and mind.

January 9

Letting the Word Live in Us

Again Paul uses the word *let*. He says, "Let the Word of Christ live in you (be comfortably at home in you). Use Godly wisdom as you encourage others in the faith. Sing and be grateful to God. Whatever you're doing or thinking, do it in the strong Name of Jesus, and give thanks to the Father through Him." (Colossians 3:16-17)

We are to *let* the Word of God live in us, take up residence in us. It's not like having the dour portrait of a long dead relative we never knew hanging on our wall. Even though great, great grandfather's image is there it makes no difference in how I live my life. But if my beloved husband is there talking and planning with me for our life together *that* makes a difference.

Like a computer program, God's Word can't be in us unless we put it there. We must know, believe and act upon what's there. When we live in it and it lives in us, it steadies and guides us, bringing strength, wisdom, forgiveness and peace. It shows the love of God through us to others. It corrects and warns us of mistakes, nudging us in the right direction. The praise it brings overflows in song from the heart.

Ever since the Christian Church was born it has been singing hymns because of its joy in the Living Christ. Rome was carefully watching the Christians. The governor of Bithynia, Pliny, reported on church activity to Emperor Trajan, AD 98-117. "They (the Christians) meet at dawn to sing hymns to Christ as God."

This is not at all unusual for when God's Word lives in us, praise always seems to follow.

January 10

Letting Our Words Count

"Let your communication with others be gracious, flavored with salt so you may give wise, understandable answers when someone asks about your faith." (Colossians 4:6)

Lord, most of us want our words to be tactful and appealing, but all too often we let the hammer and ax method take over. We must be watchful in holding anger, critical attitudes and pride at bay.

The passive sounding use of the word *let* here has a most active side. It takes the deliberate closing the mind against attitudes which can keep the light of God's Word from having access to the shadowy secrets of the inner self. Since our words can count for eternity, we pray for guidance in using tact and good-natured humor. A loving attitude may let our words help rather than irritate.

It's been said that this verse from Colossians is "a warning not to confuse loyal godliness with graceless insipidity." Too often well meaning Christian's words relating to their faith can bore or irritate people instead of causing them to seek God. Lord, our words should sparkle with Your reality. As the Holy Spirit is given fuller access in our lives, stuffiness and dullness will melt away because You, our Triune God, Father, Son and Holy Spirit, are life and light, grace, mercy, truth, humor, peace and unconditional love. Living with You, Lord, is a grand adventure in *becoming.*

January 11

A Different Story

Corrie Ten Boom, a Dutch Christian and watchmaker, with her father and sister, was arrested and sent to a concentration camp when the Gestapo discovered they were hiding Jews in the attic of their home. Her father and sister died in the camps. Corrie survived to become an internationally known writer and speaker about the grace and mercy of God. She wrote these words,

"To be above with the saints you love,
that will be glory, but to be here with the
saints you know, that's a different story."

Corrie's words make us smile. They put the "different story" in a frame we've all experienced. It's easy to think of a Christian friend who is in heaven as a saint, but as we tangle in disagreement with a mortal "saint" that's a different story.

My thoughts this morning have not pleased You or me, Lord. I had a gritty disagreement with a friend and I keep replaying it in my mind. May I hold to Your Word so I don't sin against You or her.

Paul writes that if we find encouragement or comfort in our union with Christ and His love, if we have a living relationship with the Holy Spirit, if He has shown us compassion, then God wants to give us joy by having His kind of love for others. He wants both of us to have His Spirit and His purpose. (Philippians 2:1-2)

Lord, hold me back from doing anything through selfishness or conceit. Forgive and help me consider my friend's interests too. Let the mind of our Savior be in both of us. Lord, in Your name I rid myself of resentment so I may be forgiving and tenderhearted to her as You are to me. Let us both keep the unity of Your Spirit through peace as we visit today. Thank You, Lord.

January 12

Spirit of Power

"God didn't give us the spirit of fear or timidity. He gave us the Spirit of power, love and self discipline, so don't be ashamed to speak about Him." (II Timothy 1:7-8)

Paul tells Timothy, "God didn't give us the spirit of fear." He gave us just the opposite. But Lord, many of us *are* timid, afraid to speak of our faith to others. Since God didn't send the fear, it obviously came from another source. Is it self preservation or is it sneaky old *Screwtape*, the name C. S. Lewis gives Satan in his book, *The Screwtape Letters*? Or is it a pact between the two?

O Lord, our thoughts are often warped. We try to squeeze You down to the meagerness of our understanding. We try to have full control, telling You just what we want or don't want. We offer You nice little suggestions of how You could work things around to give us what we want without causing anyone extra trouble.

"My thoughts aren't like yours. I do not work or plan as you do and My methods are not ones you would use," says the Lord. "Just as the heavens are higher than earth, so My thoughts, plans and methods are beyond your reach." (Isaiah 55:8-9)

At times, dear Holy Spirit, You are an uncomfortable Comforter! You can chop preconceived thoughts to pieces. You can breathe through our prejudiced (pre-judged) human patterns, causing shame at first, and then a surprising flood of light and understanding. Holy Spirit, I don't *want* to be afraid of having You renew and make changes in me. Help me remember You are the Giver of all good gifts and You don't give me a fearful heart. You give strength, love and self discipline. So take my fear and distrust away. Nail them to the cross of Christ and please, Lord, flood all dark and secret places of my life with Your freedom, truth and love.

January 13

A Two Story House

The owners of a house in our neighborhood transformed it by adding a second floor, making it totally adequate for the family's needs. Let's say for now the Old Testament is similar to the original one story house. It served God's purposes for His family. It educated them about Him, and about themselves. It gave His requirements through the Law given to Moses. But His people discovered they were incapable of following the Law. God knew that would happen. Neither prophet, priest nor king could keep His requirements of righteousness. They had a problem they couldn't solve. They needed a Helper, Someone to stand in the breech between God and themselves, to pay their penalty for being law breakers. They needed God Himself.

In the Old Testament God reveals that help is on the way in the person of the virgin's Son. It gives a detailed description of the Coming One, the Messiah. It tells why He is coming and how we may recognize Him. It tells where He will be born, who His human ancestors are to be. It even tells what people's response to Him will be. It reveals that He will come to earth twice, first as our sin bearing Sacrifice, God's suffering Servant. The second time He will be the undisguised King of Glory, stunning in power, wisdom, riches and honor. He will share all that He has with those who trust and obey Him.

The Old Testament shows the inadequacy of mankind to save himself. The New Testament is the second story, completing the house, fulfilling the promise made by God in the Old Testament. It tells what the True Lamb of God, Jesus, did to redeem us. It totally and adequately meets the needs of those who love and trust Him.

Old Testament Glimpses of Messiah

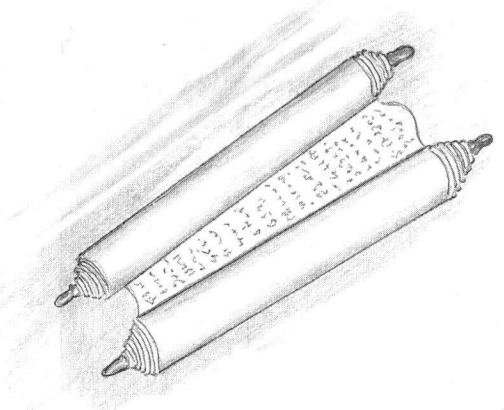

Genesis: He is the Seed of Woman
Exodus: He is our Passover Lamb, Freedom from Slavery
Leviticus: He is our Sin Offering
Numbers: He is our Establisher
Deuteronomy: He is our Choice
Joshua: He is Captain of our Salvation
Judges: He is the Deliverer from Oppression
Ruth: He is our Heavenly Kinsman and Redeemer
Samuel: He is the Oil of Anointing
Kings: He is our Reigning King
Chronicles: He is our Lord Who Hears
Ezra: He is the Restorer of Nations
Nehemiah: He is the Restorer of Nations
Esther: He is our Advocate
Job: He is My Redeemer
Psalms: He is My Song and My Shepherd
Proverbs: He is our Wisdom
Ecclesiastes: He is our Pathway through Futility

Song of Solomon: He is Lover of our Souls
Isaiah: He is God's Suffering Servant
Jeremiah: He is the Righteous Branch
Lamentations: He is the Weeping Prophet
Ezekiel: He is the Man With Four Faces
Daniel: He is the Stone Cut Without Hands
Hosea: He is the Faithful Husband
Joel: He is the Early and Latter Rains
Amos: He is the Gardener and Restorer
Obadiah: He is the Ambassador of Nations
Jonah: He is the God Who Heals
Micah: He is the Messenger of the Beautiful Feet
Nahum: He is Jehovah the Holy
Habakkuk: He is the Everlasting God
Zephaniah: He is the Lord in our Midst
Haggai: He is our Encouragement
Zechariah: He is the Comfort of Jerusalem
Malachi: He is our Promise of Blessing

January 15

I Found Jehovah-Jesus

Years ago I read the name *Jehovah-Jesus*. It so encapsulated my concept of the Triune God that I accepted the name with joy and wonder. A friend asked, "Where on earth did you get that name? Is it legitimate?" I confessed I didn't remember where it came from but surely it had to be legitimate. I would try to find out. I asked our priest if he was familiar with the name. He said no. When I asked him if he thought it was legitimate, he said, with a grin, "Theologically I believe you would say it's legitimate."

Another friend said, "You shouldn't say that! It's not possible. When God told Moses His name was *Jehovah*, Jesus hadn't even been born." That comment seemed to hit the concept of the ever living Trinity in the face. After a scrambling search I went back to Nathan Stone's book *Names of God* reprinted many times since 1991. There, in the very beginning, I found *Jehovah-Jesus*.

How appropriate! "In the beginning God..." (Genesis 1:1) "In the beginning was the Word, the Son, and the Word was with God and the Word was God." (John 1:1)

Dr. Stone says in his introduction that his purpose in writing the book was not only to show the rich significance of the Hebrew names of God but to show their fulfillment in the person and work of Jesus, the Messiah.

God represents Himself to us as a Trinity, one God in three persons, each of the Persons taking His particular part in bringing about the Purpose of the ages. We humans, in a sense, are a trinity. Perhaps this is one meaning of the Trinity's conversation at creation as He says, "Let *Us* make man in *Our* image." (Genesis 1: 26) We are each one person having three components which make up human life. We have a body in which we live and relate to others. We have a soul, mind or personality, through which we may love, hate, care and reason. We have a spirit, the deepest part of the self, through which we may relate to God and He to us.

Paul speaks of Jesus as "the exact image of the invisible God, the first born of the new creation. By Jesus all things were created ... He is before all creation and He holds all things together." (Colossians1:15-20)

Everything God is lives fully in Christ in bodily form. If God is Jehovah, then Jesus Christ, as His coequal and exact likeness, except in bodily form, is Jehovah-Jesus. (Hebrews 1:3) God the Father, God the Son and God the Spirit are the same God, with each "Person" of the Godhead having His necessary part in the eternal plan. The Father is the Father-Provider. The Son is both Sacrifice and the Priest who offered the sacrifice. The Spirit is the Indweller, the Advocate, Guide and Comforter.

Holy Father, I pray back Your words of promise from the prophet Joel. *"Pour out Your Spirit on Your people. Let Your sons and daughters proclaim You in truth. Give the old men god-dreams and the young men visions. Fill Your servants, both men and women, with the fullness of the Holy Spirit."* (Joel 3:28-32)

January 16

Know His Names

In Jesus' prayer before His arrest He said, "I have manifested Your Name to those You have given Me." (John 17:6)

In Biblical times a name was considered to be a one word resume of character or purpose. It was believed to know a person's name was to have power with or over them. Fearing they might misuse Your Name, ancient Jews designated You by the use of four unpronounceable consonants: YHWH. Later they added two vowels and thought of You as Yahweh.

Lord, throughout Scripture You've told us You want us to know You, to have power with You. The Holy Spirit, through the prophets and through circumstances, began to reveal Your character by Your multiple Names. Each Name is a God revealed facet of who You are.

Today some have the mistaken idea that the fearsome God of the Old Testament is not the same deity as the loving, forgiving Savior of the New. This confusion is due either to ignorance of Scripture or disbelief in its truth. The Bible tells that You, Lord God, Creator of solar systems and snow flakes, blood chemistry and butterflies, are changeless. You are the same yesterday, and forever." From eternity, Father, You have never changed. In Your mercy You have folded back some of the obscuring covers which concealed You from the finite mind. You chose to do this by the revelation of the full meaning of Your Word and Your Son, the Messiah, who came to Earth as the "exact image of the invisible God." (Colossians 1:15)

You have given us various ways to learn of You, Lord. One interesting way is to look at the different meanings of Your Names in the Hebrew language. No one name can sum up the meaning of a single human being, much less You, Almighty God. But each differing Name in Hebrew reveals at least one brilliant facet of Your character. You have seen to it that Your Names and their meanings are understandable in Scripture for You *want* us to

January 16

know You as well as Your will for us.

"For I know the plans I have for you," declares the Lord, "plans to prosper you and not to harm you, plans to give you hope and a future." (Jeremiah 29:11 NIV)

Note: Information on Hebrew meanings of Old Testament Names of God throughout these pages comes from a study by Nathan J. Stone. It was first given as a course on the Radio School of the Bible in Chicago. Later it was published in book form as *Names of God*.

I consider Nathan Stone, a Jew and Christian theologian, as a gift from God, for through Stone's scholarly work I have received a deeper and wider realization of God's power, purpose and dominion in individual's lives and in the world.

Elohim (El-o-heem)

Westminster Shorter Catechism says, "The chief end of man is to glorify God and to enjoy Him forever."

That is a wonderful goal, Lord, but we can only give You glory and enjoy Your fellowship as we come to know You. Our English Bibles simply translate Your numerous Hebrew names, rich in meaning, as *Lord* or *Almighty God.*

The name *Elohim* is used in the first verse of the first book of the Bible. "In the beginning *God* ..." *Elohim* carries the concept of creating and governing power. Dr. Stone says as *Elohim* You reveal Yourself as "bringing cosmos out of chaos, light out of darkness, habitation out of desolation and life in Your image." In our English Bibles the name is translated *Almighty God*, the name under which You made covenants with Abraham and Jacob. (Genesis 17:1, 35:11) It's one of the names given to Messiah-Jesus. (Isaiah 9:6-7) "...the Mighty God, the Prince of Peace." It expresses Your greatness and glory.

Elohim has the usual Hebrew ending for plural nouns, *-im*. Although it is plural in form it is used for the one God. Pronouns used with the name are plural. How consistent this is with the doctrine of the Trinity! "Let *us* make man in *our* image." (Genesis 1:26) The plural for majesty was not in use when Genesis was written.

Elohim is a wonderful name, Lord. It's a comfort and blessing. It tells of Your unimaginable power, sovereignty and glory but also of a personal covenant relationship which we may have with You. You tell us, "Don't be afraid, I'm here with you. Don't panic for I am your *Elohim*." (Isaiah 41:10) This verse gives us the right to say, with King David, "I will say of the *Almighty*, 'He is my refuge and fortress, my *Elohim*, in whom I trust.'" (Psalm 91:20)

January 18

Freshman Prayer, 101

Location: in my 'closet' with the door closed (Matthew 6:6)
Time of Meeting: first thing in the morning (Psalm108:2-3)
Subject: *Lord, Teach Us to Pray* (Luke 11:1)

Andrew Murray's books were grouped in my mother's library. Shortly after my marriage I began reading them. They fed my soul then, and they still do. This and the next four pages are thoughts from his book *With Christ in the School of Prayer*, which I have condensed and paraphrased.

Dr. Murray was a minister, a patriot of South Africa, an author of many books and a great spiritual force in this country and abroad. According to him, Lord, You want to enrol all who want to learn how to pray in Your School of Prayer. We who enrol must own up to our ignorance of Your ways, admit to being a beginner and confess we are often caught between belief and doubt.

If all the above is true, my prayer must be:
To Your glory
In surrender to Your will
In assurance of faith
In the Name of Jesus
With perseverance which does not give up

None of the above comes naturally. All five must be learned, and only You, Lord, can be our Instructor. As students we need an Instructor who:
Knows His work, has the gift of teaching
Has the patience to descend to His
student's level

Yes, Lord, You are that Teacher and more. You are our

priest who intercedes for us, who offers the necessary sacrifice and who is Himself that sacrifice.

>You teach through:
>>The urgency of our recognized need
>>Your Word
>>Testimony of other Believers
>>The Holy Spirit breathing His Spirit
>>>of prayer into us
>>The indwelling Spirit as our great
>>>Intercessor.

January 19

Praying in the Truth

" ... the time has come when true worshippers will worship the Father in spirit and in truth. The Father looks for such people because He is Spirit, and those who worship Him must do so in spirit and in truth." (John 4:23-24)

Lord, what a marvel! You seek out such worshippers and when You gather us in we bring *YOU* joy.

You are Truth so we worship You in truth. You are Spirit so we worship You in spirit. The ear is made to hear. The eye is made to receive light and to see. Just so, the worshipping human spirit is made with the capacity of receiving You. As You are, so must Your worshippers be.

Your Spirit is not bound by time, space or language. Neither the place nor the words make true worship. If we try to pray in the spirit of truth only at church but spend the rest of the week in a different spirit, then our worship is chained to a certain place (in church) and we're not free to worship with our whole being.

True worship comes from You, Lord, for only You have the Spirit to give. God the Son came here to bring us the Holy Spirit of Truth. He will shape us for worship in spirit and truth.

Jesus' earth life was coming to a close when He told the disciples, "There's much more I want to tell you but you are not ready yet. When the Spirit of Truth comes, He will guide you in all truth." (John 16: 12-13)

Lord Jesus, as You ascended to the Father in heaven taking with You the perfect sacrifice of Your blood, You sent the Holy Spirit of Truth to give us ever current access to You who will lead us into all truth.

January 20

Praying in the Spirit of Truth

Jesus said, "I will ask the Father and He will give you another Counselor to be with you forever, the Spirit of Truth." (John14:16 NIV)

Lord Christ, as You made an end to sin's dominion, through Your death and resurrection, You entered Heaven's Holiest Place with the offering of Your perfect and acceptable sacrifice. There on our behalf, You received our redemption and we received the position of the Father's sons and daughters. Worship in the Spirit is worship of the Father in the Spirit of Christ, in the spirit of sonship.

"In truth" doesn't only mean in sincerity. In the Old Testament, everything was shadow and promise of coming reality. Lord Jesus, You brought reality and substance to the prophecies. Because of You, we have the blessings and powers of eternal life as our own experience and possession. Lord, You are full of grace and truth and the Holy Spirit is the Spirit of Truth. To worship in the Spirit is to worship in truth. It is actual, living communication and harmony with God, real fellowship between the Father, who is Spirit, and the son or daughter praying in the Spirit.

Father, without Jesus, who comes with the Spirit, we cannot bring You the worship You seek. We need to confess our inability, as teachable children, and come to our Father to ask for the gift of the Holy Spirit. Then in a child's simple faith we open our lives and our living to that Gift.

To have Christ the Son and the Spirit of the Son living within us and showing us the Father makes us true spiritual worshippers so we may say, I am Your child, Father, and as Your child, I have free access to You.

January 21

The Secret Place of Prayer

"When you pray, go to your room, close the door and pray to your unseen Father, and He, who sees what you do secretly will reward you out in the open." (Matthew 6:6)

Lord, You are our Teacher today just as You were for that small group of disciples who turned the world upside down through Your Spirit. You tell us we must have a quiet place for prayer where we can be alone with You. It can be anywhere, inside or outside. It can change but it must be a place where we put our whole self and life before our Father.

The emphasis here is *the Father*. I must meet my Father to breathe in, and pray in, the atmosphere of Father love. This requires my whole hearted, childlike trust in Him.

"...your unseen Father" does not show Himself to the world but He shows Himself to the one who closes out distractions in order to be alone with Him.

He "... will reward you." Secret prayer is not fruitless. It shows in the life. Its blessings do not depend on human earnestness but on the loving power of the Father.

Realizing that I needn't try to pressure You to listen to me through a multitude of words can lead to quiet thoughtfulness in prayer. If my Father knows I need this, then I will have it. If He delays the answer, the delay too will be used to teach me. It will teach perseverance in prayer.

I know my Father sees me, knows me, hears me and I thank Him for meeting my needs. As His child I am free to bring every need to Him knowing that He will supply whatever I need from His endless riches in glory because of what Jesus has done for us. To God, our Father, be glory forever and ever. (Philippians 4:19-20)

January 22

Our Father Who Art ...

"Our Father who art in Heaven, hallowed be Thy Name. Thy Kingdom come, Thy will be done, on earth as it is in Heaven." Children may memorize this prayer but it takes a lifetime to live it.

Only You, Jesus, called God *Father*. But Lord, You came here to make Your Father our Father. You ransomed us from sin's death sentence so we could join You as brothers and sisters in Your Father's forever family.

As babies, we begin learning of love from our parents. Later, as Christians, we begin to grow in God's love. It becomes a personal relationship with the living God, a conscious fellowship with Him, and it's in this framework we learn to live by His prayer.

In prayer the tendency is to ask for our own needs and wants first; but this prayer reverses that order. First there is *Thy Name*, *Thy Kingdom* and *Thy Will*. Then forgive us. In this way we grow into thinking of others. The purpose of Jesus' prayer is to influence our personal and intercessory prayers. Unfortunately, personal prayer has the lion's share of our prayer time. Lord, You are our great Intercessor and You want us to follow Your example in order to bring Your blessings down on others by our faith and prayer. Until this becomes our goal we can't grow much in our prayer life. The toddler asks for his own wants. Soon he may learn to say, "God bless Mama and Daddy." But it's the mature son or daughter who loves his Father's work and longs to work with Him in His business. This is the one who asks his Father for things beyond his own needs and is granted his requests.

Father, may all who love You and Your ways want to pray in this way, learning Your ways and purposes. Raise up those who honor Your Name and Your Kingdom, who long to do Your will on earth the same way it is done in Heaven.

January 23

Praise

Since You came into my life, Lord, I've been thankful for Your blessings, but to actively praise You for Your attributes did not occur to me until years later. After asking Your Holy Spirit to fill me and teach me, I began to see praise as a vital force for growth. Scripture sparkles with examples; it rings with the admonition to praise You. I began to try it, almost like an experiment. At first I felt awkward, stiff and a bit hypocritical.

From that shaky start I began to see new truths becoming real in my life. As I praised You for Your mercy, I recognized Your deep mercy toward me. As I praised You for Your love and forgiveness, I found my own heart being tenderized toward others.

All of us become drained of strength and purpose at times. Perhaps some of that weakness is from an attitude rather than from hard work itself. Nehemiah, who repaired the ruined walls of Jerusalem wrote, "The joy of the Lord is my strength." (Nehemiah 8: 10) He worked long hours with his men, directing, hauling and lifting stones, mixing mortar while repulsing enemy snipers. Where did he get his endurance? Lord, the joy he had in You was his strength. And joy, when translated into action, equals energy and praise. We know this when we praise You for Your all sufficient strength.

We experience many things, joyful things, through the practice of praise but things can still go wrong sometimes. When they do, we ask ourselves, "Did I cause this somehow or are You showing me another dimension of Yourself? Teach me."

Lord, give Your people grace to hold tenaciously to faith until dark doubt is overpowered and the light of Your Presence shines on us again.

January 24

The Key to the Gate, Psalm 100

There are times when we long for God's Presence, but we can't find our way in. The gates seem to be locked and we have no key. This Psalm offers us a key. It's praise! The first verse tells us to worship God, and why we owe Him praise. His gates open to us with thanksgiving, and our praise takes us into His palpable presence.

> Sound off with Joy to the Lord.
> All lands! All peoples!
> Serve Him with a glad heart. Come into His
> presence with exuberant song.
> Stretch your mind to realize who He is.
> He is God! He created us;
> it's not the other way round.
> We are His sheep, cared for
> in the Shepherd's pasture.
> So come on in. Come through His gates
> with thankful hearts.
> Come into His courts with joyful praise.
> Bless His Name with strength
> for the Lord is always good to us.
> His faithfulness neither ceases nor hesitates.

The first objective is to go through the gates. A thankful heart is the key. We enter the King's courts with thanksgiving and go into His presence with song. We begin by being thankful which, if we are joyful because of Him, grows to be praise. Praise matures into a heart so full it pours out in a New Song which He Himself pours in.

January 25

Open the Pipeline

Jehosaphat, an Old Testament King of Judah, was terrified to learn several nations were marching against him. He gathered his people to fast and he prayed, "…we have no power against this army, Lord, but we are looking to You for help."

God gave Jahaziel, the choir director, a message for the King. "Don't be afraid or discouraged. You don't have to fight this battle. It is Mine. March toward them, take your positions and stand firm. You will see My deliverance." (II Chronicles 20:14-22)

The King prayed, admitting his helplessness. He believed God's message rather than his own fear. He brought out the Temple choirs to praise God for His holiness. "As they went ahead, leading the army and singing praises, the Lord set ambushes for the enemy and they were defeated."

Lord, we know You want Your people to praise You in all circumstances. As Judah, a name which means praise, defeated her enemies through trusting praise, so our enemies are defeated through trusting praise. Our enemies can be fear, doubt, greed, pride, anger, lust, sour moods, discouragement and self pity. Enemies of the soul are legion.

It's as though praise opens the clogged supply line from You, Lord, to us. The pipeline can easily be blocked by debris of our own making. Yet as we repent of our sin and allow You to pour in forgiveness, Your blessings of love, joy, peace and faith can once again flow through us.

Praising You in difficulty doesn't mean we are delighted by the trouble. It means we are trusting You because of who You are. No trouble on earth can change that.

January 26

Praying for Plumpkin

It was distressing when the most respected Ob-Gyn group in Atlanta, consisting of five prominent doctors told me due to damaged arteries I could not survive having a baby. I sought a second opinion in a well known clinic in New Orleans. Their report was, "It may not be *impossible* but we strongly advise against it." Hope sky rocketed. We sought the Lord's will daily for a year. No answer. It was as though He hadn't heard or He was leaving it up to us.

We decided to go ahead, praying this sort of prayer: "Lord, we want this baby and if it's Your will we can have it. If we lose him our hearts won't *stay* broken. We will trust You."

Doctors put me on a strict diet, I must see the doctor every other day and have eighteen hours of bed rest a day. The inactivity gave me much time for prayer, thought and Bible study. I decided my first desire was God's will. Each morning and through the day, I trusted the baby's life and my own to the Giver of Life. A day didn't pass without prayers for "Plumpkin." I requested that "he" would not be born unless he would come to know Jesus as Savior.

After appointments one doctor liked to say, "Now don't you blow up on me!" After hearing this several times, a flash of irritation shot through me but I managed to say firmly and quietly, "Dr. C., don't say that to me again. We can discuss 'blow ups' if one should happen."

In the eighth month the 'blow up' began. Labor was induced followed by the first pain. "Good," I said. The nurse, grumpy with fatigue, muttered, "Humph! No one in their right mind is glad for labor pains." But I was – even when they came on in earnest.

Hours passed. The warm baby boy, I had called "Plumpkin," and I met face to tiny face for the first time. It was love at first sight.

January 27

Innocent as Morning

Baby, little baby, sated with milk,
    lulled by sleep,
    who are you?
An unmarked slate, knowing no lie,
    scheming no schemes.
Your needs so many, your replies so few,
    a cry or a smile will do.

Baby, baby from God's plan
    innocent as Eden's morning.
Soft and warm, a precious weight
    filling empty arms.
Your sleeping beauty stirs my heart,
    delicate lashes on flawless cheeks.

Small, downy head of undreamed potential
    trusts upon my shoulder.
Miniature hands, tinier fingers
    holding tight.
Translucent toes on kissable feet
    working out from covers.

Sleep on tiny child, know that God
    loved and cared for you
as He knitted you together gene by gene
    and cell by cell.
Grow strong. Return His love
    and follow His guidance.
                    F.N.

January 28

"My Cup Runneth Over"

I never dreamed babies were such exquisite little creatures until we had one. We longed for another, a baby girl.

Could we risk it? Doctors said absolutely not. We thought my new status as a mother made me indispensable to our little son. The Lord nudged us to adopt, for after all, those who trust Him are adopted into His Family. (Ephesians 1:5) My longing soul heard God say, "I have a daughter for you." I prayed for her daily. She would grow not in my womb but in my heart. Baby Bill and I were examined by psychologists, questioned and tested. Our home was inspected.

After a year the Child Service Association called. The woman said they had a baby boy for us. I wanted him. He had no one to love, cuddle and teach him. I asked for the weekend to consider. A tug of war was raging in my heart. The tiny boy needed a home – but God had said a daughter! I had prayed for her, her life and health and her salvation.

Monday I called them and said we would wait for our daughter. After five more months, the Agency called saying we could come visit a tiny girl. There in the play pen sat an exquisite baby, all pink and white and blue and gold. Huge blue eyes topped cheeks as bright as sunrise. Soft golden fuzz covered her head. Bill leaned down and swooped her up high. She saw joy and love in his smile. As she laughed she dropped a dollop of saliva on his chin. With a blush and a wipe, he said she had just put her seal of approval on *her daddy*.

Here we were, a family of four. A wonderful daddy, two precious children and a mother strong enough to care for and love all three. Truly, Lord, my cup 'runneth over' filling the days with joyful amazement and praise.

January 29

An Angel's Visit

Lord, I've always been grateful for Your protection by angels and for Your letting me see "mine" when I was five. Of course I had seen pictures of them in my Bible storybook. They looked like women with heavy, chicken feather wings who wore terry cloth bathrobes. The angel who visited me looked nothing like them, but I knew instinctively what he was.

One night when the family had gone downstairs, I was in bed, frightened, covers clutched tightly under my chin. Scary, black shapes seemed to be approaching me. Suddenly, the angel was THERE! He was huge, taller than the ten foot ceiling but he didn't need to stoop. The ceiling instantly accommodated him by disappearing. Dark shadows and moving shapes vanished.

He seemed to be made of transparent power and radiant light. I had the merest impression that he had wings. Perhaps that impression came more from a sense of super human mobility than a visible shape. His hair was like spun glass the color of an amber gem and his eyes glowed from a strong, kind face. His whole being was of an unknown substance quite unlike my own. Rather than looking like flesh and blood he appeared to be visible power, color, transcendence and light.

His different and unknown quality frightened me even more than the spooky darkness. I screamed for my mother. As she turned on the sixty watt lamp, the angel and his radiance vanished, leaving the room in twilight by comparison.

Fifteen years later, as I read the book of *Daniel* for a Bible Survey class at Wheaton College, I read Daniel's description of the angel who spoke to him beside the Tigris River. I realized, with a shock, Daniel could be describing "my" angel in chapter 10.

I've asked myself why he visited me, but I have no answer. Perhaps my Father in heaven saw His frightened little child, whom He knew one day would give her heart to Him, wanted to tell her, as He has told so many others who were frightened by circumstances or the sight of an angel, "Don't be afraid for I am here with you."

     Decades have passed since then. I often sense the presence of his Master, but I've not seen the angel since our first encounter. Neither have I forgotten him. And I'm sure he has not forgotten me.

January 30

Corroborating Witnesses from Scripture

Daniel: "In April I was standing by the Tigris River. I glanced up and saw a man dressed in white linen. He wore a belt of pure gold; his skin was luminous and his eyes resembled burning coals in a face which glowed like the sun. His arms and legs were like polished bronze.
"My companions ran away and I was left alone. I grew pale and weak with fright. When he spoke I fell face down in a faint, for his voice was like thunder. He touched me and lifted me, still trembling, to my hands and knees. He said, 'Daniel, beloved of God. Stand and listen carefully to what I tell you.'" (Daniel 10:4-11)

Elijah: "Elijah had traveled all day and night. Exhausted, he sat under a bush waiting to die. While he was sleeping an angel woke him with a touch and told him to eat some food. He saw a jar of water before him and bread baking on a stone. He ate and drank and went back to sleep. Again the angel touched him and said, 'Eat again. You have a long journey ahead of you.'" (I Kings 19:5-7)

Zachariah: "...was in the Temple when suddenly an angel was there! ... Zachariah was terrified but the angel said, 'Don't be afraid Zachariah, I have something to tell you...'" (Luke 1:11-13)

Mary: "...God sent the angel Gabriel to a virgin named Mary, who was betrothed to Joseph. Gabriel said, "Don't be frightened Mary, for God has blessed you.'" (Luke1:26-28)

Jesus: "Be careful not to scorn or abuse little children, for I am telling the truth when I tell you, their angels in Heaven have continual access to My Father." (Matthew 18:10)

January 31

Angels or Daughters?

"Angels and ministers, spirits of grace, friends of
    the children, beholding God's face,
Moving like thought to us through the beyond,
    molded in beauty and free from our bond!
"Messengers clad in the swiftness of light, subtle as
    flame and creative in might.
Helmed with the truth and with charity shod,
    wielding the wind of the purpose of God!
"Earth's myriad creatures live after their kind, dumb
    in the life of the body confined.
You are pure spirit but we here below
    linked in both orders, tossed to and fro.
"You do God's bidding, unshaken and strong; we are
    distraught 'twixt the right and the wrong;
Yet we would soar as a bird from the mesh,
    freed from the wonder and weakness of flesh.
"We too shall join you as comrades in grace, here
    but a little below you in place;
Then when we move from our lowness in worth
    we too shall herald good will upon earth."
    (Percy Dearmer)

Thank You for creating angels as Your servants, to minister to us at Your command. They do Your bidding, powerful, exotic and beautiful. But Lord, I wouldn't change places with them if I could. People can never be angels, but we will always be Your sons or Your daughters.

February

February, a month still bruised by winter's grip,
    is blue, gray and purple.
Skeleton trees, tall, lank shadows,
    sway to a minor key.

Wind pipes a note. Branches start to dance,
    moving with wild abandon.
A chill creeps in, lights dim.
    A snow ballet begins.

Snowflakes swirl down in full white skirts
    covering the cold scarred ground.
Silence piles up in soft, muffled heaps,
    but my thoughts are not of winter.

Day is icy and wind is sharp,
    but in my heart is a coal of joy.
It's glowing there by the Spirit's power
    no winter storm can chill.
                            F.N.

February 2

The Eternal Road Map

"The Lord calls to us: 'Ask Me where the good road is. Walk in it and you will find peace for your soul.'" (Jeremiah 6:16)

There's much dispute today about how to find one's way to God. Some say this way, some say that. Some say, "There's no right or wrong way. All roads lead to God. Just decide for yourself and stick to it." Scripture does not teach that. Wouldn't it be irrational if a traveler, driving to New Mexico from the East Coast, chose his route by saying, "Enie-meni-myne-mo?" He could end up in Canada. All roads don't lead to New Mexico -- or to heaven.

For an automobile trip we're not sure of, we need a reliable, up to date map. We've not traveled to eternity before and we definitely need a well marked map for that. Scripture is that map. Both Testaments give necessary directions. They also describe our trustworthy traveling Companion.

Here are clues to New Testament signs posted along the way:

Matthew, You are the Law and the Promise
Mark, You are the Mighty Worker
Luke, You are the Son of Man
John, You are the Son of God
Acts, You are the Spirit of Power
Romans, You are the Justifier
Corinthians, You are Head of the Body of Believers
Galatians, You are our Freedom
Ephesians, You are the Unification of Christians
Philippians, You are our Joy and Contentment
Colossians, You are the Image of the Invisible God
Thessalonians, You are the Encouraging Advisor

February 2

Timothy, You are our Mediator
Titus, You are our Pattern for Hope
Philemon, You are our Brother
Hebrews, You are our Eternal High Priest and only Savior
James, You are the Reality of our Faith
Peter, You are our Victory in Suffering
John, You are the Author of Love
Jude, You are our Returning Lord
Revelation, You are King of Kings and Lord of Lords

February 3

20/20 Vision

Lord, You asked some Pharisees the same question You ask us today. "You have eyes, why can't you see? You have ears, but you neither hear nor remember. Why is that?" (Matthew 8:18)

John saw with perfect vision when he said in I John 3:2, "Friends, we are God's own children today, but it's not clear what we will be like in the future. One thing is sure however, when He comes back for us we will be like Him for we will see Him as He is." Paul prayed, with visionary love for fellow Christians: "I pray the eyes of your understanding will be wide open so you may know what God wants to share with Believers. I want you to realize the astonishing truth that He considers Himself rich because we have been brought to Him through Jesus Christ." (Ephesians 1:18)

Job "saw" with insight of the Spirit: "I am certain that my Redeemer lives and one day He will stand on this Earth. After my body has returned to dust, I will see Him with my own eyes. I will see Him for *myself* -- I, and not another. I yearn for that blessed sight." (Job 19:23-27)

Lord, Job wanted everyone to hear the good news and see what he saw and knew. "O, I wish my words were preserved -- that they were written on a scroll or inscribed with an iron pen or carved in stone forever!"

Father, You saw to it that Job's words were preserved for generations to come. His words are there in Scripture for all to see. You *will* stand on Earth again, Lord, and Job will see You with his own eyes, and so will I! Because of this I ask in hope and expectation: "Open my eyes so I may see (realize, understand) with 20/20 vision the powerful, eternal truths in Your Word." (Psalm 119:18)

February 4

I Want to See

Jesus said, "You have eyes, why can't you see? You have
ears, but you don't hear or remember. Why is that?" (Matthew
8:18)

Lord, at first look, Your parables seem impersonal, always
about the "other fellow." It's not long, however, before we
discover they could be about the other fellow -- but they are
definitely about me too. They're simple stories but they speak on
two levels, one earthly, one spiritual. They permeate and linger in
the mind as tenaciously as the smell of Mother's chocolate cake
lingers in the kitchen, refusing to be forgotten. Understanding
begins: Maybe eyes and ears aren't eyes and ears at all, but minds
closed against Your truth, like a turtle drawn into its shell.
Another thought nags us: Am I the weak seedling which wilts
when trouble grows hot? Or am I like the priest or Levite who
crosses the street to avoid contact with the wounded man because
I, the snooty American, don't want to be involved with the scruffy
stranger? I *want* to be like the compassionate Samaritan who
helped the needy man.

Lord, Your parables can begin to pry open turtle shell
minds, letting in the light and freshness of Your truth. They can
stretch both mind and soul, causing us to rethink situations on a
less selfish plane.

I *do* want to see clearly and I want acute spiritual hearing.
Tune these ears to Your quiet voice. The clang and clamor of our
society can be deafening, Father, drowning out Your truth. Help
me, and all Believers, for the sake of Christ Jesus who loves us and
gave His life for us.

February 5

Our Returning Lord

Each Sunday Morning we are reminded of three specific things concerning You, Lord Christ. We say, "Christ has died. Christ is risen. *Christ will come again.*" We hear much from the pulpit about Your death and resurrection, but very little about Your return.

Scripture tells about Your return to Earth, Lord. You are actually coming back but no one can know when this will happen, so guessing is pointless. Each person has an appointment with You on that day which cannot be broken. And the time to prepare is NOW. (Matthew 24:36)

Noah's experience is a good illustration of the importance of taking Your words seriously. It took him decades to build the ark to God's blueprints. Noah and his God were the joke of the neighborhood. Ridicule, snide remarks and knee slapping laughs followed him wherever he went. He endured it all and kept plugging away at his, and God's, project. Finally the rains came, and kept coming. Deluges tore away everything, but Noah was ready. The people couldn't believe what they were seeing. They ran for the hills. But flood waters swallowed them, hills and all.

People of Noah's day didn't believe God's message concerning the coming flood, so of course, they didn't prepare. Some are like that today, they believe God's Book is so out of date that it need not influence their lives. These people won't be prepared either.

There's a story circulating of Satan giving a final exam to three young devils before he sends them to earth charged with wreaking havoc on humanity. Satan's most vital question was, "How would you deceive humans and send them down here to me?"

February 5

The first replies, "I'll tell them God is a figure of an overactive imagination." Satan replies, "No. People know there's a God."

Devil two has an idea, "I'll tell them there's no Hell."

"That won't do either," snaps Satan. "They believe Hell is real."

Devil number three says, "I'll tell them, with an indulgent smile, 'Don't sweat it! You have a lifetime to prepare. There's no need to hurry.'"

Satan howls with glee, saying, "Go! You are ready. You'll ruin thousands!"

February 6

Still Waiting

Preparations were made. The groom could come at any time; bridesmaids are waiting. Five of them are ready, the other five sit chatting before they dress. Suddenly the groom arrives, the five chatty ones are stunned. What happened to the time? It's gone. While they rush out seeking fuel for their lamps, the door closed. They miss the wedding. Dismay and tears follow. They simply waited too long to prepare. (Matthew 25:1-13)

We wait for something all our lives. Children wait for Christmas, teens for their driver's license. On we go, waiting for something, the wedding, the baby's arrival, a raise. Finally we wait for inevitable death.

After all these centuries, Lord, Christians are still waiting for Your return. Time moves slowly toward history's grand finale. But You're coming, sure as morning. We can't hurry that day. All we can do is follow Noah's example. He built the ark step by step while he had time. Five of the bridesmaids prepared while they had time.

When You come back, Lord, we must have certain things ready, for we can't rush out and buy them. We must build them within ourselves, and by Your instructions. The unprepared girls' pleading at the shop keeper's door made no difference. Time was gone. The door was locked.

Of course, if we don't believe You are coming back for us, we won't prepare. If we're not citizens of Your Kingdom, Lord, we can't go with You, for we can't buy citizenship, identity, or character. We must *build* them, with trust and faith, from habits formed and the choices made, while there is time. (II Corinthians)

February 7

God's Time Clock?
A paraphrase of Matthew 24

The disciples were admiring the beauty of the Temple. Jesus said it would soon become a heap of rubble. They asked, "When will this happen? Will this be a sign to alert us to Your second coming?"

Jesus replied, "The Temple's destruction is not the sign of the end. It is only the unfolding of history. Wars, threats of war, earthquakes and famines will come, but nothing will equal the birth pains earth must endure. Evil will increase, false teachers and preachers will stir up hatred of Believers. You will be hounded and persecuted because you carry My Name. The Christian faith of many will wither because of fear. Humanity as a whole will come to resemble wild dogs slashing one another for possession of a bone.

"During this period Believers will spread the Gospel to every nation and tribe. But when you see the 'Abomination of Desolation' in the Holy Place as described in Daniel, (let readers understand) go into hiding immediately. If you live in Judea run to the mountains. Don't pack. Just leave! There will be great distress, the worst since earth's beginning. But the Father has agreed to shorten this time of terror for the sake of Believers, lest humanity be wiped out. Beware of counterfeit Christs, for they will come performing miracles great enough to deceive even the faithful if possible. If someone says, 'Look, there He is,' don't believe him, for when HE comes ALL will see Him. The sun and moon will be darkened and the stars will fall from the sky. The solar system will be convulsed and rolled up like a scroll. (Isaiah 13:10 and 34:4) Then all will see the sign of the Son of Man filling the skies with His great power and blazing glory. The unredeemed will see it and mourn for these events can no longer be ignored. Angels will sound their trumpets to gather the elect from north to south, from east to west.

"Take a tip from the fig tree. * When the fig tree buds and sends out leaves, you know summer is near. When you see these things happening you may know the Son of Man is just outside the door. Earth and heavens will pass away, but My Words will not --- not ever!"

Some biblical Christians question whether or not the modern State of Israel's occupation of Israel is partial fulfillment of Old Testament promises concerning her. Romans 11 says branches from the "olive tree," God's Chosen People, Israel, were broken off so that branches from the "wild olive tree," the Gentiles, could be grafted in. "Israel as a nation has gone through a period of rejection of their Messiah until the full number of Gentiles has come into the Kingdom. And so all Israel will be saved." (11:25) Jews have a great future as God grafts them back onto the "olive tree" from which they had been broken. (Romans 11:1-36) Paul strongly emphasizes that Christians, through their faith in Messiah-Jesus, have been grafted into God's Israel.

* Note: The fig tree is a symbol of Israel. She 'budded out' in 1948 and was reborn as a nation as prophesied. Could Israel be God's Time Clock, ticking off another milestone toward the time for Christ's return?

February 8

Our Nourishing Lord

Times were hard for Israel under the reign of Ahab and Jezebel. The people worshipped Baal and killed the prophets of Jehovah wherever they were found. The land was gripped by drought with no relief in sight. (I Kings 16:29-19)

After Elijah's confrontation and victory on Mount Carmel over the priests of Baal he was physically and emotionally drained. Jezebel threatened to hunt him down and kill him. Fear sent him running to Mount Horeb where he dropped down in exhaustion. He said, "Lord! I've had enough! Let me die!" With that he fell asleep.

An angel woke him and said, "Get up and eat." Bread was baking on a hot stone, and there was a cruse of water. After eating he went back to sleep. Later the angel woke him and said, "The journey has been too strenuous for you. Wake up now and eat again." Elijah ate and was strengthened by the food. He went on with his journey.

Lord, You nourished Elijah in this unusual way because You had another task for him. You don't change. Neither do people. Today You are the same with us as You were with Elijah so many millennia ago. We grow discouraged, and feel as though we can't go on. But when You have a task for us, if we rely on You, You nourish us, giving us strength to finish the job.

Nevertheless spiritual anemia is everywhere, even in churches. Many of us are too undernourished spiritually to face life's troubles with equanimity. We don't realize that Scripture is vital for healthy souls. Some may be too starved to meditate, to chew, swallow and digest the Word. But Lord, You and Your Word *are* our spiritual food. You are always ready to help in our time of need when we ask, listen and obey.

February 9

A Morning Prayer, Psalm 5

Lord, hear my prayer. Listen to my thoughts.
Each morning I talk to You. Yes, each morning
    I put myself on Your altar
    and await Your answers.
Almighty God, I know You hate evil. There's no room
    in Your presence for sin. Godless people
    will not be able to lift their heads in Your court.
They will be crushed by Your righteousness.

It's only because I have experienced Your mercy
    that I dare to come before You in prayer.
I worship You with reverence, hope and anticipation.
Be my Shepherd, Lord, and guide me, otherwise my
    enemies will have me.
They flatter me, seeking to manipulate my thinking.
Their advice smells of moral decay as they
    set traps for my soul.
But Jehovah, God of all faithfulness,
    welcome those who put their trust in You.
Let joyful praise rise within them like a refreshing spring
    because they are kept by You.
Bless them, Lord, with the surrounding
    shield of Your love.

David had physical enemies. We may not, but we have
enemies of the soul and they can be vicious! Society reels from
them. They are within us, in our habits, desires, attitudes and
moods. We need, must have, Your help with them, Lord God.

February 10

The Book for All People

St. Paul asks, "... How can people believe in Jesus if they have never heard of Him? And how can they hear unless a preacher or teacher tells them? And how can anyone preach or teach unless others will send him?" (Romans 10:14-17)

Nate Saint, a pilot, and one of the five missionaries martyred in Ecuador, said in Quito before going into the jungle to take Christ to the Auca Indians, "During the war (World War II) we were taught that in order to obtain our objective we had to be willing to be expendable, and many lives were spent paying the price for our redemption from the bonds of political slavery. We know there is only one answer when our country demands that we share in the price of freedom, yet when the Lord Jesus asks us to pay the price for world evangelism, we often say we can't go. It costs too much. Missionaries constantly face being cut from the church budget."

Of the five who were sent to the savage Auca Indians, three of them were my classmates at Wheaton College. Before landing their plane among the Aucas, they circled overhead for several days, lowering gifts in a basket. On the last day, as the Indians removed the gifts, they sent up a beautiful parrot. The Americans considered the parrot a sign of welcome so they landed. All went well the first day but the next day three furious natives killed them with spears. That night Betty Elliot, the wife of one of the men wrote, "Nothing was more burning in Jim's heart than that Christ should be named among the Aucas."

All Christians are not called to go as missionaries, but all who believe in Christ's work are called to help through prayer and financial help. As it is written, "Blessed are those whose feet carry them to share the good news of God's Word."
(Romans 10:15 and Isaiah 52:7)

February 10

Note: Elizabeth Elliot, tells their full story in her book, *Through Gates of Splendor*. She and Rachel Saint, sister of Nate, the pilot, returned to the Aucas after Elizabeth's baby was born, to continue the work among their husband's killers. The three natives who cast the spears accepted Jesus' sacrifice. Their lives, and lives of many others in that remote South American jungle have been transformed through the tragedy of the men's death.

February 11

The God-breathed Book

Paul writes, "All Scripture is God-breathed and is given to teach, to correct and instruct us in righteousness so that we may be properly equipped to do God's work on Earth." (II Timothy 3:16)

Critics of Scripture hold that since the Bible was written by fallible people it too must be fallible. But God doesn't reflect His creation. It is we who are to be changed in order to reflect Him.

If Paul is correct that the Holy Spirit breathed His words into imperfect people whom God Himself trusted and chose to proclaim His Truth accurately, then with God's power, the imperfect ones surely could do it. Mary was not perfect, she was human, yet God chose her to be the mother of Jesus, God's human but perfect Son.

God the Holy Spirit didn't dictate His message word for word to prophets and apostles as a business executive would. His Spirit inspired, or "breathed," His thoughts into them. The result is God's inspired Word, written down by human beings.

Scripture continues to be tested for reliability. Those who believe it and want to live by it continue to learn that God's Word can be trusted. As we fulfill the conditions God keeps His promises.

Most believers aren't scholars and certain passages are difficult to understand. We may question the Word, but we must also let the Word question us. Keep the words, and the Holy Spirit, in mind and heart, for God is all truth and He will lead and teach us.

God's "breathing into" His people began at creation. "The Lord God formed man from the dust of the ground and breathed His breath of life into man and he became a human being," so let's remember as we read what He breathed into prophets and apostles long ago, that God is breathing His words into our hearts and minds today. Lord, open our understanding.

February 12

Our Reminding Lord

Lord, I'm in trouble again. Thanks for reminding me of it. I have turned this attitude over to You. The trouble is I keep taking it back.

I have an attitude of irritation toward another Christian. From my point of view, I'm being nagged, manipulated, and pushed. I believe he thinks his motives are pure, and maybe they are. But what an iron fist! All he asks of me is that I think like he does, do what he does, be his disciple. I just want to be *Your* disciple, Lord.

Since You, Almighty God, are looking directly and clearly into both of our minds and souls, I'm asking that I may see as You see in this matter. I believe You see the two of us whom You love and You see at least one of us as being at odds with the other. Perhaps You see him as a well meaning but tactless son who has no idea that he constantly offends both me and my family. If this is so, he is surely more innocent than I, who have a spirit of resentment toward him. Forgive me, Father. Let Your peace rule in my heart.

I'm thinking that I, as a fellow Christian, should tell him that his approach stirs up my resentment. I must tell him I've asked You to forgive me and I want him to forgive me for nursing my irritation. I believe I owe him that, don't You? Now that I've poured this out to You, my foolish feelings are soothed, I can speak with love.

Peter calls us "living stones" which You use to build Your eternal home. Since we're all different, we must be trimmed and shaped by You and by each other to fit side by side in our particular places in Your "eternal building not made by hands."

Lord, forgive and purge me of ugliness before they come today. Breath Yourself into me, Breath of God. Breathe love, forgiveness and wisdom into me so we may share Your peace.

February 13

We're Under Construction

God says, "Look, I'm laying a reliable stone in Zion as the Cornerstone of My Church." (I Peter 2:6)

Lord, *You* are the Foundation of the Church You are building. It's a structure not built by people but *of* people. As strange as it may seem, *we* are Your building material. We're flimsy stuff to use in a structure which is to last forever. Yet Peter urges us to come to You, the Foundation Stone. He calls us *living stones*. As we look about us at other human stones, totally diverse in size and shape, each with individual quirks and prejudices, we wonder how, Lord, will You ever fit us together into a building of praise to Yourself?

A mental image begins to emerge from Peter's words of a building site, cleared and bulldozed. Great yellow earth-movers fill their scoops with stones, diverse stones. As the giant machines move, the stones bump, jostle and grind against one another, the scoop is tipped and the stones tumble out with a crashing roar, amid clouds of dust and chips of rock.

Lord is that what happens to us as we move together through life, grinding and bumping against one another? Do You use, among Your other shaping tools, the personalities of people we may love or dislike to knock off some of our more ill fitting, rough edges? Any part of creation can be used as tools for Your purposes. We know You make changes in us through Your Word, through circumstances, through Your Spirit living in us, guiding, correcting and encouraging us, but have You given us these fellow stones to ride in life's scoop with us, each personality knocking against the rough edges of others, to smooth and shape us into a size and shape for Your great and eternal "building?"

February 13

"Now to you who rely on Him, this stone is precious. But
to those who do not believe,
      The Stone the builder rejected
      has become the Cornerstone.
      He is the Stone that causes
      people to stumble and a Rock
which makes them fall. They fall
      under Him because they neither
      believe in Him nor obey Him."
      (I Peter 2:7, Psalm 118:22, Isaiah 28:16)

Dear Builder, I seek to fit into my place in Your Building.
Smooth out my rough places as I ride through life near anyone who
may rub me the wrong way. May love and forgiveness be the
cement which fixes me to my fellow stones.

February 14

The Sure Foundation

Lord, You are my steadfast Rock. Immovable. Secure.
You are the base to build upon, the one Foundation sure.

Age upon age comes and goes but You remain the same.
Nations ebb and flow as tides, heedless of Your Name.
But You are here, the very One who called worlds to be.

Seasons turn as kingdoms fall on the catalyst called *Time*.
Men curse You, men praise and die with their decision.

Oh, Changeless God, may I realize that frail though I am,
with You as my foundation, no wind can fell,
nor waters flood the life which is built on You.

F.N.

I've much to learn, Lord, about my relationship to You. If I can get it right with you, other difficulties come straight. Help me listen to Your voice as I build decisions, attitudes and relationships. The world's voice clamors loudly. If I heed it, Yours grows silent. This life is like a shopping cart in which we put the building materials of faith, love and character. Guide me in my choice of materials. Then Lord, please supervise my method of construction.

February 15

A Parable in a Fur Coat

Lord, You have given innumerable lovely, small blessings, that I often forget to delight in. I merely enjoy them, thinking of them as nice. That's especially true after I've been marveling on the enormous truths of Scripture, such as redemption, Your love and eternal life. I'm thinking of how nicely this cold day and a warm puppy compliment one another. Scrappy Nash, a wondrous bit of creation in herself, is ever on the alert, waiting for my daily visit with You, Lord. It's her opportunity to sit on my lap and take an early morning nap. When she sees me heading for my "prayer chair," Bible and notebook in hand, she knows it's lap time. She becomes my book rest and our respective circulatory systems keep each other warm.

I've thanked You daily for my time with You Lord, but I don't remember ever thanking You for making this dear little Scotty whom I love and enjoy. She daily demonstrates spiritual lessons. She's a teacher without words but her actions speak volumes.

By watching Scrappy
I see expectation, hope,
patience, trust, and
unconditional love
in action every day.
She is an unwritten
parable, not in a book
but in a black fur coat.

Lord, thank You for the gift of this small bit of life and loyalty, and please, Lord, remind me to learn daily from my humble little friend. Amen

February 16

Rest and Restoration

Father, I'm reaching out to You today. Be my quietness and confidence. I'm tired, achy, and discouraged. I feel alone in this battle. Good attitudes seem to have been eroded by the wash of circumstances. I've been slow in turning them over to You for cleansing and reshaping. Won't I ever learn?

Lord, You already know all this, but let me grumble quietly in Your Presence for a moment. You know, from experience in Your earth life, that even though feelings are unreliable and changeable, they have powerful influence on us. You know how things are with us because You have been where we are and have been tempted from all directions as we have. You came here as Son of Man and lived the mental, psychological and physical experiences of humanity. And wonder of wonders, Your humanity was not set aside at the resurrection or ascension.

Forgive me and restore to me the joy of Your salvation. (Psalm 51:12)

Quiet and renew my soul. Give me rest. (Psalm 23) Lord, breathe into this limp, dishrag person the joyful, yet down to earth realization of just who You are. It's in Your strong Name, Jehovah-Jesus, that I exhale my perfidious feelings and breathe in Your living Presence. You are my true place of rest, my Companion in this disturbance, my Strength, Joy and Peace. You are the Bread of Life, nourishing and fresh everyday. You are my Master and Lord, cleansing and refreshing, Living Water, cooling my fevered fears. "You satisfy my inner being with good things so that my strength is renewed like the eagles'." (Psalm 103:3-5) You have promised, "My Presence will go with you and I will give you peace of mind." (Exodus 33:14)

Thank You, Father. It's no wonder I love You. I do.

February 17

Our Caring Lord, John 9

The blind man whom Jesus healed in the Temple was being grilled by the Pharisees. His defence of the Lord made the Pharisees so angry they excommunicated him from the Temple. When Jesus heard about it, He went searching for the man and found him outside. How very like You, Lord, to go out seeking Your own. As always, You are true to character, the Shepherd of psalm and parable, seeking and finding a specific individual. You didn't leave the excommunicated one in dismay at being cut off from both Temple and God. To excommunicate means God doesn't want you any more. You are cut loose from your anchor to drift unwanted and dreary until death catches up with you.

That's not Your way, Lord. You don't excommunicate anyone until his or her final decision is made.

The healed man defended You, Lord, before the Pharisees, calling You "a good man" who did what no other could do, heal blind eyes. The Pharisee's questions plus the man's own answers led him to realize You, Jesus, were more than just a good man and a prophet. You were showing him Your true self as his Messiah, Son of the Living God and only Savior.

Throughout this story, Lord, two shining facets of Your character come through. You came from God into enemy territory to be our Savior, and now You seek us out individually and tell us so.

February 18

An Evening Prayer, Psalm 4

Lord! I need Your help! You've cleared a path for me
    before, when I was in trouble. Please do it again!

And you rebels, you listen too.
How long will you shake your fist at God?
How long will you offend Him with hypocrisy?
Your God is not the One True God, Jehovah. Your gods
    are multiple.
Their names are Greed, Lust and Power.

The redeemed are close to God's heart and He
    chooses and blesses them.
He is an awesome Helper. Call on Him.
He can hear. Let your heart be still as you meditate
    on Him before sleeping. Call Him and offer
    the sacrifice of obedience.

Today some say, "God doesn't care about us."
But Lord, when they call on You, prove them wrong
    by illuminating their darkness.
You certainly fill me with more joy and gladness
    than when funds yield interest or my stocks split.
I know I am safe with You even in unsafe times.

I know, also from experience, that I can lie down at
    night with peace in my heart and sleep,
    because You alone, Lord, are my security.

February 19

Reconciliation

"Mercy and truth are reconciled. Righteousness and peace have embraced." (Psalm 85:10)

All four of these attributes belong to You, Lord. Why do they need to meet and embrace like people who had a falling out and have finally become reconciled? A possibility begins to dawn.

Your truth is eternal, immutable and unalterable. If truth stood alone without the mitigation of mercy it would thunder out at us, "You, O man, O woman, are transgressors of God's Law! I pronounce you guilty!" But Your persistent mercy, pursuing grace, and love, answers with equal power, "That's true, you are a law breaker! But, O man, O woman, I have provided the righteous Way for you to be pardoned if you will take it for yourself."

If You were only truth, Lord, our death sentence would be irrevocable for we *are* guilty. Evidence is against us. The spotlight of truth would illuminate every fault of thought, word and deed. Our situation would be impossible.

If You could ignore Your truth and justice to govern us only with mercy, wouldn't we be too selfish and soft for the combat of life? Wouldn't we think that whatever we did would be acceptable to our over indulgent Lord? The balance between Your truth and mercy is another of Your miracles, Father. No violator of Your truth escapes unscathed. We all violate it. But on the cross, Lord, Your hard, unbreakable truth has met with Your tender, eternal mercy. The two are reconciled in the cross. The cross provides the abundant solution for our forgiveness, salvation and transformation.

Yes Lord, You are our demanding Judge and we must appear in Your Court of Justice. But our stern Judge is also our merciful Farther who because we do not have the wherewithal to pay the fine demanded by Your law, You pay it Yourself.

February 20

Chicken or Egg?

It's a joy, Lord, to be here in the warmth of Your Presence. I feel a bit like the tiny crocus might feel, if it *could* feel, as it pushes up through the snow, reaching for what it must have -- light and air. I too am pushing up through a layer of life, for I must learn to listen and understand. My desire is to be obedient to Your Word, to love and trust You more. It's not hard to love You, Lord, because You love me so much. Obedience, however, is much harder because I love ME so much.

Lord, which comes first, obedience or love? Which is more important? Love of You should generate obedience, while obeying You proclaims love. Surely they interact as twin necessities, similar to the silly question of the chicken and egg.

The Prophet Samuel says, "Do you think the Lord takes as much pleasure in gifts and sacrifices as He does in your obedience? He is far more concerned that you listen and obey Him than that you bring Him gifts. Disobedience, rebellion against His Word, is as bad as witchcraft and stubbornness as idol worship." (I Samuel 15:23)

These words are plain, and scary. Your words concerning Your love are a challenge, but also a comfort. "Because you love Me, I will rescue and encourage you. Because you trust Me, I will be with you in trouble. I will show you My salvation for you acknowledge My Name." (Psalm 91:14-16)

Lord, love for You swings the life increasingly toward obedience. You must create this in me for I am not able. I must be willing for You to make the necessary changes in my life. My obedience to You is proportionate to the degree of my love. Love of God without obedience is more a pose than a reality. Help me, Lord.

February 21

The Burden is Lifted, Psalm 32

David tried to hide his sin, thinking it would blow over. But it didn't. Finally in desperation he repented and asked God to forgive him.

Lord, what a relief it is to be forgiven, to have that
  burden lifted! When I tried to hide my sin,
  I was sick inside.
Sin is unbearable until it's confessed.
As long as I kept silent I was miserable.
Even my bones ached because Your Spirit within me
  was heavy, pressing me down,
  leaving weakness no rest could remedy.
But with confession and repentance came healing.

I came to You and said, "Lord, I must confess
  this to You. I won't hide it any longer.
I have sinned against You. Forgive me."
At that point, Lord, You forgave and cleansed me.
Whoever trusts You must ask You to forgive him.
It's then You reveal Your loving mercy to him
  in forgiveness.
All the floods of evil cannot drown him.

You are my confidence and salvation. You restore me
  and clear my conscience from distress.
I am surrounded by victory music as You tell my clean
  washed soul, "I want to counsel and protect you
  but don't be like a stubborn mule
  or a bucking horse.
They have no understanding of their master's plan.
Their kicking and charging must be controlled by bit

and bridle. You would not want that. So let Me lead you."

Lord, it's true that life's troubles wash over us
    in wave after wave. And those who defy You
    are beaten and crushed by the waves
    but those who trust You will be set
    on their feet again and blessed by You.
So come! Let's celebrate the Lord! Let's dance
    and be joyful. Let's make the heavens ring!
Let those who seek Him rejoice and overflow
    with songs of hope and deliverance!

February 22

God's Address

"....you yourselves are the home of the living God and He says it this way: 'I will live in them and move through them. I will be their God and they will be My people. So separate yourselves from compromise and corruption and I will welcome you as My sons and daughters.'" (I Corinthians 3:16, 6:19, II Corinthians 6:16)

When Your Holy Spirit lives in us, we become Your family, Your children. We are the residence of Almighty God. In a sense we are Your address!

If I were caretaker of the home of a king, I would be careful how I tended the property. Trash and cobwebs wouldn't be tolerated. It would be clean, fresh, repaired to please the king.

Yet this body of mine, this small clay pot in which the living God dwells, is often neglected or abused. The rubbish of resentment is allowed to accumulate on occasions. Some days debris from complicated relationships piles up, and is shoved into dark corners. Cobwebs of selfishness clog the windows of the soul. At times I overstuff this dwelling place with unwholesome thoughts. On other occasions I starve it by denying it spiritual nourishment.

Lord, since I'm Yours and You live in me, help me remember this body, mind and heart are Your property. Your house, Your Temple and creation. It's the earthenware container of the treasure of Your Spirit. Continue to instruct me, Lord, on the finer points of housekeeping, loyalty and obedience, so I may present my everyday life and living to You as an offering which You find pleasing.

February 23

He Talks With Me,
an exchange between a daughter and her Father

"God have mercy!" she cries in helplessness.
"My mercy is current and everlasting," He replies. (Psalm 107:1)

"Show me the way to love this difficult person," she pleads.
"I am the way to Love. Stay close to Me, Little One," says the
Father. (John 14:6, I John 4:8)

"I need wisdom for this tangled problem," she confides.
"Reverence of Me is Wisdom's beginning," He says.
 (Proverbs 1:7)

"I find no joy in this situation. I'm tired," complains the daughter.
"I am your joy and strength. Rejoice in Me," advises the Father.
(Nehemiah 8:10, Isaiah 12:2-3)

"My soul is as dry as a desert," grumbles the daughter.
"I am within you, an artesian well of Living Water, ever flowing to
refresh you. Drink deeply of Me," He reminds her. (John 4:10)

"My heart is a restless vagabond. Peace eludes me as a shadow,"
laments the daughter.
"Peace is part of My gift to you. Seek and pursue it. Catch and
hold it. It's there for you," comforts the Father. "I will give you
My peace as your mind is stayed on Me."
(Psalm 34:14, Isaiah 26:3)

"Father, sleep evades me because of these circumstances,"
murmurs the daughter.
"Don't be afraid," advises the Father, "trust Me with
circumstances. Lie down in peace and sleep. Only I keep you in
safety." (Psalm 4:8)

February 24

The Creator can be Known, Colossians 1:15-17

Paul would not have chosen to be imprisoned by Rome. But the choice wasn't his. It was Yours, Lord. You chose him to write letters which would circle the globe in perpetuity, teaching and blessing people to this very day. Paul's motto was, "For me to live is Christ," so when he was put in prison to stop his preaching, he found another way to teach. He proclaimed You through his letters.

Gnosticism had begun creeping into the church. It held that matter was evil therefore God was not the Creator. A lesser being, hostile to God, created matter. Only spirit is good, therefore God, who is Spirit had no interest in the world. Gnostics believed Christ had no material body therefore the crucifixion was an illusion.

Paul strongly refuted this heresy. He wrote, "Christ is the perfect image of the invisible God, the first born of all creation." By using the term *first born of all creation*, Paul did not mean that Jesus was the first person ever born. He was emphasizing that society of his day considered the first born son in each family to hold the highest position of all the sons. The Jews and Greeks honored the first born son in this way. It is also a title used in Psalm 89:27 concerning Messiah. "I (God) will make Him (Messiah) My first born, higher than earthly kings."

Paul says it is through the Son that all things were created. You, Lord Jesus, are not a lesser God at all but the Father's first and only Son.

All things were created by and for You. And You are before all things. "In Him (Jesus) all things hold together," things like atoms and galaxies. Natural laws which give order instead of chaos are expressions of Your mind. Laws of science, gravity, reproduction, seasons, as well as spiritual laws are Your creations as well as Your obedient servants.

February 25

Something is Missing

Lord God, help, my soul is closed up tight! I can't seem to open it to You. All kinds of temporal thoughts are holding the door closed against You. They shout and push, jamming strong shoulders against it, demanding with voices like trumpets.

The last few days I've been distracted by this almost frenzy to get on with my current project. It has happened before. But why does it pounce on me most often during my "quiet time" with You? I still follow the usual before breakfast routine. Wash face and hands, make bed, dress, go to my "quiet place" taking a cup of Bill's steaming coffee and the Scriptures. Everything is apparently the same, but nothing is the same. Something's missing. What is it? There's no deep fellowship with You, Lord, no lifting praise, or sense of peace. There's not even a song in my heart. Why? Have You given up on me? Don't You love me anymore?

At last He breathes words into my mind, "Yes, Small One, I love you with perfect love, with love you can't imagine. I am here. You aren't. Your body is here. My Word is open in your lap but your heart is closed. You're just going through the motions. Quiet time is a good habit to form but it must be steeped in reality or it is a charade, like this one today.

"Set aside those plans tumbling through your mind like dry leaves in a gale. Be honest. Quiet down. Breathe in My peace. Breathe out your anxiety. Remember My Name? It is *Emmanuel,* God with us. If you want to hear Me, know Me, and be with Me, you will put Me first. And My Holy Spirit will come along side of you to help if you ask. When He does you must listen. Today you were neither asking nor listening."

I ask You to come along side me, Spirit of God, and be my helper. And, *Lord, I'm listening.*

February 26

Today's Needs

Lord of grace, I seek You here
    among the chores of this day's needs.
I ask to walk these hours through
    and not to faint along the way.
I seek to run to do Your will
    and not grow weary with the task.

Wings of eagles lift me up
    as I await Your time.
By Your Spirit I sense Your strength,
    and spread my wings in Jesus' Name.
You are to me all joy and truth,
    the sound of music strong with peace.

I hail You now, my Lord and King,
    my true Companion
    in this day's needs.
                F.N.

What a lovely discovery! Joyful praise lifts burdens. They may be physical, like weariness, or mental / spiritual, like worry or doubt. This song came as I vacuumed the living room preparing for coming guests.

February 27

God's Mercy, Psalm 145

O Lord, my God and my King, I lift Your Name
   in praise from now into eternity!
I will bless You, day in and day out,
   as long as I have life.

No one is like You, Lord. Your magnificence
   is past comprehension. Yet we see it daily,
   on earth, in sky and sea.

Each generation teaches the next of Your awesome
   acts, Your majesty and power.
Daily I meditate on Your Word; it permeates me,
   becoming my spiritual strength.

All who love and obey You will remember
   Your goodness and Your many deeds.
They will rejoice in Your everlasting righteousness.
O Lord, You are gracious to us, and forgiving.

You give us endless opportunities and treat
   our foolish bumbling with mercy and patience.
As great as Your acts of creation and rescue are,
   Lord, Your mercy surpasses them all.

Creation throbs with praise of Your Name. God's people
   add joyful hosannas to the songs of nature.
Your eternal plan permeates centuries,
   shaping human history.
We remind one another of Your intimate works
   which mold our individual characters.

February 27

The heedless ones, godless ones, the ones who
    have no understanding of reality,
    have no place in Your Kingdom.

Merciful Father, when we fall, You lift us up,
    dust us off and set us once again
    on our feet of clay.
You nourish us, body and soul,
    from Your inexhaustible bounty.

Your ways are just and faithful, Lord.
You stand with those who call You without shame.
You listen for the call of those who love You,
    saving all who heed Your words.

I will tell this with my pen and with my voice.
As long as I have breath, I will bless
    and praise the matchless Name of *Jehovah!*

February 28

Right Now is Special

"God has said, 'I will never leave you or forsake you,' so I may confidently say, 'My Helper is the Lord. I need not be afraid.'" (Deuteronomy 31:6, Hebrews 13:5-6)

This is something we must be conscious of daily, for thoughts are flighty things. They can get off track as quickly as lightning can strike. We tend to hear what we fear. Discouraging news is rampant these days, nationally, internationally and often personally. It's strengthening and stabilizing to read Your words again, "I will never leave you; I am your helper," for when we listen to Your promise rather than the frightening multitude of words about us, we can boldly say, "...because of His promise, I won't be afraid."

When I first came to love You Lord, so many years ago, I thought You were surely going to do some special things with me. But as I've continued to grow up in You, I've come to realize what You are doing *right now* is special. You have used, and are still using, all life's events, smooth or rough, healthful or painful, sad or happy to shape and teach me. That's Your purpose, isn't it, Lord, to make each of Your people into a new person according to Your pattern for us? If we are willing, if we ask, You will do it. Some of the teaching and shaping has been difficult. Some has not. But it's *all* been good. The best part is in knowing You will not leave us. You never give up on us; for You are our great, generous Helper. It is reassuring to count on the fact that Your promise is backing us up, Your Holy Spirit is within us and Your plans are ahead of us, reminding us that we are surrounded by our God. Therefore I never need to be afraid.

As we remember this, Your strength comes through in surprising ways. Thank You!

February 29

Our Hearing Lord

Lord, when You say *no*, or *wait* to our prayer requests we sometimes think You didn't hear us, or we don't interest You. Or perhaps it's the Tempter whispering, "He's not really there, you know." But Scripture reports Your hearing is acute:

"God Himself invented the ear; do you think He can't hear? Does He who designed the intricate eye not see?"   Psalm 94:9

"The Lord's arm is never too short to reach you, neither are His ears stopped up so He cannot hear. Rather, it's your sins that have separated you from Him."   Isaiah 59:1-2

"I called out to God in distress and He heard me. My cry went straight to His ears."   Psalm 18:6

"I sought the Lord. He heard and. delivered me ... for His eye is on His people and His ears listen for their prayers."
Psalm 34:4

"I love the Lord because He has heard my prayer. Because He leaned down to hear me, I have confidence to call on Him all my life."   **Psalm 116:1-2**

"This is our confidence in Him, if we ask anything *according to His will* He hears us."   I John 5:15

"Trust God's hearing and His guidance. Listen and you will hear His voice behind you saying, 'Here's the way, walk in it.'"   Isaiah 30:21

March 1

Lion and Lamb

The lion of March
    is on the prowl
    roaring through
    the skies.
He moans and cries,
    growls and sobs,
    expressing man's
    inner hunger.
At last he's weary,
    his fierce breath
    fading to a
    gentler breeze.

The lamb steps in
    to welcome spring
    around the corner.
Spring thaws the ground,
    renews the soul,
    drops down
    crystal showers.
Hearts are lifted,
    days grow brighter,
    sensing new life
    unfolding.
                F.N.

March 2

Don't Fret, Trust, Psalm 37

My people, don't be upset because of what the ungodly do.
Their success soon withers like blossoms in the sun.
    Trust God. Stick to Him like glue.
Live faithfully where He plants you; take pleasure in His will
        and He will give you what you need most -- Himself.

A lifetime of trusting commitment to Him will cause your faith
        to shine as the sun and your decision will please Him.
Wait for God's timing; and rest in His faithfulness.
Fidgeting when schemers prosper is useless,
        so is anger. Anger only leads to trouble.
Troublemakers deceive and plot against God's people,
        but the Lord laughs at them. Their self-esteem is a joke.

It's better to forego riches than to miss experiencing His love.
Nothing compares with the adventure of being God's child.
Success of the wicked is merely show and vapor,
        but godly inheritance is solid substance.

God's enemies are seen for the moment but soon gone,
        like smoke in the breeze.
They enjoy borrowing but not repaying. Generosity pleases God.
He lights their path and delights in their way;
        when they fall, He lifts them up.

In all my years I've not seen those who trust
        the Lord forsaken. So get away from evil quickly.

Do as much God directed good as you can
and you will have Life forever.

March 2

God loves justice and never forsakes His own, He engraves
His law on their hearts. Jehovah will not
abandon them to the Enemy's grasp.

Wait for Him in trust for He is your Savior. When trouble
comes, remember He is your strength.

He delivers you from the Evil One because you trust Him.
Yes! He is trustworthy. Take refuge in Him.

March 3

The Covenant of Faith

Lord, You are God of the Covenant, God of kept promises. From cover to cover Scripture tells of Your covenants with individuals and nations.

Webster defines covenant as: "(a) a formal, solemn and binding agreement, (b) a written agreement of promise usually under seal between two or more parties especially for performance of some action."

God made a covenant with Abraham saying, "I am Almighty God. Live your life in obedience to Me and I will establish a covenant between us. I will make a great nation of you and your descendants." God told Abraham to leave his home and go to a land He would show him. He obeyed and when he reached the land, God promised the land to his descendants forever. Before Isaac was born God renewed the promise and strengthened Abraham's faith. Then step by step God led him until his faith solidified into obedience for the dreadfully hard test of sacrificing Isaac. (Genesis 17: 12 & 22)

Romans 4 tells us of Abraham's faith. He didn't doubt Your promises, Lord. By acting upon them, he moved from strength to strength, believing and praising You for the yet unfulfilled promises which he knew would be coming. By Your grace and teaching, Father, he became absolutely convinced that what You promised You would bring about.

I want to grow in faith, Lord, but I'm learning it's no bed of roses. You often ask us to leave our "land," our pre-Christian way of living and thinking, to go live in the land of Your promises. You ask for changes in our inner self, and as we obey, You work through the open door of our obedience, forming an even more pervasive faith within us, just as You did with Abraham.

We could liken faith to muscles used in any skill or sport. Regular exercise gradually strengthens muscles so we may run faster and longer. Similarly, exercising faith, not doubt, builds stronger, more confident faith.

Lord, Your faithfulness has not changed in all these millennia. When we today believe and trust Your promises enough to act on them, we can rest assured that You will follow up and our faith will be strengthened.

March 4

David's Pain: a Prophecy of Messiah, Psalm 22

This psalm was written by David when he was in desperate
straits, yet it leads beyond anything David experienced. His hands
and feet were never pierced and no one gambled for his clothing.
He vented his pain and dismay, and in doing so he prophesied of
the Coming One, the Suffering Servant of Isaiah 53 and John 19.

My God! My God! Why have You forsaken me?
Why don't You help me?
I call for Your help day and night.
You lived in the midst of my forefathers' praise,
        and You rescued them
        when they called for Your help.

I too am a man, Lord, yet these people think I'm a worm,
        a reproach, something to be despised. They circle
        me and smirk. They shake their heads and say,
"All right, He's been bragging about God as his deliverer.
Let's watch and see if He will get him out of this mess!"

Lord! You brought me to birth and laid me on my mother's
        breast. As a child You honored me for my faith.
Don't leave me now. I have no help but You.
They watch like lions, salivating over red meat.

I'm as weak as poured out water.
My bones are dislocated; my courage and strength
        have melted within me.
I hang like a wet rag. My tongue is so dry
        it sticks to my teeth.
They circle me like wild dogs, watching,
        snarling, mocking.

March 4

They have pierced my hands and feet.

They divide my clothes among them
    and roll dice for my robe.

Save me, Lord, so I may live to praise You,
    to proclaim Your Name to all people.
Your sons and daughters will glorify You,
    for You do not forsake us.
My praise will ring aloud as I carry out
    my vows to Your people.

The humble shall be satisfied and the
    strong shall worship.
Nations will yet be filled with joy,
    as they remember God and adore Him.
They will recognize Him as the True
    and Eternal King.
They will kneel before Him.
Children of generations not yet born
    will bow low before Him
    in joyful, continuous and exultant praise!

March 5

Making of a Soldier

The church at Ephesus was young, struggling and small. Its communicants were an unlikely mix of Roman and Greek pagans recently converted to Christ. Some were slave, some free, very few were wealthy. There were also Roman soldiers, religious Jews and proselytes. Their only bond was their faith in the risen Christ.

Paul sees the vulnerability of this incompatible group trying to survive Rome's hatred and persecution. Old prejudices must be changed. Hearts must be melted and reshaped for the situation is a tinder box which Satan is working to ignite.

Paul compares the military equipment of his two Roman guards to what God gives His people. Earnest Christians are, in a very real sense, soldiers; therefore Paul warns us to prepare for the battle ahead. He writes the Church at Ephesus, "Your strength must come from the Lord's mighty power within you, not from your own strength. You can't win the battle without Him, so win with Him. Put on all of God's provided armor so you can survive the diverse strategies and sneak attacks of Satan. Remember our struggle is not against flesh and blood people but against non-material beings, rulers of the unseen world, against vast swarms of evil spirits of Satan's kingdom." (Ephesians 6:12-18)

Paul considers the soldier's sturdy belt. When buckled securely it encircles him. It holds his weapons, keeping them close at hand. Paul sees the belt as God's absolute and unchanging Truth. God's Truth encircles the Christian, his plans, relationships and his living. It holds the sword, the Word of God close, always ready for use, to guide, protect and teach.

March 6

Fitted for Battle

On the first reading of Ephesians 6 we may think it doesn't apply to our current age but all we need do is remember past experiences in order to see the commonplace foes we must fight. This very day three old, familiar enemies of my soul are harassing me: Discouragement, Fear and Doubt, a deadly trio, lurking, circling, and waiting for their opportunity to strike.

Is it just a natural human mood, just a vulnerable spot in my personality? Well, perhaps. But Lord, Your arch enemy knows me and if I'm not watchful he will wreak havoc with my weaknesses. As the Old Testament puts it, he will plow up my soul with my own oxen.

Paul sees his prison guard's belt as representing the Christian's most basic need -- to *know* God's Truth. Our plans and actions are based on what we believe is true. Today God's Truth is under fierce attack. It's being drowned in lies, half-truths, and by the discard of Christian belief and morals.

The belt doesn't stand alone. God's armor includes the breastplate, sturdy sandals, shield, helmet and sword. To be fully protected we must use each provision.

Your righteousness, Lord, is our breastplate protecting the heart, the seat of all human emotion. Solomon tells us, "Guard your heart, your affections, carefully, for it governs your life." (Proverbs 4:23) True faith and love come from the heart and direct our goals.

Paul studies the guard's heavy leather sandals and tells us to lace them securely. For the Christian soldier the sandals, knowledge of God's Word, protect the soldier from falling in rough terrain, keep him balanced and moving in the right direction.

For the good news of the Gospel to do its work in us, we must know we can't win the battle alone. We must have and use all Your provisions, Lord. When we go into battle we will be hit by

the enemy's arrows. Satan can make arrows from almost anything.
He uses thoughts, perceptions, moods and our wants to lead us into temptation. We must have a shield. Therefore, Lord, You have provided one. It's up to us to use it.

The Roman battle shield was made of wood, covered with leather and soaked in water before battle. The wet leather often quenched the fire of the enemy's burning arrows. The Christian's shield is his faith in our faithful God.

"Faith comes through hearing God's Word." (Romans 10:17) Since faith is living, it must be nourished like all living things in order to live and grow. The written Word, the Living Word and the Holy Spirit are nourishing foods of faith.

Lord, as I study, pray and read continue to open my understanding for I do believe. Help my unbelief!

March 7

Provision for Protection

Truly Lord, You provide us with absolute truth. You protect our hearts with Your own righteousness. Our "sandals" keep us on the right path. Your Word and our faith are our shield.

The mind, the battleground for our souls, is protected by the Helmet of Salvation. Ideas and plans are born and develop in the mind. Imagination, like wind, may move anywhere. Thoughts can be instant. Holy or evil, right or wrong, they flash in the mind like unexpected lightening bolts. Don't we ask ourselves at times, "Now where did *that* come from?"

Salvation is a strong deterrent against having unwanted thoughts take root in our minds. As we open our minds and hearts to You, Lord, drawing You in, Your Spirit is born in us and we are born again, as You told Nicodemus he must be. If we want to grow it's at this point that salvation begins to cost us something. It costs dedication to new citizenship, new loves and goals – loyalty to a new Master .

God supplies us with two offensive weapons. One He calls the Sword of the Word of God. "The Word of God is alive and active. It's sharper than any material sword for it cuts between the soul and the spirit, the bone and marrow. It clearly shows us the intentions of our own hearts. Nothing is hidden from God's sight. All cover is removed. Everything is laid bare before Him with whom we must settle our account." (Hebrews 4:12-13)

God's Word is like a laser beam. It can do delicate surgery within us, successfully cutting away malignancies of mind and soul. It can mend deep gashes or replace stiff scar tissue from old wounds with healthy flesh. It lifts low spirits, restoring enthusiasm.

Lord, if *You* needed and used the Sword of the Spirit to overcome Satan, how can we frail creatures, created from the dust

March 7

of the earth who crumpled before the Tempter's power, even hope to survive Satan's traps without the mighty Sword?

You provide another weapon for Your soldiers. Paul calls it *prayer*. Father, we talk to You through prayer; and You talk to us through Your written Word and the Holy Spirit who is within us.

I ask You, Lord, to bring these last two powerful provisions together in my life and the lives of Your people everywhere.

March 8

The Wedding Dress, I

Yes, my wedding dress has walked down the aisle seven times, with seven brides. In 1949 I was the first. After that came friends and finally daughters. Originally the dress was sleeveless ivory satin with matching jacket. The bride before our daughters shortened it two inches. My daughter, Kakie, wanted to wear it for her wedding, but she wanted me to remake the bodice, cut up the jacket and sleeves. My sewing skills were sufficient for family needs, but for this job, with no pattern, they were totally inadequate. Since dry cleaning didn't remove the mark of the alteration, I plunged it into a tub of hot soapy water, saying, "Okay, dress, you have a choice. You can come through this ordeal like a trooper, live to walk the aisle again, or you can retire to the attic." With a final, "Help me, Lord!" I pushed it under the suds. It came through its scrubbing undamaged, but the fold line remained.

I had the well preserved, handmade lace veil of my great grandmother, Nancy, who had purchased it in Paris for her wedding in 1865. Lace from her gown was usable to appliqué over the dark fold line at the hem.

Somewhat to my own amusement, I prayed earnestly about the dress project. *Doubt* immediately spoke up, "You silly little fool! God doesn't listen to prayers like that!" *Faith* replied, "Yes, He does! He's our loving Father, and like good earthly fathers, He enjoys giving gifts to His children. And in the midst of this project maybe, just maybe, He will teach me more about Himself."

Each piece fit together slowly but smoothly. No rip-outs necessary. Both dress and bride were beautiful and elegant. It was a gift from my Father in Heaven. With the gift came the assurance that nothing is too small for His love and nothing is too large for His power.

March 9

In Blue Tissue Paper, II

The dress and I had another adventure. Laurie and Bill were to be married two years later. I was delighted when Laurie said she'd like to wear the dress and veil. It fit perfectly. But, there was a problem. It was December; the sleeves had been used in remodeling. And I had no fabric to make them.

After taking the lack to my Father in Heaven, I began the long search for fabric. Nothing I found came close. What to do? Yes. Pray and wait.

Doubt agreed with the results of my fruitless search, "There's no fabric or lace in Jacksonville which will do. Just give it up." *Faith* said, "No. My Father knows every inch of the cosmos, knows where each atom spins and He can certainly solve my wedding dress problem."

I continued working until all was finished except the sleeves. I awoke the next morning haunted by an undefined memory -- something about blue paper and *cedar chest*. I began emptying it, layer by layer. There on the bottom lay a nine inch flat package wrapped in blue tissue paper. Clear memory flooded in. It was the wedding veil of my great grandmother's close friend and sister-in- law, Sally Porter. The two girls had gone to New York and Paris, with Sally's parents, to shop for their trousseaux. The veil had lain forgotten in my cedar chest for thirty five years. Here then were the missing sleeves!

I cannot remember this lovely gift from God without the sting of tears rising in my eyes. The teary eyes were not as much for the solution, as for the glimpse of the Fatherhood of God. It's as if He said to us three women, "I'm here with you, loving you, wanting you to come to Me as a little child comes to her father's knee and asks for her needs."

March 10

You Must Remember, Psalm 103

David is talking to his own soul, reminding himself to engrave God's gracious mercy into his memory forever.

Listen, my soul, I want to remind you of something vital. Never forget to bless Jehovah. Praise Him with all you have. Remember who He is and how He blesses you. Make a list of His blessings and keep it handy before you.

My soul, try this list for starters:
He forgives your countless sins.
He heals diseases of soul and body.
He buys you back from Satan's destructive ownership.
He pours His love and mercy upon you.
He satisfies you with every blessing so you may fly
like the eagle and not slither like the slug.

We don't merit His compassion but He always gives it.
His anger is slow in coming. He is patient and forgiving;
however, never dare to presume on Him
for He will not hold back his anger forever.
Remember this, the Lord doesn't give us what we deserve.
No, His store of merciful forgiveness is higher than the sky
for those who love and obey Him.

He takes our sins as far away from us as morning's dawn
is from the setting sun. He is our Father,
with more compassion for us than
earth's best fathers show their children.
Although He knows us through and through,
backwards and forwards,

yet not for a moment does He forget that our substance
    is earth's crumbly clay.

Our life is short, but God is in control.
Compared to time it can be likened to bright flowers
    popping open on the hillside.
A hot wind blows and the petals drop.
Soon they wither and fall and no one remembers
    where they bloomed.
But the Lord remembers. His love for us began
    before time existed and continues after it ceases.
His salvation is waiting for each new individual who comes
    to Him in faith.

The Lord is King; His rule is established in eternity as
    Ruler and Creator of all things.
Natural and supernatural, material and spiritual laws
    are His to command.
So praise Him, angels and archangels! Bless Him, you
    myriad hosts of Heaven!

Let all creation under His rule everywhere bless and praise
    His Name!
And you, my soul, never, never fail to bless Him with
    joy and in truth!

March 11

Praiseworthy Benefits

David made his list of God's best benefits, listing them in the order God gives them: He forgives, heals, redeems, crowns, satisfies and renews. Forgiveness is the first gift we must have. "He forgives all your iniquities." Iniquity isn't simply a quick mistake. Jesus died for more than our mistakes. He died for our deep, ground in mulishness and our consistently "me first" attitude which is the root of all sin.

Satan, who is our prosecutor, doesn't tell God lies about us. He doesn't need to. He accuses us only of what he knows we have done. Our Advocate, our Defender, Jesus Christ, says, "No. No sin here! I carried it to the cross. Your sins are paid in full."

"He heals all your diseases." David is talking to his own soul when he says *your* diseases, meaning "He heals all my soul's diseases." Diseases of the soul are as common as those of the body, like greed, unforgiveness, pride, lust, fear, depression and hate. The Lord sets about making us whole, freeing us of these diseases.

"He buys back your life from destruction," or He keeps it from wasting away. Sometimes we hock our souls for a mere pittance only to spend it on empty things. But the Redeemer is ready to redeem us from the cheap pawn shop and set our feet on the road to His Kingdom.

"He crowns you, my soul, with loving kindness and tender mercies. He satisfies your mouth (the soul) with good things so that your youth (strength) is renewed like the eagle's." The *satisfied mouth* and *renewed strength* feed the soul the same way wholesome nourishment strengthens weary muscles and bodies. Jesus, the Bread that Lives, lifts body and soul into praise and thanks.

Each soul-blessing is a praiseworthy gift of incomparable worth. Not one can be lost, stolen, burned up or washed away.

March 12

Lord of the Morning

Look out the window. Morning's a'borning!
    Color is rising from sky and from sea.
Sun lays a pathway over the water,
    birds have their flutes out,
    announcing the day.

People are waking, joyful or grumpy,
    making decisions. How shall it be?
What will I give or what can I get?
    Praising or scheming, which shall it be?

God's in His heaven projecting His glory,
    shining it through sunrise and sea.
His Son, never leaving, is never forsaking;
    bringing me courage, bringing me peace.

O Lord of the daybreak, Lord of the night,
    Your Spirit within me, helping me see.
For it's You I would worship.
It's You I would praise, so guide me
    this new day, now and always.

F.N.

March 13

Of Dust and Glory

"And God made man from the dust of the ground" (Genesis 2)

It's a pensive moment as we kneel before You, Lord, on Ash Wednesday. The priest marks us with the symbol of the Cross. It reminds us of what we are made, and at death the body returns to its original form, dust.

As ashes are put on my forehead in the shape of the cross, symbol of Your awful but precious death, I feel deeply the stillness and solemnity of this moment of remembrance. It's a deep, aching sadness because of what You endured.

Suddenly, You turn on a light within me which becomes a song rising up and flooding my heart: "And God made man ... and breathed into him the breath of life and he became an everlasting soul." Your message dawns, bright as returning day: "Yes, daughter, made of dust. But what's the other ingredient? It's the very breath of My Spirit. You are not merely clay; you're earth and heaven. You are dust and glory. Because of My sacrifice you have the capacity for Heaven, but through Me, only through Me. Each person must choose dust or glory."

Lord! Your truth comes at the precise moment of need. May I liken it to a powerful, eternal generator? You are always ready to create power whenever one of life's storms knocks the lights out.

Remind me daily earth is not my home, and this body is soon gone. But the best thing to remember is while You made us *of* dust You did not make us *for* it. You made us for glory!

March 14

Temporary Endings

"As for man, his days are as grass, he flourishes like a flower of the field; the wind blows over it and it is gone and its place remembers it no more." (Psalm 103:15, NIV)

The church calendar tells me it's Lent. My life's calendar of years says it's winter, reminding me of life's brevity. Nine friends and family members have recently left us. The last of our combined parents has graduated from this planet. The first two of our eight siblings are gone. My brother, a surgeon, was killed by the knife of an addict, seeking drugs. My brother delivered his own killer by C section free of charge, twenty years earlier.

The death of my mother-in-law takes me back in memory to my own mother's death, for I prayed the same prayer, with tears, for both: "Take her quickly to Yourself, Lord." He granted the request both times.

The night before my mother died, words of the spiritual, *Swing Low Sweet Chariot,* replayed in my mind until it became a prayer image. Next morning while having breakfast with my sister, the phone rang. As my sister answered it my eyes fell on the words of the calendar, "I have seen your tears, heard your prayers and granted your request." (Isaiah) Immediately I knew my prayer of the previous night had been answered. Hurrying to the bedroom I found it was so. The swift, silent chariot had come for her. My sister and I stood on either side of the bed holding her hands, singing *Praise God From Whom All Blessings Flow,* while silent tears flowed.

Years later, as Mother Nash was at the end of her life, the chariot again became the image in my prayers. I sang the song to my husband as we prepared for bed. He awoke at 4:00 A.M. with the song playing through his mind. He too envisioned the chariot sweeping down for her. Turning out the light at 4:25, he slept until

March 14

the phone woke him at 6:00. The call was from his sister in Ohio telling him their mother died in her sleep at 4:25 that morning.

One more precious saint was transplanted from earth to the Kingdom of Light where she will bloom eternally. Praise!

March 15

A Garment of Shining Light

This is a prayer which came from my heart and pen as the Angel of Death came for my mother.

Chariot of Fire, unseen, not heard,
  sweep through light years of space.
Transcend time that binds us here,
  pull in beside her bed.

She'll spring right up from her empty shell,
  leap in with joyous step.
Drive straight and true, O Angel of Death –
  through into Heaven's realm.

There in God's Kingdom she'll drop off the old
  and slip into the new,
  like a garment of shining Light.
Daddy will be there, bright with glory,
  smiling with joy.

Together they'll sing a brand new song;
  like praise we've never heard.
So, Angel, swing low. In the flash of an eye
  come down for her tonight.
                                    F.N.

This prayer image came to me both nights preceding our mothers' deaths. My mother's in 1974 and Mother Nash's in '94.

March 16

Lord of the Living

"Where now is your sting, O Death? And where, dark Grave is your triumph?" (I Corinthians 15:5)

When my father died I drew some consolation in knowing he was with You, Lord. I knew the tarnish of humanity had been buffed off and he was like polished sterling, "bright, shining as the sun." But Lord, he was gone and the sting was there. Your Word insists the separation is only temporary for believers and our victory is permanent. But oh, how it hurts for now! Our very souls are bruised.

The term 'communion of saints' was not unfamiliar to me. But for years I assumed it meant either the bond between earthly Christians or the bond between Christians in heaven, but between the two groups? No.

Then one Sunday the often heard words of the Eucharist exploded with new insight. I seemed to participate in a God given scene in which earth and heaven respond in tandem. The priest said, "It is right, and a good and joyful thing, always and everywhere to give thanks to You, Father Almighty, Creator of heaven and earth. Therefore we praise You, *joining our voices with Angels and Archangels and all the company of Heaven* who forever sing this hymn to proclaim the glory of Your Name."

As we sang the hymn, my spirit was lifted and I was praising You, with pew mates and with the "great cloud of witnesses" (Hebrews 12) banked about us like towering clouds. For a moment I sensed I was joined with dear ones, both the heaven dwellers and mere mortals together, sharing praise to our God.

Lord, this experience has pulled some of the sting from Death. Thank You for being Lord of the Living, whether we live in heaven or live on earth. (Matthew 22:32)

March 17

New Life Pictures

Joyful praise from hearts ascending
to our Lord who made this day.

Spring is born. All Nature sings it,
in color, growth and freshness.

Earth is drawing resurrection pictures
filling eyes with beauty.

Memories of amazing grace wake
my mind to hope anew.

Jesus! Jesus! Life's creator, flow through me
with signs of Spring.

Like the sap in leafless branches
You are shaping a fruitful tree.

Mold this flighty, stubborn will so
it becomes transformed.

Cause it to grow and have no Winter
because its roots are deep in You.

F.N.

March 18

The Water of Life Poured Out

Each year the Feast of Tabernacles commemorates Israel's years of wandering in the wilderness where God supplied them with manna, quail and water from the Rock. Every adult male within fifteen miles of Jerusalem gathers for the feast, as did our Lord. Yearly they camp out in hastily built huts for seven days. It is to remind them of their long years of homelessness.

On the eighth day of the celebration they gather in the Temple. Choirs sing and musicians play. A priest brings water from the fountain, and as he pours out the water, symbolic of the life saving water from the rock, he cries out, "Lift up your hands!" With lifted hands and thankful hearts the people shout, "With joy you will draw water from the wells of salvation!" (Isaiah 12:3)

It's in this setting in the Temple, with these words on the lips of the people, that Jesus calls out, "If anyone has a thirsty, dissatisfied soul let him come to Me and drink. Whoever trusts his life to Me will have streams of fresh, living water flowing from within him." (John 7:37-39)

In the story of the woman at the well, the woman asks Jesus to give her His living water. He was not referring to natural water, essential for physical life but to spiritual water necessary for Eternal Life. As we "drink" Him into our living, God the Holy Spirit becomes within us a spring bubbling up, refreshing our lives. He invites us to sink our life roots deep into Him so we may flourish like a tree planted by the river. (Psalm 1:3)

Jesus poured out His life at Golgotha to atone for our sin. Today He pours His Spirit upon us as we ask for Him.

References of God pouring His Spirit upon us may be found in both Old and New Testaments. Examples may be seen in Joel 2:28-29, Acts 2:17-18 and Acts 10:45-46.

March 19

A Donkey Ride

During Passover Jerusalem and nearby towns were overflowing with pilgrims. A city of tents surrounded Jerusalem's walls. The grapevine broadcast that Jesus had raised Lazarus from the dead and Jesus was coming to Jerusalem. There was a rumor that He could be the Messiah. Could this really be true? Everyone wanted to see Him.

Jesus knew He couldn't be heard over the crowd but He could be *seen* on a donkey's back. Riding on a donkey conveyed Scripture's message concerning Messiah: "People of Zion, celebrate! Cheer! Look, here comes your King, riding a donkey, bringing you salvation. He is gentle, riding the foal of a donkey!" (Zechariah 9:9)

People shouted *Hosanna* (save now) for they counted on the Messiah to free them from Rome. He would become their conquering military hero.

Most Jews knew their Scripture. By fulfilling this prophecy Jesus was declaring Himself the long Expected One. The people liked part of the message for it agreed with their hope. But there was a second message which confused them. In ancient Israel the bearer of a message of peace rode a donkey. Everyone understood the message: *"I come in peace."* If a messenger bore news of war, he rode a horse. The people wanted a warrior king, one who would free them from Rome, not one who would make peace with her.

Lord, some call Your entry into Jerusalem the Triumphal Entry. But Your true triumph lay ahead. It came as You shouted from the cross, "It is finished!" What You did riding a donkey into Jerusalem, knowing what would happen that day, took determination and premeditated courage!

Ah! Jesus, Son of Man, what a courageous Man You are! Lord Jesus, Son of God, what a great God You are!

March 20

Eternity in the Balance

"Jesus took His disciples to the Garden of Gethsemane. He asked Peter, James and John to stay close for He was in agony and dread… 'Stay and keep watch with Me'" (Matthew 26:36-46)

Lord, You needed the support of Your friends for what lay ahead. But they only wanted sleep. You told them You came to earth to die, but that wasn't what You feared most. You were both Son of God and Son of Man. As Son of God, You knew that Satan could not change God's Eternal Plan. But what of Your humanity, inherited through Your mother, Mary? The first man, Adam, failed the test. It was through him that humanity inherited sin. You, the 'Second Adam,' Son of God and Son of Man, were anxious in Your humanity. Could You go through with it? Satan kept slashing You with that question. Could You complete the Purpose of the Ages as Son of Man while carrying the sin of all humanity?

You knew Satan. You had fought him before. Scripture describes an earlier experience where You and he faced each other in the wilderness. (Matthew 4:1-11) When You were a baby in Bethlehem, he tried to kill You through Herod's furious purge of babies. (Matthew 2:16) Satan wanted You to die before the crucifixion. Anything would have been better than having You fulfill God's plan for our redemption by dying on the cross.

And now, in the Garden, Satan attacks with all the power of evil. This was his last chance to keep You from fulfilling Your destiny as Savior. Yet You, Lord Jesus, never crumbled before him.

What would have become of us without Your obedience to the Father and Your resistance to Satan's full power of temptation?

Note: This and the following are in a booklet called *The Seven Stations of the Cross* which I compiled for Lenten meditations.

March 21

Our Praying Lord

In the garden Jesus said, "Father, I'm praying for those You've given Me and not only for them, but also for those who will come to believe in Me because of their message." (John 17:9-20)

Lord, You prayed alone and with the disciples. Whatever the situation, You prayed. Prayer was as necessary as breathing to You. Without it You could not carry out God's plan.

Your prayer in the Garden, while struggling with what You knew lay ahead, still comforts and strengthens us today because Your prayer was for US!

Your earthly work was almost completed. Soon You would be with Your Father in heaven again. The cross loomed darkly before You. But even knowing what lay ahead, You were concerned for Your followers.

Your prayer begins, "I am not praying that You, Father, take them out of the world, but for Your protection of them from Satan's power. Make them clean through Your Word of Truth. You sent Me here with a purpose to fulfill as I'm sending them out with a purpose. It's for their sake that I consecrate Myself so they too may be dedicated in truth." (John 17:15-19)

Jesus, You came here to earth and dedicated Yourself to the Father's Eternal Purpose. You prayed that we might believe in You. In acting on our belief we carry out Your purpose. One of those purposes is to do for others what You, willingly and sacrificially, did for us, to pray for them. Lord, may we Christians not sin against You, or others, by failing to pray for each other. (I Samuel 12:2)

Give us faith and perseverance, for without faith in what You have done, are doing, and will continue to do for us individually, we cannot grow as Christians.

March 22

Without Defense

The Jewish rulers carefully schemed to get rid of Jesus. They paid Judas to point Him out to the Temple guards that dark Thursday night in Gethsemane. Lord, You were arrested and spent that awful night of torture in the Roman prison. You had just come from the Sanhedrin, the high court of Jewish law. They charged You with blasphemy. But the judges knew Governor Pilate would not try a religious case. Since only Rome could pass the death sentence, the success of their plot depended upon having Pilate try the case. They wanted You dead. So they changed the charge of blasphemy to a triple charge, each a lie, but charges Pilate would be required to try, since each was against Roman rule. First they said You were a revolutionary against Rome, second You urged withholding taxes from Rome, and third You claimed to be a king.

False witnesses accused You, but You had no lawyer and You made no defense. Pilate asked, "Don't You *hear* what they are saying against You?" But You didn't answer. Pilate was puzzled and startled.

Isaiah, centuries before Jesus' birth, wrote, "While being bullied and tortured, He stood silent before His tormentors. As a lamb at its slaughter ... so He made no reply." (Isaiah 53:7)

Pilate wanted to let Jesus go but as he saw the happy crowd of yesterday become an ugly mob screaming, *"Crucify Him! Let His blood be on us! He deceived us with His donkey ride! He is an impostor! Crucify! Crucify!"* Pilate was afraid and capitulated and washed his hands of responsibility.

Lord Christ, with today's hindsight we know why You did not speak that day in Your defense. For the purposes of God the Father, You, God the Son, were carrying the enormity of human guilt Yourself. So You had no defense. You took the guilt of our sins to death with You.

March 23

On Your Shoulders

Lord, the long Roman whip, studded with bone and iron pellets, curled around Your body mercilessly, ripping out skin and muscle with each lash. Most lost consciousness or died under it. Isaiah spoke of the lashing of the Messiah:
"We thought God was punishing Him for *His own sin.*
But it was *our* grief He carried. His wounds should have
been *ours.* The price of *our* peace and forgiveness was
laid on Him and we are healed as the whip cut His flesh."
(Isaiah 53:4-5)
After the beating You were taken from judgment hall by the soldiers. The whole detachment gathered round to watch the sport as they "worshipped the king." They stripped You and pulled a dirty red robe over the torn shoulders. A thorn "crown" was crushed into Your head. Kneeling before You, amid raucous laughter and lewd jokes, they aimed blows and globs of spit at Your head.

The long night of torture finally over, they turned You over to four soldiers who were just coming on duty fresh from a night of rest. At sunrise they put the cross on Your shoulders. With muscles trembling from blood loss, weakness and torture, You started the winding route to the killing field.

Crowds followed. Some jeered, some grieved. Words of the prophet must have come to the minds of some as they watched You stagger under the weight of the cross: "Many were shocked by His appearance that day. His face and body were so mutilated, more than the others. This is My Servant, pierced and bloody, who shall cleanse many nations." (Isaiah 52:14-15)

Jesus, You are the Father's beloved Son. On earth You were His Servant, the "Second Adam," who would obey His Father's purpose even to the laying down of His life to redeem His creation.

March 24

Simon

The long walk with the cross began. Each step must have been torture for You, Jesus, to force Your body to take one more step. Then another.

The four Roman soldiers supervising the crucifixion must make sure the criminal lived until they could kill him in the prescribed manner. After all, they could not crucify a dead man.

Lord, as Your strength continued to fail, the weight of the cross became too much. The centurion saw You trembling, staggering, barely conscious. Realizing You might die too soon, he looked for someone to carry the cross. Roman officers had the authority to order anyone into service as needed. That Friday morning Simon of Cyrene was chosen by Centurion's command.

Simon was born in Cyrene, or modern Tripoli in North Africa. He later moved to the countryside in Palestine, and came to Jerusalem to celebrate Passover. St. Mark tells that Simon was the father of Alexander and Rufus who worked in the first century church. Paul must have known Rufus well for he writes that he was one "chosen of God." He mentions that Rufus's mother, probably Simon's wife, was "like a mother" to him. (Romans 16:13)

Lord, we don't know whether Simon believed or hoped that You were the long awaited Messiah. He may have heard You preach. But this execution was a totally unexpected turn of events, *the Messiah being marched off to be crucified! How could this be?* He had to have been completely confused. Maybe he had only heard rumors about You. Either way, it's unlikely that he realized You were "Christ our Passover" on Your way at that very moment to be sacrificed for Simon himself.

How he must have marveled later at the honor bestowed on him in carrying Your cross!

March 25

Sounds of Weeping

The street was a tangle of people following the four soldiers, the two thieves with their crosses, and Simon, who now carried Your cross, Lord Jesus. A mixed crowd followed. Interested spectators were there, shocked Believers and sweating soldiers, grim and irritated by their gruesome task, and by the shoving of the crowd.

Lord, Your enemies gloated. Disciples followed from afar. The women, stumbling along behind You, were openly crying. You turned to them and said, "Women of Jerusalem, don't weep for Me. Cry for yourselves and your children. Worse days are coming to Jerusalem, days when people will say, 'Women who have no children to care for or babies to nurse are fortunate.' They will call to the mountains, 'Fall on us and cover us from this horror!' If people do this to One who is innocent, what will become of those who are guilty?" (Luke 23:28-31)

Lord, when You told the women this concerning Jerusalem, were You looking ahead to the total destruction of the city by Rome in AD 70?

It was the custom for Jewish men not to speak to a woman in public -- not even their wives or daughters. It was considered "politically incorrect." But Lord, what You care about is *people*, not social taboos. When You heard crying behind You, You turned and spoke to the women, wanting them to know You cared that they were hurting, even in the midst of Your terrible thirst and pain. You cared two millennia ago and You haven't changed a bit. You still hear, still love, still care today about people, men, women and children, black ones, white ones, good ones and bad ones.

"Jesus Christ is the same today as He was yesterday and He will *never* change." (Hebrews 13:8)

March 26

The Place of the Skull

"When they came to the place called *the skull,* they crucified Him, along with the two criminals...." (Luke 23:33)
The name, Golgotha, was derived from its appearance. *Calvary* in Latin and *Golgotha* in Hebrew have the same meaning: "the place of the skull." There's a place just outside the Old City that fits the description. It's a high rounded knob, like a gigantic skull. Two caves appear to be eye sockets and a jagged depression suggests the nose. In appearance, in name and in purpose it seems a fitting place for terrible things to happen.

Before the crucifixion, Lord Jesus, the soldiers tore away Your outer garments, reopening wounds which had partly coagulated and adhered to the fabric. The clothing was carelessly dropped in a heap until the work of the crucifixion was done. They offered You wine drugged with myrrh, reputed to be a painkiller. (Remember the wise man's gift at His birth? Significant? Yes!) You refused it, knowing excruciating pain and thirst lay ahead of You.

David wrote: "Lord, I'm as weak as poured out water. My bones are dislocated. My strength and courage have melted within Me. I hang like a wet rag. My tongue is so dry it sticks to my teeth." (Psalm 22)

Lord Jesus, in Your thirst, weakness and pain, You refused the offered opiate. Why? Was it because Your plan, made with the Father in eternity, was to have You experience in body, mind, emotions, and spirit the *full extent of* our death penalty? You took it ALL, Lord, no short cuts. No relief in the substitution of Your guiltless self for our guilty selves.

We bless and praise You, Lord God, Father, Son and Holy Spirit, for Your gifts of forgiveness and salvation, so exorbitantly costly to You, yet freely granted to "whosoever will."

March 27

Pierced

The Time had come. They nailed You to the cross, Lord, and hauled it upright between the two thieves. As it dropped into the hole they had prepared for it, the wounds in Your hands and feet tore open. Horrible though it was, Lord, Your death is precious to the millions upon millions of us who accept what You have done for us.

Pilate's notice of the charges, JESUS OF NAZARETH, KING OF THE JEWS, was written in three languages, Greek, Latin and Aramaic. Surely this is one of the infinite details, visible for all "who have eyes to see," that the three great languages in use at the time should pronounce You *King*.

The soldiers could relax now. The "king" was up there, out of their way. They could joke with the crowd about the king who "refused" to come down off the cross. Now they could throw dice for the robe.

King David never experienced what he wrote in Psalm 22 although he wrote it in the first person singular. It describes One whom the Old Testament calls "David's greater Son. "

> "These men circle me like wild dogs, watching,
> snarling, mocking. They have pierced my hands
> and feet. They divide my clothes among them
> and roll dice for my robe."

The robe was unique in that it was seamless, woven of one piece, like the High Priest's robe. Your mother, Mary, wove it with love. But its pattern is significant for more than the fact that Your mother loved You. The function of the High Priest was to be the intercessor between God and man. He sacrificed a lamb for the sins of the people. This is what You do for us, Lord. You stand in the breach between us and the Father. You are both the Priest who offers the sacrifice and the Priest who is *Himself* the sacrifice.

March 28

Planned From Eternity
Paraphrase of Isaiah 52:13-15, 53:1-12

Look at God's Servant. The day will come when He will prosper and be greatly exalted. Kings will stand speechless before Him when they understand what He has done. Many were shocked that day, His face and body were so marred, more than the others. But this is God's Servant, pierced and bloody, who shall heal many nations. Did any believe the reports foretold by the prophets? Only very few took them seriously.

He grew into manhood before our eyes like a fresh green plant springing from arid soil. We saw nothing appealing in Him. We ridiculed Him and turned from Him so we did not have to hear what He said. We thought God was punishing Him for *His* sins. That's backwards. It was *our* grief He carried. Those wounds and bruises should have come to us. The ransom price of our peace was paid by Him and we were healed as the whip cut His flesh.

Like straying sheep, we turned away, each choosing his own direction. Nevertheless, God heaped our sins on Him. While He was being bullied and tortured, He stood silently before His tormentors. Like a lamb being slaughtered, or a sheep during shearing is silent, so He said nothing in His defense. From prison, to an illegal trial where sentence was passed, He was led out to His death. They killed Him between two common thieves, then buried Him in a rich man's tomb. There was neither evil nor violence in Him, yet it was God's eternal plan that He be crushed.

God's righteous Servant left no physical progeny, yet by making Himself our sin offering He shall see untold numbers of His spiritual children, and He shall be satisfied. Millions upon millions from future generations shall be counted as righteous before God because His righteous Servant stood in our place, poured out His life for ours, and prayed for us sinners.

March 28

Note: Isaiah wrote this chapter describing God's purpose in sending the Messiah to earth to be our sacrifice 700 years before His birth at Bethlehem. The following references deal with a few of the New Testament fulfillments of Old Testament prophecies: Matthew 26:57, 59, 67,   Matthew 27:14, 24, 30, 58, Mark 14:57, John 19:1-4, 34.

March 29

"IT IS FINISHED!"

From the cross, Lord, You saw Your mother with John Ben Zebedee. Their pain and confusion showed on their faces. Your concern for them both led You to give John a new mother and Mary a new son. From then on Mary lived with John and his family.

One of the thieves mocked You, saying, "If You really *are* a king, as they say, save Yourself and us!" The other, who had obviously had a change of heart, said, "Shut up! We deserve this, but this Man hasn't done any wrong." Then he looked to You and said, "Lord, when You come into Your kingdom, remember me." It was truly a last minute conversion, yet You replied, "I promise you, you will be with Me today in paradise."

From about noon until three o'clock an eerie darkness covered the land. It was as though nature herself mourned her Creator. In the darkness You called out those agonized words, "My God! My God! Why have You forsaken Me?" Father, Son and Spirit are One, indivisible. Yet at this moment the indivisible was divided. Our sin, which You, Jesus, were carrying, ripped You from the intimate Presence of the Father and the Spirit.

All had been fulfilled. You could let go of Your life now, Lord. Gathering Your last vestige of strength, You pushed up on Your bloody feet in order to draw one final breath. With that breath You shouted, "IT IS FINISHED!" It was no whimper. It was a shout of victory. In effect You were saying, "Father! It's over! We have done it! Now Our people may come to Us freely, boldly and with confidence." (Hebrews 4:15-16)

Jewish law demanded that the victims be dead and buried before the start of the Sabbath at 6:00 p.m. on Friday. The soldiers agreed to break the legs of the three to speed the death. With broken legs they would be unable to push up on their feet and relieve pressure on the diaphragm thus making breathing impossible. They would suffocate. But when the soldiers came to You, Lord, they found You dead. They did not break Your legs, but to be certain their job was successful, they ran You through with a spear. *

Yes, it *is* finished. All blessing, praise, honor, glory and power to You, Father, who reign over past, present and future, and to the Lamb forever and ever. Amen!

Note: Before the first Passover in Egypt God told Moses in Exodus 12:34, "Do not break the bones of the Sacrificial lamb ...They must not leave any of the sacrifice till morning or break any of its bones." (Numbers 9:12) "He protects all of His bones, not one of them will be broken." (Psalm 34:20)

March 29

March 30

Torn Body, Torn Curtain

Yes, it was finished but because the work of the cross is eternal its results continue bringing forgiveness, new starts and eternal life to billions.

After the crucifixion, memories must have flooded Mary's mind as she held Jesus' body briefly in her arms. Surely she recalled Gabriel's announcement of the conception of her Child by the Holy Spirit, the shepherds with their story of angels' visits, foreigners kneeling before her baby Son while presenting their gifts. Perhaps she remembered how old Simeon held the tiny Boy in his arms when she and Joseph took Him to the Temple for dedication. Her heart must have lurched as she saw, in memory, Simeon's wrinkled, old face alight with the glory of recognition as he told Mary, "... He is to be a Light to the Gentiles and the glory of the Jews ... He will give His people knowledge of salvation through forgiveness of their sins, but, the sword of sorrow will pierce *your* soul." (Luke 2:35)

Lord, the moment You laid down Your life, the Father illustrated the meaning of Your sacrifice in an astonishing way.

The innermost room of the Temple where God's Presence dwelt was known as the Holy of Holies. Only the High Priest had access to it. Once a year, at Passover, the High Priest entered to present the blood of the sacrificial lamb and the prayers of the people. The Holy of Holies was closed off from the people by three heavy layers of drapery. When the Son died, the Father tore the separating draperies from top to bottom, from Heaven to earth. (Matthew 27:51) The significance of this event is clear.

Lord Jesus, Your sacrifice tore away the barrier of separation between God and humanity, giving all who seek You free access to the very Presence of the Living God. All praise and thanks go to You, Holy Lord!

March 31

A Sealed Tomb

"As evening came, a wealthy man from Arimathea, named Joseph, who had become a disciple of Jesus, went to Pilate and asked for Jesus' body. Pilate had it given to him. Joseph took the body, wrapped it in linen strips and put it in his own new tomb that was cut from the rock. He had a large stone rolled over the entrance to close it before he left.

Here the centuries old words of Isaiah leap up from memory: "He made His grave with the wicked (the two thieves) and the rich (Joseph of Arimathea) in His death although He had done no violence, neither was there any deceit in His mouth." (Isaiah 53:9 KJV)

By Saturday morning the chief priests and Pharisees were still agitated even though Jesus lay dead in His tomb. They had seen Him just yesterday as the soldiers took Him down from the cross. Death's pallor was obvious. They felt relief of accomplishment as they checked carefully to see that the heart was no longer pumping. Blood no longer flowed from the wounds. It had dried. Yes. He was dead, truly dead.

But something bothered them. They had heard, Lord, that You said You would die, but You would rise from death. They knew that was impossible but impossible things often happened when You were around. The rumor nagged them until they went to Pilate and told him they feared the disciples would steal the body and spread the rumor that He had risen. They wanted Pilate to seal the tomb and set soldiers there to guard it. Pilate agreed and it was done.

The Pharisees probably slept well that night, smug in their confidence that they had seen the last of Jesus of Nazareth.

Little did they know. Little did they dream what the coming days would bring.

April 1

April's Dawn

May God be praised in Heaven and Earth
    this shining April dawn.
Earth has heard Your great command,
    "Rise up from winter's tomb!"
Trees respond with colorful cheer,
    twigs grow bright with sap.

Tiny creatures tune their fiddles
    as soon as darkness falls.
All nature sings in joyous rhythm
    with chirp, or croak, or whistle,
For winter's grip has lost its hold
    and life breaks free at last!

O that mankind would praise You so
    for all Your wondrous ways,
Our dark depths would heed Your call,
    "Turn to Me and live!"
The chains of night would fall away
    and man would be reborn!

F.N.

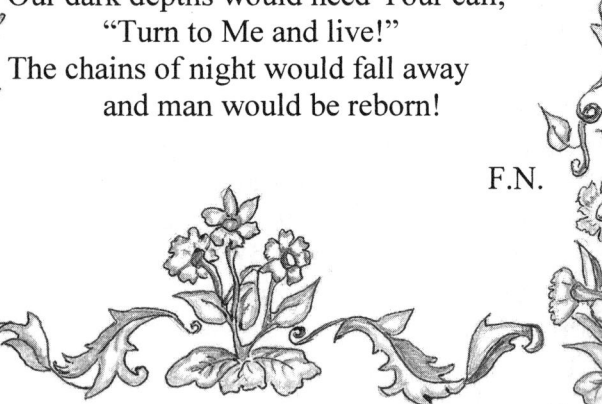

April 2

The Pivotal Point

Creator God, You programed spring in Your cosmic plan at creation. In spring Your Son, our Redeemer, gave us His life. According to Scripture, nature was distressed that day. Earthquakes shook the land and darkness fell at midday, lasting until our Savior shouted from the cross, "It is finished!" It was three o'clock when Jesus laid down His life. The darkness must have been caused by a total eclipse as Jesus' sacrifice totally eclipsed the horror of permanent death for Your people.

It's a marvel, Lord, that spring and the crucifixion came at the same time on the calendar. One is so beautiful to see, the other so horrifying. In spring nature is doing all its lovely warming, cleansing and blooming. Winter is over. Spring wraps round us with beauty. There's color everywhere, brightened by sunshine. Fragrance rides the breeze. Bird song fills the branches and diamonds dance on the river.

Redeemer Christ, it was during this season of irresistibly beautiful new life that Your earth life was torn from You. This pivotal point of eternity came in the midst of spring's colorful resurrection from the dead of winter. Nature bursts into new life just as You burst from the tomb. Your death and resurrection provided Resurrection Life for "whosoever will." Stir up our understanding, Lord, so we may see the vivid connection between spring and Your Resurrection.

"Death, where is your sting now; where is your victory? Death's sting is sin ...but thanks to God who gives us victory over it through our Lord Jesus Christ." (I Corinthians 15:55-57)

April 3

Lord, Was It A Good Day?

The day of Your death is awful to remember Lord, full of intrigue, brutality and betrayal. I can almost see, hear and smell the dirt, sweat, blood, the buzzing flies, labored breathing and groans, taste the tears. But, Lord, Your death is our salvation. Even so, we cannot help but mourn on that Day. We strip our churches. Hearts are awed and heavy for what You endured for us. We mourn for the One we love, for the One who loved us first. But mixed through our sadness, lying over and under it, is pure praise and sure knowledge that it was the very best thing that has ever happened for us.

But Lord, was it a good day for You? You are Spirit and we humans are unable to grasp the concept of invisible Spirit, so You came here as Jesus that we might see You in human form, fleshed out and standing free, You, the living, breathing, image of the invisible God. (Colossians 1:15) You, Jesus, *gave* Your life freely. Neither Rome's might nor zealous Jew's fear or hatred took it from You. They did not win out over You. God merely used them to implement His plan, made before Creation.

You told Your disciples Your death would be similar in some ways to a woman in labor. When a woman holds the little one in her arms she knows the pain was worth it. A new life! In the same way, Your life, death and resurrection brought new and everlasting life to Your children.

And so, back to the question: was it a good day for You, Lord? It was as hideous a death as could be devised by the mind of man, yet I believe it was a good day for You, for this is why You came here. You accomplished Your mission. Christ our Passover is sacrificed for us!

April 4

Why Did Jesus Have To Die?

On Friday night after Jesus' burial, His disciples huddled together in fear and frustration. Tears flowed. Questions rose. Why did He have to die? The answer begins in a book we don't read often, the Old Testament. God chose the Jews as His vehicle to carry His truth to the world. He inculcated them with the necessity of a blood sacrifice to atone for sin. God accepted Abel's bloody lamb but rejected Cain's beautiful fruit and vegetables. Cain tried to improve on God's plan. He may have been sincere in his attempt to help God with His planning but if so, he was sincerely wrong. Only the specified blood sacrifice of the lamb would do. (Genesis 4:1-9)

God tested Abraham's obedience when He told him to sacrifice his son, Isaac. God knew Abraham would obey. He just wanted Abraham to know also. As Abraham raised the knife, God stopped him and *provided a substitute* for Isaac. A ram was caught in the brambles. God told him not to harm the boy. With great joy Abraham named the place *Jehovah-jireh* meaning Our God Provides. God was teaching him that a life must be given to satisfy the debt resulting from our sins. If we won't accept God's provided blood sacrifice for ourselves, then we ourselves must pay the debt with our own life. (Genesis 22)

All Israel took part in enacting God's atonement on the eve of their departure from Egypt under Moses' leadership. Each family slaughtered a lamb and marked the lintel and sides of their doors with blood. They were to eat a hearty lamb dinner and stay in their houses (under the blood) as the angel of death swept through Egypt. The angel *passed over*, or skipped, the houses marked with the blood of the lamb, therefore the Jewish Feast was named *Passover.*

So why, Lord Jesus, did You have to die? You were not guilty of sin; we are. But You loved us more than You loved Your own life. Each of us is guilty (Romans 3:23), therefore each must pay our own debt or else accept Your offer to be our substitute. You died for us because You love us and there's no other means by which we can be saved. (Acts 4:12)

We're sinful and condemned. Reality tells us that unpleasant fact. No amount of scrubbing can clean us up. No whipping or torture can drive it from us. We may tell ourselves we are a "nice, reputable person, not nearly as bad as Mr. So-and-so." But if we're honest we must admit we do and think many bad things. "So what?" some may say. "Everyone does. We're all in the same boat." True, but God wants to take us out of that boat. Compared to His standards we fall impossibly short. Our sin and rebellion comes from deep inside us. (Mark 7:20-32)

Yes, Lord, You paid for our redemption from sin's powerful grip. You see us struggling, sinking, dying and You love us too much not to pay the ransom price for any who will let You. You are the only One who has the price of perfect holiness to pay for us unholy ones. You *love us that much!* Amazing!

April 5

Our Risen Lord

Earth is dressed in the stunning beauty of new life. It is Resurrection Day! Dogwood, redbud, azaleas, jonquils and tulips are wearing their best blossoms. Lilies trumpet Your Name, Lord God, in high exultant praise!

Just as light was bleeding upward in the east, three women made their way to the tomb. They carried mixed spices to prepare the body. Rather than finding what they expected, they saw the broken seal and empty tomb! Two shining beings, looking like men, asked, "Why do you seek the Living One among the dead?"

The women's news of the empty tomb brought Peter and John running to investigate. They saw the linen strips, not in a jumbled mass as if they had been unwound, but undisturbed in their folds. Your resurrection body, Lord Christ, had passed through the linen leaving them wound intact.

When Mary Magdalene realized no one had actually seen You, she ran back to the site to hunt for You. Tears blinded her as she searched the tomb. Then You spoke her name and she knew it was You! She ran back to the others and breathlessly gasped, "I have seen the Lord!"

Some will ask, "How could this be?" But Lord, isn't it more reasonable to ask, "How could this NOT be?" Death could no more hold You, God Incarnate, than a mouse trap could hold back the rising sun. It's true that death gripped You that Friday, for God the Father ordained this death. But He also ordained Your resurrection. You *are* life, the very essence of God life. You live, our Master and Redeemer, and so shall we! HALLELUJAH!!

April 6

The Hunt

It's a golden day. The sky is as blue as a sky could be. A breeze sends silver shivers over the river. Its banks are bright with budding trees. A hot air balloon begins its ascent, soon to be followed by others. They are like giant Easter eggs in bright designs.

Yesterday's Easter egg hunt flashes through my mind. Happy squeals followed the children's discovery of each treasure. When all the eggs were found, I heard our oldest grandson ask, "Mom, is that all?" My daughter replied, "That's all, David. You found the very last one."

The egg hunt was over too soon, but that's not true of the hunt You, Creator God, planned for Your children at creation. You hid an endless treasure trove for people to search out and "discover." You tucked away minerals, jewels, chemicals and formulas, facts and hints deep in the earth, sea and sky. You hid principles and truths, moral, natural and spiritual laws, for in Your understanding of us, You knew how delighted and challenged we would be by both the search and the discovery.

Into space You flung planet sized "eggs," invisible until night covers everything, then they glimmer, glow and shine causing us to ask, "Who made that? How can we reach it?" That's just what You want -- to show Yourself to us.

As long as humans exist, Your marvels will beckon us. You let us find what You put here. You let us know some of what You know. We are truly blessed if we come to understand that You Yourself, are the greatest treasure hidden from our eyes. You, Lord, are the only way to satisfy the deepest longing of the soul and fill the hungry heart with lasting joy.

April 7

The Hush of Your Presence

Sleep refuses to answer my call
and hours grind slowly.
Why not desert the hot, twisted covers,
sit by the window
and watch for morning?

Outside my tower it's black and still,
no traffic sounds
on road or river
no voice of shrilling phone.

Here in the dark aloneness
wrapped in silence
clothed in awe,
breathing seems an intrusion,
as restless time stands still.

There's only quietness, peace,
and the hush of Your Presence,
O Emmanuel. * My soul drops to her knees
before Your blazing Holiness.
F.N.

* God With Us, Matthew 1:23

April 8

Lessons From A Squirrel

What an invigorating day for a walk! Dogwood, red bud and azaleas are bright with color. Vivid new green, spotlighted by sun, compliments the sky. An inky blue river flashes lacy petticoats as it dances with the wind. Even an experienced grump would be compelled to change complaint to song in a setting like this.

While walking under the oaks I see a squirrel emerging from a waste receptacle. We both stop and eye one another with interest. Finally he comes out carrying a long, limp french fry by one end. Wisely, he shifts his grip to the center before scurrying up a giant oak. On my next lap around the park I notice he has shared his good news. Three others have located fries and are participating in an unexpected but satisfying feast.

The book of Proverbs reminds us to take lessons from the ant about work and preparedness. (6:6-8) The first squirrel reminded me to take a lesson from him. He shared his good news with his companions in the oak tree. There was satisfying food available to those who would go to the *right place* to get it.

We have heard it said of Christian witness, "It's simply one beggar telling another beggar where to find bread." All human souls, without the Bread of Heaven, are empty. And an empty soul, like an empty stomach, must fill itself with *something*. We humans often try to satisfy our hungry souls by feeding on power, wealth or pleasure. All too often Christians, fearing to be thought "different," hide their true source of nourishment: "Christ in me, the hope of glory." (Colossians 1:27) Are we ashamed to share the great Source of our satisfaction and joy?

Jesus says, "If anyone is ashamed of Me and My message, I will be ashamed of him when I come in glory. (Luke 9:26)

Lord, thanks for Your message from Your tiny gray servant.

April 9

The True Vine

"I am the vine and you are My branches. Stay firmly connected to Me and all that I am will flow into you." (John 15:1-17)

All winter my spirit was hungering for a closer walk with You, Lord. I was reading an old, small book, *The True Vine* by Andrew Murray, which added fuel to the fire You were already kindling within me. While wrestling with the concept of the vine and the branches, I asked Your Holy Spirit to be in me in a fuller way. You did, and I became awash in joy, wrapped in Your peace and filled with a new song of praise.

My goal for spring gardening was to rip out four grape vines which had gone wild in our old but new to us back garden in Summit, New Jersey.

Each morning before pulling on my jeans I asked You to open any areas within me that were closed to You. After prayer and breakfast, the battle with the vines began. One particularly tough old branch ran for yards, partly over, partly under the ground. I pulled. It clung. I hacked with the hoe and tugged until I came to the joint of branch and gnarled root. With foot braced against the root, teeth gritted, I pulled with all my strength. Suddenly it tore loose and I, with the branch still clutched in my hand, tumbled head over heels down the sloping ground. I crashed with a stunning thud into the sun warmed trunk of a great oak tree. Covered with leaves, twigs and soil, and seeing stars from the impact, I also "saw" Your point, Lord. If the branch has life, it is only because the vitality of the vine pulses through it. The branch in my hand would never again be able to produce a single leaf. I threw back my head and laughed in pure joy at the wonder of it all. You, Creator of vines, oceans and galaxies, are concerned enough with me, a small "branch," to collate my days, first with

April 9

the inner longing for a closer walk with You, then with the right books, the Holy Bible and *The True Vine*, and next with the timely illustration from my own back garden.   Still dizzy but with delighted earnestness I said aloud, "Yes, Lord, I see! Without You living in me, and me living in You, I am not really living. Help me, Lord, to cling to You as tenaciously as this sinewy old branch clung to its vine." (John15:1-17)

April 10

You Are The Supplier

Jesus said, "I am the vine and you are My branches. If I live in you and you live in Me, your life will be fruitful. As a branch broken off from the vine can bear no fruit, so it is with you. Unless you remain attached to Me, you can't produce a thing." (John 15: 5) Lord, Your illustration is dynamite. Only a Creator God who truly wants His people to know Him would plan for a grapevine and Himself to have a common denominator.

Productive vineyards have an orderly, disciplined beauty. They resemble an army of small, green and brown soldiers standing in formation. Their careful upkeep is not only for beauty for if it's left untended the rapidly growing branches will sprawl across other plants, cutting off their light and consuming their nourishment. Grapevines and Christians require constant pruning. It's only with vigorous pruning that either can reach its potential.

Lord, surely all earnest Christians know how it is to become detached from You. Joy and peace begin to wither. Ripening fruit of love for You starts to drop off. Any number of silly or serious things can nudge us from You, for we are "prone to wander." Detached, we must struggle along on our own dwindling reserves when we could be partaking of Your infinite resources.

With You our lives will begin to yield the fruits of faithfulness, patience and kindness, love, self control, gentleness, joy, peace and goodness.(Galatians 5:22) As we remain in You, You bring us what You said You came here to give us, "I came so you could have life, and have it *abundantly*." (John 10:10)

You are the Supplier, we the receivers. Our lives, firmly attached to You, have the very Life of the Vine nourishing and producing within us characteristics of Your Kingdom.

April 11

Why Should I Fear? Psalm 56

O Lord, give me Your mercy! I'm in prison. Caught! Beaten up.
    They would love to see me go to pieces.
But I can't do that, Lord, even though I'm trembling from fear
    and fatigue.
This is the very time I need to cement my confidence in You.
I won't dwell on my fear but on Your strong promises.

I'm proud to trust You, my God, for You are my Redeemer
    and Savior. Your eyes see and Your ears hear me.
You even know the number of tears I've shed in private over this.
I will take courage in what I know of You. I know Your
    love surrounds me. Your power protects me.
That's Your promise to me. When Your Word and my trust
    are mixed, why should I fear?
How can a mere man harm me? It is YOU who are Almighty
God.

My gracious Lord, it is Your strength which has kept me
    from falling apart. Not my own.
I will walk with You, Lord, through this, in both praise
    and confidence.

      David is fleeing King Saul's armies which were much larger and better equipped than his small group. This is his prayer for deliverance and his statement of faith in God. He decides to look at the trustworthiness of God rather than dwelling on his fear.

April 12

Ol' Man River

Sitting at the breakfast table with my second cup, I find watching the river stirs my thoughts beyond the waiting dishes. I think of the song, *Ol' Man River* which claims "you must know somethin' but you don't say nothin,' you jes' keep rollin' along."

I'm caught up by the tides and Ol' Man River begins to talk to me in parables. Since he speaks no words, I'll say back to him what he shows me.

Ol' Man River, you remind me of the great River of God's love which continually flows through human lives. God's love, like you, Ol' Man River, is too deep for me to see its depths, too wide to see the other side and too long to see the beginning or ending. Only your surface, with its infinite ripples, is visible. I liken the ripples of water to life's ups and downs. It's the very roughness of the water which catches the light, making each ripple sparkle. Ol' Man River, my Lord's love is like that. If we trust Him with life's difficulties, the light of His presence can cause them to be points at which new understanding is born. And that new understanding brings surprising blessings.

Boats move easily and freely across your surface, Ol' River, but out of the water a boat is a clumsy thing; it's out of its element. When we Christians are out of God's will for us, when our love has grown cold and our sin is unconfessed, we are out of our element. But progress toward Christian maturity is sure and purposeful when "we live and move and have our being in Christ." (Acts 17:28)

So Ol' River, for one who has the reputation of being mute, you have stirred up some happy morning thoughts. Thank you for your parable on God's ever flowing mercy and love. And thank You, Lord, for making the river and letting me see more than just its beauty.

April 13

Jesus Is Our Bridge

While musing on the river I notice the sturdy steel and concrete bridge arching high over it. The bridge is a way to go from one bank to the other. This brings me a strong mental image of God the Son, who is our bridge to God the Father. Jesus tells us how to reach the Father. He says, "I am the way, the truth and the life. No one comes to the Father except through Me." (John 14:6)

The builders of the steel bridge spared no expense in making the bridge safe. Huge steel beams undergird and suspend it. Reinforced concrete is planted deeply beneath the river's shifting muddy floor.

Neither did God spare any expense in providing the Way for us to cross the uncrossable chasm from death to life. "God did not spare   His only Son's life, but freely gave Him up to death for all of us." (Romans 8:32)

Concerning this Bridge from man to God, Peter writes, "God didn't pay your ransom with perishable things like silver and gold. He redeemed you, bought you back, from your sinful, empty life ... with the innocent blood of Jesus Christ, God's Lamb. He, Jesus, was chosen for His redeeming work before creation of the world. God's plan of redemption is now shown in these last times for your sakes."(I Peter 1:18-20)

Believers through the millennia have crossed the dreaded Dark Valley by way of this Bridge, with joy and confidence, to find themselves in the Presence of the "High and Holy One who inhabits eternity." (Isaiah 57:15) Jesus' cross is God's Bridge. Its base is planted securely in eternity, stretching from the banks of Time into the Kingdom of Light. There is no toll to be paid. It's an invitation.

April 14

Praise Brings Joy, Psalm 92

Lord, it's a joy to sing praise to You, the Most High God,
    to celebrate Your love in the morning
    and rejoice in Your Presence at night!
Your mercy fills my heart with music so that it spills out as I
    remember Your mercy and Your deep-rooted plans.
Many seek wisdom in the wrong places and truth evades them.

Even though evil grows like weeds, its followers perish forever.
They grow strong in Your sunlight and fresh air but they
    don't see light and air as Your gifts.
Their lives slowly add up to destruction. But Lord, You see all this
    and never miss a beat of what's going on.
Understanding escapes them, but not You! They will be blown
away
    like thistledown but You remain steadfast, unchanging.

Thank You, Lord for strengthening me and refreshing my soul
    with Your justice.
Those who reverence and obey You grow and mature
    like sturdy trees in Your garden.
Even in old age they stay green and fresh, flourishing
    and bearing fruits of God's Kingdom . *
They announce with joy "Our Lord is righteous and just.
He is our unshakable Rock in whom we may safely trust."

* Note: "... the fruits of the Spirit are joy, patience, love, peace, kindness, goodness, faithfulness, gentleness and self-control." (Galatians 5:22)

April 15

Hard Evidence

"Without faith we can't please God. Whoever comes to Him must believe that He exists..." (Hebrews 1:6)

Lord, it's plain that You require our faith. But we aren't born with it so how do we get it? Your answer is, "If you ask, you will receive, if you look for Me, you will find Me, if you knock, I'll open the door." (Matthew 7:7)

We know from experience we can't create faith ourselves, but here's where Your mercy and provision come in. Your first goal for us is that we come to You, like a child comes to its father and *asks* for what it needs. You gave us this need of faith just so we will come, ask and receive it from You.

At times we read a passage from Scripture we don't understand, so we ask You to explain it. Instead of deciding, "That can't be true," we bring our question to You and accept it for now. That's a bit like planting a seed. Before long it takes root, and sends out shoots. The intangible begins to jell in the life, making a difference, becoming an unmistakable force in our living. "Faith is *substance*...: it is *evidence* ..." (Hebrews 11:1)

Faith can't be held in the hand. But it's real -- a spiritual reality. It has power. Like electricity, God's power can *do* things. God-given faith can remake lives and relationships, turn us around and influence all areas of our lives. Faith could be called a "mind altering substance" because over time, it changes us. It can turn our resentment into forgiveness and joy. It can replace fear with trust in Your guiding wisdom.

"This tiny seed of faith, if nourished, grows into hard evidence. It's invisible to the eye, but recognizable in the lives of those who have it." (Hebrews 11)

April 16

Faith is a Gift

"It's by God's grace you are saved through faith and not through your own efforts. It's a gift from God. It's not by your good works, so none of us can brag." (Ephesians 2:8-9)

Lord, Your Word stresses the absolute necessity that we Believers have faith in You. Our faith may be as tiny as a seed but it must exist and it must be alive. Paul calls it a gift. We can't buy, inherit or borrow it. If we lack what You demand of us, we ask You for it, Lord. We seek it, and You develop it in us. So -- *how* do we ask? We ask earnestly, persistently, in faith believing.

The King James Version of the Bible describes faith as "...*substance* of things hoped for, the *evidence* of things not seen." (Hebrews 11:1) *Substance* is matter, reality, core or meaning, essence, foundation. *Evidence* is a clue or a key, a confirmation, sign, a brand, a fingerprint.

St. Paul says faith is a "fruit of the Spirit." You, Holy Spirit, are known as the Indweller, the One who lives in us after our spiritual birth. Could we liken the fruits the Spirit produces in our lives to a peach tree producing peaches? Every fiber of the peach tree is imprinted, or programmed, with the demand to be a peach tree. It can be nothing else. It can only produce fruit "after its kind."

If God's Spirit lives in us, we produce "fruit" with the recognizable traits of the Indweller, "after His kind." Those in God's family begin to take on an obvious family resemblance.

If a tree is producing peaches we know it is a peach tree. This is true of people too, whether godly or worldly. "By what their lives produce you will recognize them. One cannot pick peaches from a thorn bush or pears from an ivy vine." (Matthew 8:16-19)

Dear Lord, please strengthen and increase the Gifts of Your Spirit in Your children. Bring godly fruits from our lives. Amen

April 17

Where does faith come from?
1. Jesus is the Author and Perfecter of faith. Hebrews 12:2
2. It comes from Him to us. Acts 3:16
3. It comes from heeding His Word. Romans 10:17
4. It comes from asking God for it. Luke 17: 5, Mark 9:24
5. It comes from Jesus' prayer for us. Luke 22:32
        and John 17:6-20

What is faith?
1. It's a living thing -- a seed, not a stone. Luke 17:6
2. It's our way of access to God. Romans 5:1-2
3. It's our shield of protection. Ephesians 6:16
4. It's our protecting breastplate. I Thessalonians 5:8
5. It's substance and evidence. Hebrews 11:1 KJV
6. It's necessary if we are to please God. Hebrews 11:6
7. It's precious -- to God and to us. I Peter 1:7

Why do we need it?
1. It does for us what we can't do for ourselves.
        Matthew 17:20
2. It counts for righteousness; we have none of our own.
        Romans 4:5
3. It helps us live the Christian life. II Corinthians 5:7
4. It brings us to salvation, allowing Christ to live in
        our lives. Luke 7:50 and Ephesians 3:17-19
5. It justifies us before God. Galatians 2:16 and 3:24
6. It sanctifies us -- causes us to mature. Acts 26:18

April 17

How may we encourage our faith?
   1. Stay close to God.
        a. Through prayer. I Thessalonians 5:16-18
        b. Through reading the Word of God, for "It is
           alive and sharp as a surgeon's scalpel,
           cutting the false from the true in our lives."
           Hebrews 4:12
        c. Through confession to God and repentance.
           James 5:16, I John 1:9
        d. Through praise. Ephesians 1:5-6, Hebrews 13:5
   2. "Be on guard, stand firm in the faith, keep up your
courage and always act in love." I Corinthians 16:13,
Matthew 26:41

April 18

The Covenant of Love

"Only Jehovah is God. You must love Him with all your heart, your soul, mind and strength." (Deuteronomy 6:4-5)

Moses said this to the people of Israel. Centuries later Jesus said it was the first and most important commandment of all, for as we keep it, the other eight will follow. It's a command, not a suggestion. It's here that we find the joyful purpose of life. We know it's our duty to love You first, but Lord, Your Spirit must create that special love in each of us for it to be there.

Great promises go with loving You loyally and deeply. You promise to forgive us, heal our souls and redeem our lives, strengthen us, satisfy our needs and put Your godly love in us. Paul, who knew You well, writes that You will free us from wrong desires and responses, not by the Jewish requirement of circumcision, but by *spiritual surgery* from the hand of God so we are capable of loving You with the whole self. (Colossians 2:11)

The promise refers to the New Covenant Jeremiah spoke of: "'The time is coming,' says the Lord, 'when I will make a New Covenant with My People. It will be different from the one I made with your ancestors who broke it. I will put this New Covenant and My laws in their minds and engrave them on their hearts. They will be My people and I will be their God.'" (Jeremiah 31:31-33)

This is Your most important requirement of us, Lord. You are worthy of all love, praise, obedience and honor, therefore You demand it. Since we cannot, of ourselves, create this kind of love within ourselves, You bring it about in willing, seeking hearts. No one else can work it into us. Only You, Lord. So we come, waiting hopefully, expectantly and with the belief that You who demand it and promised it will also provide it.

April 19

Only the Spirit

Lord, Scripture tells us what Your purpose for us is, but at times we wonder, puzzle, pray and study, trying to discover why You do things the way You do. We're not unlike Cain in this. He wanted to change Your demanded sacrifice of a lamb to vegetables. (Genesis 4:2-5)

We have been known to offer You nice "little suggestions" on how You could improve Your public relations.

"My ways and thoughts aren't like yours, neither are yours like Mine," says the Lord. "Just as the heavens are higher than earth, so My ways and thoughts are higher than yours." (Isaiah 55:8)

We simply do not have the mental or spiritual capabilities to understand Your ways and thoughts. An earthly simile comes to mind concerning the relationship between my dog friend, Scrappy Nash, and me. I often talk to her. Tell her things. She listens as best she can, cocking her head this way and that and watching me intently. Scrappy loves me and knows I love her. She trusts and obeys me. But she does not understand me. She does not know what my motive is for putting tooth paste on a brush and jiggling it around in my mouth. She has no idea what I'm doing when I pray or why I make up my bed in the morning only to tear it up at night. She would need a human spirit in order to understand human ways and motives.

We Christians must have the Holy Spirit. Only He can bring us to faith and reveal what God wants us to know. Eugene Peterson says of Him, "Spirit is the scriptural word for God sharing His life with our lives. It means that God is not an anonymous somebody 'out there' or an idea explained in a book, but a living presence whom I experience in the life I live day by day." *

The Spirit teaches and guides us. He gives us what we need for now. But Lord, life still puzzles us at times. St. Paul's comment is a comfort, "Now we see through a glass darkly, but

April 19

then face to face.   Now we know in part: but then we shall know
even as we are known." (I Corinthians 13:12)

Help me, Lord, and all Your people to leave what we can't
grasp to You, so we can concentrate on what we do understand.

* From *Living the Message* by Eugene Peterson
used with permission

April 20

Many Crowns

Crown Him with many crowns, the Lamb upon His throne;
Hark! how the heavenly anthem drowns all music but its own:
Awake, my soul, and sing of Him who died for thee,
And hail Him as thy matchless King through all eternity.

Crown Him the Lord of love; behold His hands and side,
Rich wounds yet visible above, in beauty glorified:
No angel in the sky can fully bear the sight,
but downward bends his wondering eye at mysteries so bright.

Crown Him the Lord of life, who triumphed o'er the grave,
and rose victorious in the strife for those He came to save:
His glories now we sing who died and rose on high,
Who died eternal life to bring, and lives that death may die.

Crown Him of lords the Lord, who over all doth reign,
who once on Earth, the incarnate Word, for ransomed sinners slain,
Now lives in realms of light, where saints and angels sing
Their songs before Him day and night, their God, Redeemer King.

Crown Him the Lord of years, the Potentate of time:
Creator of the rolling spheres, ineffably sublime.
All hail, Redeemer. Hail! For Thou hast died for me:
Thy praise shall never, never fail throughout eternity.

Matthew Bridges, 1851
George J. Everly, 1868

April 21

The Song Tells the Story

Hymns can be vivid and explicit praise, similar to the Psalms, which were also written to be sung. In addition to praise, hymns from standard hymnals are mini-courses in theology. For example *Crown Him With Many Crowns* is an excellent declaration of just who Jesus Christ is. Each verse speaks of His Kingship.

In verse one we see the sacrificial Lamb of God reigning as all heaven salutes Him with ringing praise and joyful thanksgiving. This matchless, one-of-a-kind King died in my place.

Verse two names Him as the Lord of love. The wounds He took for us, because He loved us, are still visible but they are no longer gory; they have become beautiful in glory. Heaven's angels still divert their eyes from the His scars, the shining evidence of His love for us.

Verse three shows the redeemed rejoicing over the fact that His death and resurrection triumphed over death. We too will die but because He rose we will follow Him into real and everlasting life.

In verse four we see Him as the Incarnate Word, reigning over all lords and rulers of earth. His ransomed ones are with Him in incomparable joy and praise of their King and Redeemer.

Verse five shows Him as the absolute Ruler of time – past, present and future. He brought the blazing galaxies into being by His word of command. All intricacies of human mind, body and spirit came from His knowledge and wisdom. He draws whosoever will come to Himself and pours His love upon us preparing us for eternity with Him. Is it any wonder that praise and worship flow, all unbidden, from hearts and lips of those who love You?

April 22

The King's Banquet, Matthew 22

As children we were taught in Sunday School that the word *parable* means "an earthly story with a heavenly meaning."

The Psalmist writes: "I have important things to tell you so hear me well. What I say is in parable, so listen with your mind as well as with your ears." (Psalm 78:1-2)

Often Jesus uses parables in His teaching. At first they seem to be about everyday things, like bread, water or coins but as the meaning of the parable becomes clear, we see it's really about an attitude which can prod us into action. Parables are like mirrors, in that they can reflect our own attitudes, causing us to ask ourselves, "Do I do that?"

This parable of the King's Banquet *seems* to be a story of a king who plans to give a dinner party to celebrate his son's wedding. Servants deliver the invitations but the people won't accept. The king sends other servants to tell them the dinner is prepared, everything is ready. Again they ignore the invitation. Perhaps some planned to accept but waited to see if something more interesting came up, or time slipped by and they weren't prepared. Others became so irritated by the repeated invitations that they beat up or killed the king's servants.

The king, now infuriated, sends soldiers into town to kill the offenders. Realizing those he had invited didn't deserve to come, the king sends invitations indiscriminately to all the street people, good, bad, clean or scruffy. Ultimately, the king's invitation includes everyone but only those who accept it and get ready for the party are allowed to stay and enjoy the banquet with the king and his son.

"Jesus came to His own people, but they didn't want Him. Yet to all who believe in what He said, He gives the privilege of becoming His own children." (John 1:11-12)

April 23

They're Coming In

The King in this parable is God the Father. He's preparing a wedding banquet for His Son. He has been sending out invitations since Creation. He wants us to join Him in celebrating His Son.

Today we receive countless invitations to join, support or contribute to various organizations. It's easy to put other invitations before His. Just send money and we're in. Our King doesn't charge dues. He only wants us to come to Him and learn what celebration is *really* like.

The King's first invitation went to the Jews. He gave them many advantages, His covenants, His commandments, the prophets, the Temple with its rich symbolism, and the Old Testament. But those who were asked first said, "No thanks, too busy. Maybe later."

But the King's invitation is to come NOW. "TODAY if you hear God's voice, don't turn away." (Hebrews 3:7-8) He may not send another invitation. He doesn't owe us one. In fact, He doesn't owe us the breath in our lungs at this moment. The parable tells of Israel's rejection of God's gift of the Lamb of God. They didn't just say, "No thank you," they beat up or killed His prophets. God sent other servants, His disciples and apostles. Again God's invitation was refused, so He sent invitations into the world's streets and alleys, gathering those whom the Jews scorned, Gentiles, Roman soldiers, heathens and slaves.

Human rejection by some cannot foil God's plan. In this case, it implemented it, for He extended His invitation to include you and me and whoever would come of any race or color. Many came, and they are still coming to gather round the King's table awaiting His arrival.

April 24

The Open Door

The rest of Jesus' parable could be another story, but it's like another chapter. Together they tell the whole story. Without understanding both parts of the story we could misunderstand the King. (Matthew 22:11-14)

The servants follow their master's instructions and gather any who will come to the King's banquet: the good, bad, rich, poor, religious or pagan. They come to the great hall and wait expectantly for the King's arrival. Finally he comes in and stands quietly, observing each guest. He sees something he won't tolerate at his wedding feast, a dirty person. The guest is not wearing a wedding garment and this is a *royal* wedding. He obviously came directly from work for he is grimy, stained, and smelly. His hair is tangled and his nails are dirty.

The King asks, "Why are you here dressed that way? You haven't even washed. You're dirty! And where is your wedding garment?"

The worker is ashamed. He sincerely thought he could eat at the King's banquet table just as he was. But he was sincerely wrong and the King has the man thrown out into the night.

Jesus' parables aren't told to entertain the crowds. He's not nearly as interested in our amusement, wealth or happiness as we are. His purpose is to show truth and prepare all who will listen for what the future holds for those who are prepared and for those who are not. A requirement for attendance at the King's banquet is that we come, repentant, allowing Him to wash us clean in the sacrificial blood of the True Lamb of God. Then we are "ransomed, healed, restored, forgiven ……." and ready to dine with the King.

April 25

The Divine Laundryman

What does it mean that the King throws out an invited guest because he is inappropriately dressed? None of those from the streets are well dressed, but they seem acceptable in the King's palace until one person is turned away without dinner.

The parable is called the parable of *The Open Door* because when Jesus came to earth the Jews were invited to follow Him but they would not; they denied Him. So the Father invited everyone, pagans and Gentiles, people who never expected an invitation. Concerning God's invitation it is important to know that while we may come to Him *just as we are*, we can not stay that way in His Presence. His grace is free but we must pay the price of following Him in spirit and truth. Dressing up is not the issue. Cleaning up is. We confess our sins, making them right. We forgive others and accept their forgiveness. It's about letting God into our living and thinking so He can begin to clean up our hearts and minds.

Both David and Isaiah knew God as the Divine Laundryman. Both saw his own sin, and asked God to clean him up: "... in Your mercy blot out my sins. Wash me as white as snow. Make my heart clean, O God, and give me a willing spirit." (Psalm 51)

Isaiah quotes God to the people: "Come, let's reason this out. Even though your sins are scarlet, they can be white as snow. They may be deep crimson, but if you repent, they shall be clean as newly washed wool." (Isaiah 1:18-20)

The necessary wedding garment is clothing of mind, heart and soul: repentance, new birth, faith, love, hope and reverence for God. These gifts from the King are given to us at the time of our cleansing. When He demands something of us which we are unable to give, He Himself begins to form it within us if we are willing and obedient.

April 26

An Acceptable Covering

God's plan and purpose of salvation for individuals was made before He laid earth's foundation. He invites us, undeserving as we are, to come to Him through the sacrifice, resurrection and glorification of Messiah Jesus. Through God the Son, God the Father will restore creation to its original perfection. (I Peter 1:19-20)

Beginning with Genesis, Scripture speaks of God clothing us, covering the shame of our sin. Adam and Eve became sinners through their disobedience to God. They tried to hide their disobedience from Him by covering their nakedness with leaves sewn together. They knew their bodies as well as their souls stood shamefully naked before Him. The Lord made coverings for them of animal skins. And here is the first blood sacrifice: the innocent life of an animal given as covering for the sins of the guilty. (Genesis 3:21) Few believers know of this theologically important event.

We're still sinners. We still need a covering acceptable to God. Christ's death is our covering. As God the Father looks at those who come to Him in spirit and in truth, He sees their covering -- not our sin, for His death covers them.

About 700 BC Isaiah spoke these words of the long expected Messiah:

"I take great delight in the Lord. My soul rejoices in Him for He has clothed me with salvation and covered me in a robe of His righteousness." (Isaiah 61:10)

The robe of Christ's righteousness is the perfect covering for our sin. It alone gives complete coverage. When the King looks at those assembled for the coming Feast of the Lamb, He will welcome those who are covered by the robe of Christ's own righteousness.

"Happy are those whose sins are covered." (Psalm 32:1)

April 27

You Are Invited

The Lord says, "I invite all with thirsty souls to come to My refreshing Spring. Those who have no money, come to My Banquet. Yes, come on, drink wine and milk. Money is not required.

"Why spend money for that which brings no satisfaction? Write My invitation down in ink and come. Your hungry, thirsty soul will be overjoyed with My abundance. Come. I will make an eternal contract with you. The same sure mercies I showed to David, I will give to you. (Isaiah 55:1-3)

"Come, while the invitation stands. Call My Name while I am near you. Those of you who are far from Me come, set aside ungodly plans. Come, I will forgive you and be merciful to you.

"Remember, my plans are not like yours, neither are My methods human methods. Aren't the heavens higher than Earth? In the same way My ways and thoughts are higher than yours.

"Earth is watered by rain and snow, bringing harvest and bread to the table. So it is when My Word goes out. It doesn't come back to Me without accomplishing the purpose for which I sent it.

"With My Truth, you will go out in peace and joy. Crops shall burst out upon mountains and hills with praise. Trees will clap their hands in time with nature's thanksgiving song. Instead of briars and thorns, flowering trees and evergreens will cover hills and valleys with new growth. This is the everlasting sign of your God's power and mercy." (Isaiah 55:6-13)
You are heartily invited. So come.

April 28

I Accept

Hymns which teach and encourage are a tremendous blessing to Christians. And they are a refreshing way to praise You, Lord, to answer Your invitation in a way we may not be able to do in our own words.

In answer to Your invitation of Isaiah 55, the hymn *Come Thou Fount of Every Blessing* seems the perfect response. What follows is my paraphrase of parts of it. Paraphrases aren't as beautiful as the original, but I find that by struggling to say an idea in my own words, it becomes, in a sense, mine.

> Come into my life, Lord God, Source of
>   all blessing.
> Tune me, like a violin, to join with Heaven's
>   hosts in towering praise.
> It's Your Name I cling to -- the Name
>   of Redeemer's love.
> Your love has led me here and I know Your
>   grace will lead me home;
>   for You sought me out and claimed me,
>   even before I knew You.
> Your redeeming blood bought me back
>   from eternal death.
> I can never pay the debt I owe You for
>   Your love and mercy.
> So let Your faithfulness lock my unfaithful
>   heart to You.
> I'm giving it to You, Lord. Take it and put
>   Your seal of ownership on it.
>   F.N.

April 29

The Polluted Man, Psalm 14

David had so many disappointments at the hands of people he knew and trusted that he became conscious of the widespread corruption of people as a whole.

People without God easily lose their way.
> They grow warped by their own lack of wisdom.
They put God down and their own egos up – on His throne.

God looks to see if anyone seeks Him with an open heart,
> but most have turned to their own evil ways.
They rot at the core, like an apple with a resident worm.
They become bloated with self-importance,
> all gas but no substance.

They devour God's people like french fries
> and reach for more.
Do they really believe they can spoil His plans?
Well, they can't. Neither human from Earth,
> nor demon from Hell, can destroy
> the God-dreams of His people.

But who will make their hopes a reality?
You will, Almighty God! You will do it.
How I pray You will do it NOW!
Then the joy of the Lord will fill Your people
> with praise songs.
It will spill out in ringing worship for all
> the nations to hear.

April 30

Gumption and Grace

O Lord, You absolutely do marvel and delight me! Your greatness cannot be contained in infinity, and yet no created thing is too small or too large to carry Your undeniable fingerprint. It's seen on blackberries ripening along the mountain road and the moon's power to lift ocean tides.

Why does such a large proportion of humanity ascribe Your masterpieces, great or small, to "laws of Nature" or *any* source other than You? Natural law was planned, created and is maintained by Your command.

It's puzzling how the discovery of the most rudimentary sketch by one of Earth's great artists can send spasms of excitement through the art world, yet the same critics can walk through a velvety night hung with eon ripe stars and not acknowledge the God behind it. They believe an impersonal law of nature caused it. Isn't it more likely that Michelangelo's *Pieta* evolved without the touch of human hand or human mind behind it, than to think there is no personal Intelligence behind the universe.

I believe You create and sustain all creation, whether atoms or galaxies, raging storm or downy wee chick with the mystery of its small life inside. If I believe this Lord, why does worry keep sneaking into the mind concerning this new difficulty? Help! I want to acknowledge You in all things. The mind knows nothing reaches me, of either pain or pleasure, without Your permission. I also believe and know from past experiences that whatever You allow comes with the powerful potential for good and for growth. Therefore, I rest in that realization and give You thanks.

Please Lord, give me the gumption and the grace to turn true head knowledge of You into living faith and give me an elastic soul which stretches in trust, rather than shrinking in fear. Amen.

May

May is morning
  dipped in coolness
  tender fresh.

May is fragrance
  breathing out
  intoxicating senses.

May is opal dawning
  from blackest night
  hung with stars.

May is crystal rain
  blessing earth
  bringing life.

May is promise
  from life's Creator
  of grace bestowed.

May is hallelujah!
  HALLELUJAH
  and Amen!
          F.N.

May 2

Peter's Restoration

Lord, You knock persistently on our door. You want us to bring our needs to You. There's only one door separating us, but the handle is on our side. We must open it from our side.

Peter had a desperate need to be forgiven, for he denied even knowing You after Your arrest. After the Resurrection, he and the other disciples were fishing in the Sea of Galilee when they noticed a man on shore building a fire. The man shouted to them where they might find fish. They followed his directions and caught so many fish the net began to tear. When Peter realized the fire builder was You, Lord, he dove into the water, racing the boat to shore.

Lord, John's story of Your healing of Peter's deep inner wound (John 21:15-19) indicates he was hurt because You asked him *three times* if he loved You. The first two times You used the word *agape*, which means perfect love or God's kind of love. The third time You asked, "Peter, do you love Me?" You used the word *philio,* which means to care for or brotherly love. Lord, You knew Peter's human frailty and loved him enough to settle for lesser love. You love us that way today.

Feelings must have run high in both men. A mental image begins to form. There's Jesus, His earnest eyes reflecting deep tenderness. And there's Peter, the rugged fisherman, his leathery, sun baked face streaming with tears, sitting, shattered before his omnipotent Friend.

Lord, Your forgiveness restored Peter's self respect and deep- ened his commitment to You. He writes, "Be humble under God's mighty hand so He may lift you up ... Put your worries on Him for He cares for you." (I Peter 5:6-7) Peter opened the door to Jesus' forgiveness from his heart. So must we. Thank You, Lord Jesus, for making the gifts of forgiveness and restoration possible for us.

"If You Love Me, Speak Up"

We all affiliate with Peter's restoration. It hits us hard enough to wake us up, not knock us out.

Some Christians are ashamed to mention their faith in You, Lord. Faith is the most precious gift a person can have. It doesn't diminish when we give it away, yet we hold back on sharing it. We're fed media straw so often and Scripture so seldom that our spirits are malnourished. Godless groups persistently say it's "politically incorrect" to speak of one's faith. They say faith should be private. Like sheep we tag along with the majority. Scripture teaches that remaining silent is *eternally incorrect* and we will be held accountable for our silence! All too often we swallow the drivel spewed out by the mind benders. Then we puff up with pride because of our "fashionable modernity."

Three times Peter denied You, Lord. Three times You asked if he loved You. With his every affirmation, You gave the same command, *"Feed My sheep."* Just before Your Ascension You told Your followers, "Be My witnesses in Jerusalem (at home), in Judea and Samaria (our neighborhood) and in the farthest parts of the earth (wherever you are)."

I love and enjoy my husband. I can't be with others long before I mention him or something he said or believes. His love lives in me. He makes a huge difference in my life. We share thoughts, plans, joys and sorrows.

It's this way between You and Your current disciples, Lord. You said, "You love Me? Then speak up." It's not a suggestion; it's a principle. If we don't love You we can't be a witness to You. If we don't tell others of what You have done in our lives, we have very little love for them or You. So Lord, open the hearts of those who love You, so we will open our mouths in joyful witness to Your awesome love.

May 4

The Trinity Speaks, Psalm 2

There are four singers here: David, vs.1-3, God the Father, vs.4-6, God the Son, vs. 7-9, and God the Holy Spirit, vs. 10-12.

David:
"The nations of the world rage like fools! Do they honestly think
    they can outwit the Almighty?
The rulers of earth are but small chess men placed on a board,
    yet they arrange summit meetings; they scheme. They
plan. They cheat and lie. And what's the purpose of their foolish
frenzy?
Their pompous motto is: 'Down with God! Free our courts,
    schools and homes! No more slavery to old time religion!'"

God the Father, Ruler of Time and Eternity, roars with laughter:
"Foolish pawns of Lucifer! My Son is being crowned.
    The coronation is currently in progress!"

God the Son affirms the Father's decree:
"My Father has said to Me, 'You are My begotten Son,
    My Heir. All earth is Your inheritance, nations, islands,
    seas and skies. Break them if You wish.
You own them lock, stock and barrel. Crush them into
submission.'"

God the Holy Spirit speaks:
"So rulers, prime ministers, presidents, dictators, congressmen
    and commoners, listen to Me while Time is in existence.
Get wise. Turn around. Bend your knees to Messiah-Jesus!
Celebrate His holiness. Exalt His Name! Your lives depend on it!
God's anger is lethal, but His blessing is Life, eternal,
    abundant and free!"

May 5

A Foolish Decision

"The fool has decided there is no God," Psalm 14:1

Lord, today groups of people are fighting against You with surprising vehemence. But that's not new, is it? Lucifer, the great deceiver, has been fighting for dominance of the human mind since time began. Today's media provide powerful ways for him to thoroughly infect earth with his deadly virus.

Psalm 2 refers to nations and rulers who rage against You. They try to make You illegal and to wipe the knowledge of You off the map. Certain groups are in a frenzy to lock You out of schools. Deranged artists paint You as a homosexual or as a preserved fossil floating in a tightly capped bottle of urine.

It's puzzling, Lord. If they really think You are a farce, a powerless nothing, why do they spend so much time, money and passion bombarding You? How does one nullify nothing? They must be afraid of You, for if You are real and true, then they are false.

According to Psalm 2, You "hold them in derision." (KJV) You scoff at the absurdity of the created fighting the Creator.

Lord, strengthen Your redeemed ones of this Earth. Help us recognize the fact that Satan's tools, with all their propaganda, their ranting and subversive efforts to wipe You out, don't change You one whit. They may bash their heads against the Rock of Ages until they are bloody, but You are God. You remain the same. Immortal. Invincible. Almighty. Victorious! Amen *

* Amen does not mean The End or *that's all*. It is a prayer in itself expressing hearty agreement, meaning may it be done or it will be done by Your power.

May 6

My Grandson's Letter

This is a part of my grandson's letter from college. He describes a problem he is having after leaving his home environment.

Dear Nannie,

I love the University of Georgia so much! I love the air and hills, and the fact I can find books in the library about my ancestors. I love my friends and Brothers at SAE but when you don't have the same priorities and standards as the majority, it can be a challenge. It's hard to know and believe what I do about Christianity and marriage and live in this largely pagan world. I know I'm no better or wiser than my friends but they are so far from Christian thinking. I can't blame them. If it weren't for you and Papa, Mom and Dad, I'd be right there with them.

My girl and I are in a hard place for people to relate to us. We believe in abstinence until early marriage, lots of children, and orthodox interpretation of the Bible. The form of worship we like is not popular with young people.

The Christians our age are in youth groups who play lots of guitar, sing lots of songs followed by a pale message. I find I'm "too Christian" for my friends and "too pagan" for the youth groups.

I'm not really unhappy. I just wonder where the young C.S. Lewises and Tolkeins are? Where are serious Christians who can tell a good joke, enjoy a cigar and a stiff scotch while maintaining truth and faith? The two of us often wish you and Papa, Mom and Dad were here to go out with us and then go to our church with us.

.	I've been praying about this and your letter was an answer to prayer. With God's help I'm figuring out what to make of this situ- ation. I'm not going to abandon my friends and brothers I live with for people I hardly know or like. But rather I'm going to stand my ground and try to set an example. I just pray God will

May 6

give me the courage and ability to resist sin.

I'm eager to continue my walk with the Lord. I don't pray as much as I should. I read the Bible but can't seem to do it daily. The more I read and learn about Christianity the more I see how much of myself needs to be changed. I'm not doubting my faith. I know Christ is Lord of all and I want to serve Him. I also believe *faith* is *obedience* and I'm not a very obedient servant.

I want to be like you and Papa. You seem to have mastered greed, lust, materialism and PRIDE. C. S. Lewis says, "Pride leads to every other vice. It is the complete anti-God state of mind." You, of all people, people know how prideful and arrogant I am. But I want to *act* Christianity not only *think* that way.

Enough serious stuff! I'll be home this weekend and I look forward to seeing you. Share my letter with Papa, if you want, and tell him how much I love him. He was my best friend this summer.

Much love from
your Grandson

May 7

Believe. Believe. Believe.

"Those who believe in what the Son of God has done for us have eternal life but those who don't believe do not have eternal life." (John 3:36)

The word *believe* is an every day word used by all people. We say, "I believe I'll read this book first, then the other," or, "I believe it's going to rain."

We've heard church members say, "Sure, as church members, we believe in Jesus. I guess we're supposed to, aren't we?" But to believe, in the biblical sense, is not simply going along with what's being taught. It's not simply believing that long ago a man named Jesus lived on earth and taught some good things which we would do well to emulate. Belief makes changes in lives. Explorers set out on dangerous ventures on uncharted seas and skies because of their deep belief that this or that was an actuality. If they are wrong it could mean catastrophe. Scripture tells us Christian belief is the difference between salvation and eternal death. That's a difference!

Lord Jesus, in order to believe *on* You we must believe *in* You. We are to trust You with our lives, to put them in Your hands, to honor, love and obey You. But why should we? You lived two millennia ago. You're gone and we're left. Human reasoning would call it absurd to trust ourselves to You.

To be Christian we are called to trust You and Your Word. But before we dare trust You, we must know who You really are.

Scripture says You, Jesus, are the Son of God, equal with God the Father and God the Holy Spirit. You make that claim Yourself today as You say, "My Father and I are one." (John 10:30) You told the religious Jews, in John 8:56-58, "Abraham...saw My day and was glad." Your words stirred great indignation to which You replied, "Before Abraham was, I am!"

May 7

Again, as Philip had questions concerning Your teaching he asked You, "Show us the Father and that will satisfy us." You answered, "Don't you know me after all this time, Philip? ...Any one who has seen Me has seen the Father." (John 14:9-10)

Before C. S. Lewis knew who You were, he determined to disprove Your existence. But Lord, You mercifully planted a deep curiosity in his atheistic heart and mind about the "Man who turned the world upside down."

Lewis didn't want Your claims to be true but he *did want to know the truth.* He used his razor sharp reason to try to hold onto his comfortable unbelief. But in the end the pure logic of Your plan of redemption backed him into a corner with no escape. In the book, *Surprised by Joy,* he describes himself as entering the Kingdom of God, a most "reluctant convert, kicking and screaming."

Lord, You've brought thousands of unbelievers to true belief through the words of this once unwilling convert.

May 8

What to Believe?

John the Apostle says if all Jesus said and did were written, earth couldn't contain the volumes. Lord, we don't know all Your plans but Scripture tells us all we need to know for now.

To claim the name *Christian*, which means to be *in Christ*, we must know You, Jesus, are "very God of very God, begotten not made, of one Being with the Father." You have the very mind of God. The relationship of Father and Son is so constant, that You reflect the Father perfectly.

We know we are separated from You by our sin. It's when we ask Your forgiveness, turn away from sin and toward You, that You provide, through Your cross, the *only* way to come to You,.

You knew when You gave us free will, we would abuse it. You want us to come to You because we love and honor You, not because we are marionettes on a string. In foreknowledge You planned before creation to pay our penalty Yourself as the True Passover Lamb. (1 Peter 1:18-20, Ephesians 1:4) We are invited and strengthened to live Your way instead of ours. As earthly parents yearn to bring the runaway child home, You want to bring us home -- forgiven and restored.

These are non-negotiable tenants of Christianity we must be-lieve or we are fooling ourselves concerning our position *in Christ*. When we believe, love, obey and trust You, You give us the very Life of God – Eternal Life. Peace which comes with this gift is beyond comprehension. Neither life nor death can remove it. It's from this position of forgiven sons and daughters that we forgive others, making peace with them, for the Father has forgiven us for the Son's sake. In spite of our tendency to wander, we can forgive ourselves for Your forgiveness is stronger than our weakness.

May 9

The Way to Life

St. John's gospel says, "In Christ there is *real life* and His *life* is the light by which we can see (understand)." (John 1:3-4) John speaks often of the themes of life and light in his Gospel and first letter. He tells why he writes: "I'm writing so you may believe that Jesus is the Messiah, Son of God, and that by believing you will have real and everlasting life Jesus speaks of so often." (John 5:13)

Lord, You tell us why You left Heaven and came to earth. "I have come here so you may have life and have it more abundantly." (John 10:10 KJV) It's not skimpy life, lived fearfully or in cloudy confusion, not with a shrunken spirit but with ABUNDANCE! "I give you life and you will never perish. You are safe with Me and nothing, no person or circumstance can snatch you from Me. (John 10:28) I am the Way, the Truth and the Life. There is no other way to the Father except through Me." (John 14:6)

This life need not fear death, destruction, or dreary monotony. John's words make it plain that You, Lord Jesus, are the only way to real life and You have the Father's seal of approval.

Eternal life isn't everlasting earth life. It's the life that God lives. Lord, You invite us to enter it so we may share Your life as beloved sons and daughters in Your Eternal Family.

We must each decide about You, Lord. Scripture describes You. The Holy Spirit is ready to clarify our understanding if we ask. God's Word and the Holy Spirit together will draw us to the undeniable conclusion You are who You say You are.

May 10

Light is the Theme

"In Christ there is real life and His life is light by which we can see." (John 1:4)

Jesus is the Way to life eternal. He is also the light by which we can understand His Way. In His light the false fades and the real is seen more and more clearly. Just as physical light is necessary for plant, animal and human life, so You, Lord Christ, are the *must* for our spiritual life. You said, "I am the light of the world. Those who follow Me won't be left in the dark but will have the very light of My life living within them." (John 8:12)

When God said, "Let there be light," the newly created light drove out the darkness. It's just that way when God the Holy Spirit comes and shines His light into our individual darkness. He can bring order out of the chaos of our lives. Left to ourselves we are a jumble of fears, circumstances, emotions and mistakes. When the light of God comes in He lights a path for us.

Physical darkness can be uncertain for we can't see what's around us. When night falls we use whatever means are available to dispel the darkness, to chase it away with light.

Your light guides us. It shows events, motives and situations for what they are. It distinguishes truth from the false. Lord, we need Your light to recognize our own motives at times. When our false intentions are revealed to us we may go to You for forgiveness and help.

The Apostle Peter says, "You Christians are called by God to be holy people, belonging to Him. He called you to come out of darkness into His light in order to praise Him." (I Peter 2:9)

May 11

The Enemy of Light

"The Light shines on in the darkness, for the darkness has never overcome it (put it out, or absorbed it). Light is unreceptive to darkness." (John 1:5)

Lord, we know spiritual darkness is in this world just as surely as spiritual light. John's Gospel tells us You are that spiritual Light. It also tells us there is an Enemy of Light, a darkness which has tried for millennia to extinguish Your Light. But You, Lord, are undefeated. The darkness of evil may hate You but it can't do away with You. Even total blackness doesn't hide the light of the smallest candle. Its light penetrates the darkness. John urges us to choose You, Lord, in the ongoing conflict with darkness by believing and trusting You.

Physical eyesight is a precious gift. You not only created eyes to respond to light, You made the "eyes of the soul" to be able to respond to Your Light. You want us to "see" You, Lord, because You love us individually and want us to love You back!

It's easy to lose our orientation when the electricity goes out. Everything disappears. We feel helpless, groping in the dark. We may stumble or go the wrong way. A rustle or creak runs shivers up our backs. When lights go on, we may see what we heard in the dark was no danger. But if it's threatening we can see to escape it. Lord, Your Light also lets us see life's dangerous traps so we may avoid them.

Help us to realize we don't have to live in spiritual darkness. You came here to light up our lives and minds, to forgive us, give real joy and peace, to give us a worthy purpose. You, Lord, have promised, "I am the true Light of the world. Whoever follows Me won't stumble along a false path but will have the Light of My Life within as their guide." (John 8:12)

May 12

To See or Not to See, That is the Question

After telling my fourth grade Sunday School class about Jesus as true light and life for each of us, I told them this home made parable to help them understand Jesus as the light of the world:

"Imagine a world of total darkness. There's no sun, moon or stars. No fire, electricity, no batteries or light bulbs. No candles. No matches – not even lightening bugs. Everyone was born in the dark. They lived and died in the dark. Many children were lost. Knees, elbows and heads were always scraped and sore because no one could see where he or she was going.

"Once long ago in the blackness a ray of light flashed over head, leaving behind a large glass ball filled with glowing particles of light. As it fell to the ground, people gathered around, wondering what it was. Some thought it was beautiful. For the first time they saw themselves and the faces of neighbors and families. But they also saw the dirt and disorder they had accumulated in the darkness. With the light, they knew they could make changes in their lives and clean up the mess they had made. Some liked the idea.

Others hated and feared the light. They didn't want anyone to see them as they were, neither did they want to clean up the way they lived. If they accepted the light changes would be necessary. And change frightened them. If they could only destroy the light, their world could be black again. So they attacked the shining ball with clubs and stones. As it began to crack, light particles spilled over the ground. Some people stamped on them, trying to extinguish them. Others gathered them to take home and scatter them about. The world would never be totally dark again. Light had come into the world. It began to spread until people had the choice of living in the light or in the darkness. In order to live in the dark all they had to do was keep their eyes tightly closed against the light.

"Each of us has a choice somewhat like that today. We can open our lives to the light of Jesus so we can see His love, His help and His care. Or we can close Him out of our lives and choose to live in the dark."

One boy said, "Wow! I never heard that Bible story before!" I explained the story was like a fairy tale. It was a made up story to draw a picture with words rather than pencil and paper to illustrate the necessity of light. Without light from the sun, there could be no life on earth. In the same way without the light and life of Jesus there would be no eternal life with God.

An interesting conversation followed. Fourth grade minds were stretching toward the concept of the great mercy and love of God. Some children got it. Others did not.

May 13

Though and Yet

Abraham didn't doubt God's promise of a son by Sarah in his old age. He believed it because God said it and God strengthened his faith. God would make the impossible possible. (Romans 4:20-22)

Lord, it's when we take Your words as truth that we have faith. When we claim Your promise of salvation, through Christ's death, we become new born Christians. You give us Your Spirit when we trust Your promise that You will do for those who ask. (Luke 11:13) Victory over doubt comes when we rely on Your Word.

Faith is a living gift which You want to strengthen in us, so You test us. Richard Wumbrandt, a Hebrew Christian and pastor, had his faith tested daily for fourteen years in a Romanian prison. He tells of Job's faith shining through two words he used during his testing: "*Though* He (God) slay me *yet* will I trust Him." (Job 13-15)

Habakkuk, the prophet, writes during a severe famine: "*Though* fig trees don't bud and no grapes form, *though* the olive crop fails and other crops wither, *though* the ewes don't lamb and cattle stalls are empty *yet* will I trust the Lord." (Habakkuk 3:17-18)

Abraham and Sarah's *though* and *yet* are amazing. You promised them a son through whom the Messiah would come. Abraham was seventy-six and Sarah was sixty-six. They waited *twenty-four more years* for Your promise to materialize!

My mother prayed for her children while standing firmly on this fact: "Believe on the Lord Jesus Christ and you will be saved *and your household.*" (Acts 16:31) She prayed sixty years for my oldest sister. What about me, Lord? Can I say, "*Though* this event is scary and painful will I *yet* trust You with it?" Is my faith built on the Rock of Ages or will it be eroded by sweeping tides of fear?"

May 14

Disguised Blessings

My father had been in hospital for almost five months fighting a losing battle with an infection caused by the removal of an irritating mole on his thigh. Neither sulfa drugs nor antibiotics had appeared on the medical horizon at the time. The five doctors on the case would have removed the leg but the wound had spread beyond the hip joint. All skin grafts became infected.

Mother was frightened and exhausted from living at the hospital, only going home to bathe, change clothes, and kiss her four children. One sleepless night in the hospital she prayed, "Lord, I know You are here with us. You may want to take my husband or You may want Him to live. I'm willing either way, but Lord, will You please just -- just let me know?" Not knowing what to do after her unusual request, she sat, limp and numb. Taking up her Bible she opened it at random. The words she read startled her: " Be of good cheer, it is I," (Matthew 14: 2) Next she read, "Believest thou that I am able to do this? According to thy faith be it unto thee." (Matthew 9: 28-29)

"O yes, Lord! I know You can do it!" she said, "My question is, will You? Please let me know."

She read on at random. "Why are ye fearful, O ye of little faith?" (Matthew 8: 26) "With man this is impossible, but with God all things are possible... Go thy way and as thou hast believed, so it shall be done unto thee...I will come and heal him." (Matthew 8: 13, 19:26; 8: 6)

Mother said the real clincher came with John 11: 4. "This sickness is not unto death but for the glory of God, that the Son of God might be glorified thereby."

Late that afternoon Dr. Roberts came into my father's room with a long face and dreaded news for my mother. "Mrs. Johnston, I'm sorry to have to tell you but the infection has reached the blood stream. There is no possible way Dr. Johnston can survive

May 14

the night."

Her heart lurched with fear, her revived faith forgotten. She hesitated a moment, then was surprised to hear herself saying with calm confidence, "Dr. Roberts, there's a higher Physician on this case who tells me Harry will live. I believe Him."

My father lived through that night and through all the rest of the nights for the next sixteen years. He lived to bring glory to God through his witness to the healing power of God. He lived to prove to and share with the medical and dental world the formula God had given him. My Dad named his process *endodonture*, or "root canal."

When he entered the hospital the process had not been totally accepted by the scientific community but because of God's power to heal, my father lived to prove it beyond a shadow of doubt. The world has been using this gift to great physical benefit ever since. People are also in the Kingdom today because of my father's open and unashamed praise of God who extended his life against "the odds" of the best minds of Emory University Hospital to complete His purpose. Another long lasting bright gleam of God's glory, is that the four of his children learned early of God's healing power.

That year seemed, to my twelve year old mind, like an ugly, threatening giant. It was frightening, painful, upsetting and expensive. But my mother believed Romans 8:28. "For we know that all things work together for good to them that love God, to them who are the called according to His purpose."

God's plan was to bless and strengthen, not wound or weaken. It came to us disguised as an "ugly, threatening giant," but when its masque fell off, there stood God's blessings.

Note: Verses here are from my mother's King James Version.

May 15

Four Hundred and Ninety Times?

Peter asked Jesus, "Lord, how many times shall I forgive a person who hurts me, as many as seven times?" (Matthew 18:21)

We like Peter. He seems so "human," making mistakes like we do. He doesn't always get the point, but he's not too proud to ask questions. He thought his suggestion that we should forgive seven times was most generous when Moses' law said three was enough.

Your reply must have shocked Peter. You said, "No, not seven times but *seventy times seven*." Before we could ever keep track of four hundred and ninety times, we would lose count. But that's the whole point, isn't it? Don't keep score.

Lewis Smedes, in *Forgive and Forget* reminds us that some relationships mend themselves but if they won't, forgiveness is the only way. He calls forgiveness "God's own invention to stop reruns of resentment." When "forgetting," we still know the unpleasant event occurred but we don't call it up and rehearse the hurts. Forgiveness removes malignant growths from the inner life. It frees the forgiven one from the mental replay of guilt and bitterness. As we forgive the other person, it's not long until we realize we ourselves were bound by our own lack of forgiveness. And now both are free.

No matter how tactful we try to be, we can't be with people long before differences develop – some small, some serious. Lord, You began, and clearly illustrate, the process of healing through forgiveness. You are our shining example and You expect us to follow Your example. If You only forgave us four hundred and ninety times, all our "forgivenesses" would have been used up long ago. Then where would we be?

May 16

Jesus Had A Need, John 4:1-9

While on Your way to Galilee, Lord, You said You "needed to go through Samaria." The disciples knew that was a dangerous place for Jews to go. Samaritans and Jews had had a running feud since 720 BC and the two groups despised each other. It was not considered respectable for a Jew to go there. But Lord, You "needed" to go anyway. Why?

It was about noon when You arrived at Sychar. The disciples went to the village to buy food, leaving You and John sitting on the edge of Jacob's well, waiting. At last a woman came to draw water and You asked her for a drink. That doesn't seem like an unusual request but it amazed her. "Why ask me? A Jew asking a Samaritan for anything is unheard of," she said.

John's story is brief and we wish it was more detailed. It tells several things about You, Lord. You were hungry, thirsty and tired, three very human conditions. If we read between the lines we see You as a barrier breaker for You spoke warmly to an unacceptable person, a Samaritan woman of questionable character.

It was unheard of for a rabbi to speak to a woman in public, even if she were his wife or daughter. But although it was socially unacceptable according to Jewish religious law, You, the long awaited Messiah, talked with her. You sat there in the sun, sweat running down Your face, and started a conversation to show her she was acceptable to You. It's the same today. You want to talk with us and have us talk with You.

She was the reason You *needed* to go through Samaria. Her need drew You there. You tore down walls that day, racial walls, as well as those of gender and tradition. Instead of walls, which sep-arate, You build bridges to unite us. Lord, You are showing us God loving His world, not only with words but with strong actions.

Living Water

Jesus said to the Samaritan woman, "If you knew the truth about God's gift, and who I am, you would ask Me and I would give you Living Water." (John 4:10)

Lord, You caught this woman's interest by nudging her toward seeing her own needs, not only for water but for a different life and future. You didn't confront her with her sin. You wanted her to see it for herself. Not realizing You were speaking of spiritual things, she challenged You. To her *living water* meant fresh, running water rather than ground water which seeps into the well. She replied, "You can't get running water from this well. Even Jacob couldn't do that and he dug this well. Can You do something he couldn't?"

If she were a Jew she would have known the Scriptural meaning of living water. Isaiah writes, "God's people will joyfully draw water from the wells of salvation." And again, "God will pour water on the thirsty land." (12:3 and 44:3) The psalmist tells of his soul being thirsty for the Living God. (Psalm 42:2) Scripture tells them there is no satisfaction except from the Living Water Himself. (Isaiah 55:1)

But she was not a Jew and Your words puzzled her. She knew no water can satisfy thirst permanently. Jews knew only Messiah could do that. By telling her this You were telling her who You really were, God's Promised One ushering in the New Covenant. (Isaiah 43:18-19)

Samaritans only believed the first five books of the Bible and they altered them to fit their life style. With possibly a bit of sarcasm she says, "Alright, give me Your water so I won't have to come here in this heat every day." Lord, since You know exactly what it takes to satisfy spiritually thirsty souls, You did not leave her wondering.

May 18

"Bring Your Husband"

As the Samaritan woman talks with You, Lord, she seems to be thinking things she never thought before. She asks for Your Living Water. You tell her to go bring her husband. She says she is unmarried and You agree with her saying, "You are right. You've had five husbands and the man you now live with is not your husband." How does she feel knowing You know about her? Does she feel a jolt of shame and emptiness, or just surprise? Your comment causes her to realize there is something unusual about You and she says, "Sir, I think You must be a prophet." Next she asks a question, "Should we worship in Jerusalem or in this mountain?" Does she ask this to change the subject? Does she think, *I've never found God anywhere, not even on Mount Gerazim? Where is He anyway?*

Samaritans changed their place of worship from Mount Zion in Jerusalem to Mount Gerazim in Samaria. They built their temple there and considered it to be the true place of worship.

Lord, You tell her, "God is Spirit and whoever worships Him must do so in spirit and truth." You are telling her, if God is Spirit, then He is everywhere. With the true spirit of worship we may worship wherever we go.

May 18

The woman says, "I know Messiah is coming and when He does He will explain all these things to us." Lord Jesus, as You tell her, "I am He," she puts down her water jar and hurries to her village where she excitedly tells her neighbors, "Come see a man who told me everything I've ever done. Could He be the Messiah?"

Curiosity led the Samaritans to follow the woman back to You and the disciples. When they heard You, they wanted to hear and learn more themselves. They urged You to stay with them.

How very like You, Lord, not to hurry off to be about Your other business but to stay two days in enemy territory with them. But after all -- people *are* Your business.

Many Samaritans believed and agreed they had come to hear You because of what the woman said. But after they heard You for themselves they said, "We know this man is truly the Savior of the world."

May 19

Choose to be Thankful

Lord, there seems to be only one sure formula for having one's prayers answered as we want them to be. That is to pray "Your will be done." We don't always see why You answer our prayers the way You do. We think we have a prayer which is in accordance with Your will. But You may say no or wait.

Some prayers are prayed in ignorance. After time passes we may be sincerely thankful that You said no to that one. A yes could have caused serious trouble. After this happens several times it underscores our growing awareness that You, Lord, know what's best for Your own and if we seek Your will in trust, we will find it.

Paul tells us in Corinthians of his earnest request, made three times, to which You said no. From what we can see of Paul after his conversion, he obeyed You. Your will became his will.

You blessed him abundantly, but not with the healing he requested. You gave him breathtaking visions of heaven which he found no adequate words to describe. Yet You didn't grant his request. He writes, "I pled with God three times to take this problem from me, but He said, 'No, My grace is sufficient for you and My power in you is made more obvious because of your weakness.'" (II Corinthians 12:8-10) Paul accepted that and chose to be thankful.

There is disagreement concerning Paul's "thorn in the flesh." Some think it was near blindness. Others believe it could have been epilepsy, or possibly the virulent form of malaria which was present at the time.

Lord, You have answered many of my prayers, for which I am thankful. But the answer You have given me concerning the prayer closest to my heart is "wait." You have assured me on several occasions over the last five decades when *the time is right* the answer will be a resounding *Yes!* So I wait choosing to be thankful for what I'm sure will happen.

May 19

St. Augustine's mother was terribly disappointed when her prayer for her son was not answered as she wanted it to be. She prayed he would stay with her and remain under her Christian influence. But he left and lived a wicked life.

While in Milan, Augustine met Ambrose, the Bishop of Milan. The Bishop was the key to Augustine's conversion and under his teaching Augustine became a great Christian teacher. God's answer to Monica wasn't *no*. It was, *"Wait*. Wait until the other parts of My plan are in place. Then it will all work together for good."

What an encouragement to faith. We are expected to wait for Your timing – until all pieces of the puzzle are in place. The King James Bible calls it "the fullness of time." Help me, Lord, and Your people everywhere to choose to be thankful for Your ways with us.

A later note: Since the completion of this writing I can say after fifty-one years of prayer and expectation, my great and merciful Lord has *answered my prayer with a resounding Yes!* And His timing was absolutely perfect.

May 20

An Unexpected Cameraman

"We are not fighting against flesh and blood people but against rulers, against authorities, against dark powers of this world and against evil forces in heavenly places." (Ephesians 6:12-18)

Lord, Satan knows us so well, better than we know ourselves. It's as though he planted a spy in our minds to take notes on unspoken thoughts or to unexpectedly record the surges of pride, doubt, faithlessness or grouchy moods.

He can use our victories as well as our defeats to trip us. Tests come daily. At times they are large, other times they are small, but come they will. If we have just come through a crisis successfully, the Tempter tries to twist the victory into pride. We may find ourselves congratulating ourselves, "Well, self, see how smoothly you did such and such! You're okay! You have proven your courage and loyalty once and for all! You're a mature Christian now. No need to ever doubt your own strength again."

Or when friends say nice things about our "Christian attitude," it's easy to forget how we pled with You, Lord, during the crisis, to be our courage, strength and joy, and how *You did just that*. Unless we set a guard over our attitudes, we misplace the credit and smugly wear it like the Medal of Honor, rather than giving You thanks and praise. As Satan sees his spy's video, he must say, with a sneer to his demonic accomplice, "Aha! Look at the little peacock, strutting and spreading her feathers. How easily she forgets and ignores *That One* she says she loves and wants to honor. Her pride is the weapon we'll use against her this time. The really juicy part of the whole episode is the little fool thinks *she* deserves the credit when actually it was *That One* who took her through it."

May 20

Lord, even though I'm ashamed I've paraded about in undeserved pride, I am thankful Your Spirit showed me what I was doing. Tests continue to come. Sometimes they are so small I think they're not worth bothering about. But if I fail the tiny tests, am I not letting my guard down? Give me insight and wisdom to realize my frailty is no match for Satan's strength. I must have Your Holy Spirit constantly living freely in and through me, giving me light so You may change the shape of my soul.

May 21

Direct Me, Lord

"Trust in the Lord with all your heart and don't rely on your own understanding. Acknowledge Him in everything and He will direct your decisions." (Proverbs 3:4-5)

These words are plain but hard. I'm to trust You, Lord, listen to You and not overestimate my understanding of situations. It's humbling to admit I can't solve my own problems, that real wisdom is not mine. It's Yours.

Humility and trust are not "in words" today. Society urges people to trust ourselves. Best selling books tell how to get our own way, crush opposition, intimidate the competition, be first in line. But Lord, You are not surprised by society's new ideas, are You? What's new about *me first* thinking? About pride itself? These have been the natural human response since Adam and Eve. It's easy to become snarled in the tangle of choices, to convince ourselves what we want must surely be what You want too. But Lord, I know I need Your direction. I want it. The psalmist gives good advice, "Stop fretting and realize only God can be God." In order to still the mind's tumultuous rush, I am to hush and listen. When I'm quiet and waiting before You, You reclaim me from distracting worries. You can tune me in to the mind of the Father. And when I'm in tune with You, You direct me.

A small porcelain figurine of a baby bird in a shop window in Bermuda caught my attention. Its mouth was wide open, tiny wings thrown back in utter abandonment to its need. It was hungry, pleading to be fed. Psalm 81 popped into my mind: "Open your mouth wide and I will fill it, says the Lord." Today that baby bird gapes hungrily at me from the bathroom shelf, reminding me to be open to You and Your direction with the eagerness of a hungry little bird.

Lord, I marvel at Your methods of directing Your people. Scripture may be the most frequently used method. Giving us peace when our decision matches Your decision is another. Mature Christians can help by agreeing with or challenging a decision. At times You use circumstances, opening one door while closing another. Regardless of the means of Your guidance, we can wait in trust with open and expectant hearts.

Father, may I seek Your wisdom in this decision, realizing it will come as I earnestly ask and then wait for Your answer?

May 22

What Requirements?

"What does the Lord require of you but to behave justly and mercifully and to follow Him with humility." (Micah 6:8)

Lord, it's a shock to see all the rules and regulations in the first five books of the Bible. But after all it is more than a book of religious regulations. It is Israel's health and moral code, its national laws.

Just before Joshua led the people back to the Promised Land after four hundred years of captivity in Egypt, Moses wrote down what You wanted of Your people, so they wouldn't forget. He knew their perfidy and it worried him. He realised he didn't have much longer to stand in the breach between God and the willful people. Wisely, he gave them the common denominator, the foundation of obedience and truth. He commands: "Love the Lord your God with all your heart, soul and strength." (Deuteronomy 6:5)

Lord Jesus, when asked which was the greatest commandment, You replied, "The greatest commandment is to love the Lord with all your heart, mind and soul. If you do this the second greatest will follow. Love your neighbor as much as you love yourself." (Mark 12:30-31)

These requirements are as current today as when You gave them to Moses millennia ago. You and Your law are the same yesterday and forever ..... so teach us to love You, our Lord, with all our heart, mind and soul.

May 23

Song of Moses, Exodus 15:1-18

After God had taken Israel across the Red Sea safely, Moses was so filled with praise this song seems to have simply burst from him:

I lift the Name of the Lord in song for He has triumphed
    gloriously!
By His power He has thrown horse and rider into the sea.
He, the God of my Salvation, is both the source and the
    object of my joyful song.

I will praise and exalt Him, the God of my salvation.
He is a warrior, fighting all evildoers.
Pharaoh's chariots and soldiers sank, like rocks,
    into the depths of the sea.

Because of their opposition to You, they are no more.
Your breath, like a powerful wind, piled the waters into
    walls on either side, making a path through the sea.

The enemy assumed it was safe to follow. He rode onto
    the path, bragging of what he would do to us.
But he assumed too much! One command from You,
    Almighty God,
    and the waters crashed over Egypt's armies.

Who among the gods of Egypt is like You, O Lord? None!
    There is not one like You!
Your consuming holiness, Your awesome glory and the
    wonders You perform are unique to You, only You.

With love which never fails, You lead those You have
  redeemed.

By Your indescribable strength, You guide them to Your
  Land.

You will bring Israel into the Land and plant them
  like a vine on the Mountain of the Lord,
    the place of our inheritance,
    the place You have chosen as Your Land.
By Your will, Jehovah-God, You have reserved it
  for Your eternal reign!

We may ask ourselves, Does this ancient prayer of praise
have any real meaning for us today or is Moses merely a
superstitious man ascribing the name *God* to simple good luck?

The character of God does not change nor does He change
His Name of *I AM*. In the New Testament God in Christ is the
same yesterday, today and forever. He is the great I AM. His
promises are as good today as they were in Moses' time.
Hallelujah and Amen!

More Than Millions,
Proverbs 31:10-31

King Solomon is describing the perfect woman. No one is
able to live up to perfection but it's a worthy goal.

A good woman is worth more than millions.
Her husband never has reason to regret
his complete trust in her.
Peevishness has no part in her character
and she always treats him lovingly.

She seeks good workmanship and spends
carefully.
She rises early, prepares a family breakfast
and plans her day.
Before the others are up she's dressed
and prepared for work.

She realizes the value of time and uses
her skills diligently in caring
for the family and home.
She is always ready to help the needy
and encourage the downcast.

When cold weather comes, warm clothing
is ready for the first cold snap.
She is neat and well dressed, always
bringing honor and respect
to her husband.
Tomorrow's cares don't worry her;
she faces them with good cheer.

Her advice is well worth hearing
    and is spoken with kindness.
She watches over her household
    and keeps the children wisely occupied.
They respect and honor her, knowing
    they are blessed in their mother.

Her husband says of her, "There are many good
    women, but you are the best!"
Charm can deceive and beauty fades
    but the woman who honors God
    is to be praised and admired.
Give her the love, honor and thanks
    she so richly deserves.

May 25

Two Way Stretch

"Respectful fear of the Lord is the beginning of wisdom, and knowledge of Him is light on a dark pathway." (Proverbs 9:10)

Not many people read Proverbs today. It doesn't fit our *Me First* philosophy. It's a shame to ignore it for it gives strong, practical help and rich spiritual insights. The words *practical* and *spiritual* are a good combination.

The writers ask us to stretch in two directions, like the fat lady's girdle. First we stretch toward You, Father, for You are to be our center, our beginning, not only at conception and birth but in the way we live and choices we make. As You become our core, our target, we begin to stretch in a second direction, toward others. You become not only our center but our circumference, our outreach.

I love Proverbs. It reminds me of dangers and wonders so basic they slip quietly into my life, such as laziness, the disasters of gossip and the unending benefits of living God's way. It reminds us of the strong, bitter chains of unforgiveness.

Proverbs explains what You, Lord Jesus, said when You were asked which commandment was the greatest. You said to love God with heart, soul and mind is first, and the second is to love your neighbor as yourself. Then You added, "If you keep these, the others will follow easily."

The writers of Proverbs set us on the path of true wisdom. It's not book knowledge but it is the realization of Your life and love within our hearts, minds and souls. Lord, as You live in us we are cleansed, moderated and expanded. You stretch us, toward You and then to those in our life's circumference.

It's You first, then others. Not me. I'm to be third. Lord, I have a long way to go!

May 26

The Gift of Wisdom

Amid great fanfare Solomon is crowned King of Israel following his father's reign. He realizes he needs help and asks God for it. In a dream, God appears to him and says, "Ask Me what you want, Solomon."

Solomon answers, "Lord, You showed mercy to my father, David, because he was faithful to You. You have made me king in his place. But Lord, I don't know how to govern. Give me wisdom in making decisions."

The Lord says, "I will give you wisdom as well as riches and honor. No other ruler will be your equal in these. And if you obey My Word, as David did, I will give you long life." (I Kings 3:5-15)

Solomon awakes realizing God has spoken to him and given him the gift of wisdom. With the gift he begins writing what God is showing him. Many proverbs, at least one psalm, *Ecclesiastes* and *Song of Solomon* are in our Bible today because of God's gift to him.

Proverbs is written in the form of a letter to Solomon's son. It consists of common sense advice for living every day with confidence and satisfaction. It tells the importance of wisdom, the moral, physical and spiritual benefits of following "Lady Wisdom." Solomon realizes early in his reign the task God set before him is too large, but God knows what He is doing. Along with the task He gives Solomon what he needs to complete it. He supplies him with wisdom, discernment, riches and honor. God gives them, Solomon uses them, practicing and developing them.

God supplies the tools we need to finish the tasks He gives us. It's our responsibility to use them, sharpening them under His guidance until they become efficient tools to use in our life situations.

May 27

Seek Wisdom

Solomon's letter to his son, Proverbs 1

"My Son, the purpose of this letter is to steer you in the direction of wisdom and self-discipline. It's necessary for you to understand the basics of a moral, just and prudent life. These words will teach discernment to the inexperienced and discretion to youth. Even adults, if they will listen, will add to their understanding.

"Remember to practice your father's instructions for they will grace your life with beauty as a golden ornament about the neck enhances one's appearance.

"A Ph.D. won't bring wisdom. But the Lord will, if you listen. Wisdom begins with reverential awe of the Lord, the recognition of His infinite wisdom and transcending power. Only fools mock wisdom and resent God's discipline.

"Ungodly people will invite you to follow them. Don't. They may say, 'Come join our adventure. It's fun to see who we can trick, either with a weapon or a clever scam. Think of the valuable things we can acquire for nothing! O yes, and of course we will -- er -- split the profits with you.'

"Small crimes lead to larger ones, until at last the perpetrator will lose his freedom, or his life.

"There *is* a better way. It's the way of level headed Wisdom. Wisdom makes herself * available to all who seek her. In fact she calls out at life's crossroads: 'Why do you mock me and scorn morality? If you listen to me, I will fill your minds with understanding and your blind eyes with beauty. But if you reject me when I call, trouble will sweep you away in its rip tide. You may call but I will no longer answer, for you must eat the fruit you planted and cultivated in your life. Your greedy schemes and destructive complacency will make a bitter meal. But eat it you shall, every bite.'"

"But whoever seeks Me will find Me when he looks for Me with all his heart. Whoever heeds Me need have no fear of being overthrown." (Jeremiah 29:13)

* When Solomon refers to wisdom, he uses feminine pronouns. David also uses feminine pronouns in referring to his own soul in Psalms. "My soul shall make her boast in Thee, Lord." (34:2, KJV) Of course, wisdom and human souls have no gender. Neither do nations, ships and planes but when referring to them we use the feminine pronouns.

May 28

Some Beneficial "Don'ts," Proverbs 3

"Son, keeping my advice current in your mind will enrich your life and the lives of others. Take love, faithfulness and honesty with you wherever you go. Better yet, engrave them on your heart. They are friends of your soul and will endear you to both God and man.

"Trust God with your life and possessions and be thankful. Don't count too heavily on your own opinions for they may be wrong. Only God is perfect. Talk things over with Him before you act and He will direct you.

"*God* put you here. Be proud of *Him*, not yourself. Obey Him. Give back to Him a portion of what He has given you. Don't skimp. Give from the first of your wealth, not from the leftovers.

"Concerning God's discipline, don't resent it. As our good Father, He corrects and trains the child He loves. His purpose is not to hurt, although at times it may hurt. His purpose is to teach and to equip us for good living.

"The benefits of Lady Wisdom surpass any other investment. She is more precious than fine jewelry. More to be prized than riches. She provides a rich lifetime income of contentment.

"God in His wisdom laid earth's foundation. By His understanding He flung the stars into orbit. He divided the sea from the dry land and governs seasons, clouds, rain and sunlight.

"If you are in a position to help those who deserve it, do so. Don't hold back. When you owe money to a neighbor, pay it, if you have it at hand. Don't say, 'Come back tomorrow.' Don't envy the riches of the wicked, or follow their example, for God's judgment will fall on them without your help. He ignores the wicked and without Him they will come to shame. But He blesses the families of the upright and gives them grace and honor. Bless His Name." Thank You, Lord, for Your merciful generosity.

Shaping the Future, Proverbs 4

"Listen, Son," writes Solomon, "when I was still a tender child, and my mother's only son, my father began teaching me certain principles. Now I'm teaching you. Gather up my precepts in your heart and practice them.

"Learn Wisdom. Cherish her and she will protect you. Whatever goals you may have, let Wisdom be first on your list. She will bring you honor.

"Let me guide you, Son, toward Wisdom's path for she shapes thoughts and thoughts shape actions and actions shape character and the character you build becomes your destiny. Wisdom leaves no blots on your past.

"There is another path which may look inviting but it leads to disaster. Avoid it at all costs. Those who follow it stumble and fall. Evil's insidious trap snaps shut on them and before they know it they become its slave. Those who take that route find pleasure only in deception, cheating, theft and destroying. They would enjoy bringing you into their evil ways. It would be a feather in their cap, but once you're involved in evil it is difficult to extricate yourself. "As you walk the route of Wisdom, it's like seeing the first light of dawn. Its light grows brighter as you go, bringing fuller understanding until you move into full, clear daylight.

"For those on the downward spiral of evil's path, it's another story. The light continues to fade until they can't even see the thing which made them stumble. So, dear Son, keep all my instructions, for they protect the health of your body and they turn on the light of understanding in Your soul."

May 29

This is a picture of a loving earthly father giving counsel to his young son. Most parents can see themselves in this role, because they've been there. But the letter goes deeper than that. It's also a picture of our Father in Heaven, our God of all healing counsel, speaking to His sons and daughters, inviting them to let His Word become woven throughout their minds and character until they are of one piece with His Word.

May 30

Wisdom's Call, Proverbs 8
a paraphrase and condensation

Do you hear Wisdom's voice ring out in challenge? Do you hear her invitation? She stands at earth's crossroads and calls, "All you foolish people, listen to me. Come, open your minds, listen and gain understanding from me. I despise evil and injustice. You will hear no shady deals or cheating schemes from me. Wise people recognize my worth and earnestly seek my ways.

"Choose to learn reverence of God, fair treatment of all. I teach self discipline and thought of the consequences before taking action. Come learn common sense and discretion. It's of more worth than earth's millions. Steer clear of bribes. Offering them or taking them is a slippery path ending with a trap.

"I live with virtue and prudence. I have knowledge, good counsel and insight to give. To honor God and fear Him is to hate evil, pride, arrogance and dirty, subversive talk. I have power, understanding and good judgment. By me rulers serve well, making good laws. I care for those who honor me, and those who seek me will find me. (verses 1-21)

"I, Wisdom, was with God before creation. He appointed me before the world began, before mountains pushed up or hills and valleys unfolded. I was there before oceans were made and assigned their territory. Before God stretched out the heavens or flung the glittering stars out into space, I was there. As He established laws governing all created things, seasons, tides, boundaries, plants, animals and humanity, I was the craftsman by His side rejoicing in His presence at creation.

"Don't ignore my words. Be wise. Seek me early. You will find life and blessing from the Lord. To ignore me damages yourself and others. You will find only bitterness and trouble." (verses 22-26)

May 31

Filled With Joy

Reading and thinking of Proverbs 8 reminds me of parts of the Gospels and Paul's Letters. A new thought begins to form in my mind which makes me glad.

When Christians say *God* we are referring to the Trinity, God the Father, God the Son and God the Holy Spirit, "One God in Three Persons," indivisible. Lord Christ, You did not come into existence at Bethlehem. You were with God the Father and the Holy Spirit before creation.

Solomon's "Wisdom" says in Proverbs 8 many of the same things as You say about Yourself, Lord.

"Wisdom" calls for all people to come to her. (verses 1-4) Your call, Lord, is for all who are weary or thirsty to come to You. (Mathew 11:28-29, John 7:37) Both say come and learn of me. Both say those who seek me will find me. (Proverbs 8:17, Matthew 7:7) Both were there at creation. (Proverbs 8:22-23, John 1:1-2) Both participated in creation. (Proverbs 8:30, John 1:3)

I do not believe that Wisdom is Jesus, any more than I believe that love is God, but truly God is love. Total wisdom and perfect love are among Your many characteristics, Lord.

The verse which I revel in is verse 30 of Proverbs 8. "I was the craftsman by His side. I was filled with delight day after day, rejoicing always in His presence, rejoicing in His whole world and exulting in the creation of mankind."

This new insight of the Trinity, celebrating "together" at creation, fills *me* with joy. It gives a fleeting glimpse, a tiny peep, into what You did in eternity before Your incarnation, full of joy, happy and celebrating. It brings tears of joy to my eyes just trying to imagine it.

May 31

Lord, this makes Your willingness to move from eternity's joy into humanity's suffering even more powerful, more poignant. I love and praise You for Your wisdom and Your astonishing love.

Joyful, joyful, we adore Thee,
God of glory, Lord of love;
Hearts unfold before Thee,
Opening to the sun above.

Melt the clouds of sin and sadness,
Drive the dark of doubt away;
Giver of immortal gladness,
Fill us with the light of day.

Mortals, join the happy chorus
Which the morning stars began;
Father love is reigning o'er us,
Brother love binds man to man.

Ever singing, march we onward,
Victors in the midst of strife,
Joyful music leads us sunward
In the triumph song of life. Amen.

(Henry van Dyke)

June 1

Surrounded by Love

The green and gold scene in morning's new light
    looks in the window at me
and I look back with wondering eyes
    to watch You unfold the day.
Your Presence is here in rustling high leaves
    as well as the forest's depths.
What it says to me, Lord, makes my heart leap up
    with assurance of Your love.
Your love surrounds me, I know;
    it's deep in the future unknown.
Behind me it's there, like comforting years,
    solid beneath my feet.
I lift praise for Your love, and thanks
    to my King.
Here's worship with love returned,
    for I revel in seeing Your work.
So work, dear Lord, in the inner me
    and create a loving heart.   F.N.

June 2

Our Liberating Lord

"While Jesus was praying, His face changed. His clothing blazed like lightening. Moses and Elijah stood there with Him talking of His coming death in Jerusalem." (Luke 9:29-30)

Lord, what must Peter, James and John have thought when You, their day-in-day-out Friend and Teacher, were *transfigured* before their eyes? Why were Moses and Elijah there? They had been "dead" for centuries, yet there they were! Why were they chosen? Why not Abraham? Abraham was called "the friend of God." He followed You into an unknown land. He was prepared to sacrifice his own son if You had not provided a sacrifice. Why wasn't he there? (Genesis 18:22-39)

Or how about David? He was "a man after God's own heart." He wasn't perfect, but You loved him. At times he wasn't even good, but he was full of praise for God through every difficulty. He fought Israel's enemies for his faith. He fought his own doubts for his faith. He reasoned with himself, advised himself, questioning his doubts: "Why are you doubtful, my soul? And why are you so restless? I am putting my hope in God and will praise Him for His coming help." (Psalm 42:5)

Adam could have been there. He was earth's pattern for humanity. Then there was Isaiah to whom You gave the exalted vision of Yourself. It was he who wrote about Messiah as God's Suffering Servant.

It must have been because You, Moses and Elijah had a great mission in common. Moses was to liberate his people physically from slavery and to lead them to the Land of Promise. Elijah was to free them from false gods. This was liberation of the mind. And Lord Jesus, Your purpose in coming here was to free us spiritually, mentally and physically from the bondage of false philosophies, from sin and death and to lead us to Heaven.

You three liberators met to discuss Your coming death at Jerusalem. (Luke 9:31) Your death and resurrection, Lord Jesus, means eternal liberation. No wonder the glory of God shone from You! No wonder the disciples were stunned!

Lord, You bought us and brought us the choice of freedom from the bondage of false philosophy, from servitude to current finite standards and from the pain of sin and death. For all of this and more we praise You today!

June 3

Ears that Hear

Scripture alerts us to the necessity of having healthy spiritual "ears." Without them how can we hear when the Spirit of God speaks to our spirit? He teaches us, His Spirit to our spirit.

Jesus asked His disciples: "Can't you understand Me? Are your hearts so hard that you cannot hear? You have eyes. Why don't you see? Don't your ears work either?" (Mark 8:17)

"Whoever has ears let him understand." (Matthew 11:15)

"Whoever will hear and heed a life-giving rebuke will be made all the wiser because of having heard it." (Proverbs 15:31)

"Ears that accept sound criticism are a lasting gift to the owner." (Proverbs 25:12)

"Listen carefully to Me with open ears," says the Lord, "Take in, understand and absorb, My words so your soul may live." (Isaiah 55:2-3)

"The Lord wakens my ears each morning to listen like a student being taught. The King of all Creation has opened my ears so that my spirit hears." (Isaiah 50:4-5)

Lord, You and I both know I don't always listen carefully. Am I so set on what I'm doing, I don't want to hear? Forgive and help me.

June 4

Distractions

Jesus said, "The most important commandment is this: Love the Lord your God with all your heart and soul, mind and strength" (Mark 12:29-30) and "You shall put no other gods before Me." (Exodus 20:30)

Lord, You know what a project oriented person I am. When I'm all wrapped up in something I need to stop and ask myself, "Self, are you worshipping this project? Are you honoring the project or are you honoring God through it? It seems to be mastering your time, thought and energy, rather than you mastering the project." This is one of those times, Lord, when praying "in spirit and in truth" is hard. Distracting thoughts, like a better way of phrasing a paragraph, or even the thought that I'll soon need another ink cartridge, slip in from the wings of the mind, almost unnoticed, claiming center stage, demanding the spotlight.

It's because of this difficulty that I need to pray, worship and listen with a pen. The pen acts as ballast in the midst of runaway thoughts. It helps me return You to center stage, Lord, and let other "projects" play only bit parts. Work with me on this, Father, and accept these jottings as prayers, loving meditations and praise.

Lord, my knowledge of myself is incomplete, but I can see You are planting the seeds of love, peace, joy, patience, faithfulness and self-control within me. Some have begun to sprout and they're growing. But Father, all too often the Tempter slips in tampering with my prayer time, distracting me by nudging me with details which must be seen to – but not now! Lord, please take care of the seedlings You've planted in my soul and keep them growing.

June 5

Lord, I'm Only Human

Yes, Lord, I'm only human and human is what I want to be, with the Holy Spirit guiding me. The words human and humble sound so like the word *humus,* meaning the crumbly, earthy soil from which You made us, that I'm taking the liberty of equating them. Soil is pretty humble stuff, so how does pride sneak in?

At times my mind wanders, but not this time! What I read today stopped me cold. Before me was *Living The Message* by Eugene Peterson. Jesus is speaking, "I can see it now -- at the Final Judgment thousands strutting up to Me and saying, 'Master we preached the Message, we bashed the demons, our God-sponsored projects had everyone talking.' And do you know what I, Jesus, am going to say? 'You missed the boat. All you did was to use Me to make yourselves important.'" * (Matthew 7:22-23)

Lord, for decades my favorite projects have been Bible study, teaching and writing. I can't keep from writing of what You mean to me. I want to share You. But I want to do it for reasons which please You. Do I do that? I know I'm only human and as a human, I'm flawed. Sometimes I'm so uncritical of myself that I can't, or won't, know my own motives. Since this question came to mind yesterday and the reading from Dr. Peterson's paraphrased New Testament today, I'm suspicious of my attitudes.

I do like it when someone tells me what I wrote helped them. It makes me feel special. But Lord, You are the special One. You constantly pour loving mercy on me and You do it so I can share with others.

I like being human, it's another gift from You, Lord, but I always need Your Spirit to keep my humanity under Your direction. Along with that thought came Your message to my heart: "Daughter, we both know you're human. But you're mistaken in using the word *only.* You have God-life, Salvation-life

June 5

within you – My very Life. Be glad you are human but don't dwell on the *feeling* of helplessness.

"Feelings are relatively unimportant. They are flighty things, forever changing shape. Put your mind on what you *know* of yourself and Me. You know you are weak and human. So what? So is all humanity. *Humus,* remember? What do you know (not feel) about how I love you? It's all written down in My love letter to you, the Holy Bible. I love you, chose you, redeemed you, have taken up residence within you. My very Life is in you. Yet you *feel* distant from Me, like I wandered off and left you alone. Dear Child, you have it backwards. I was not the one who wandered off. You have let yourself become entangled by the subversive power of fear rather than being lifted by knowledge and trust. My Adversary has great success in toying with human feelings. It's when your knowledge of My Word carries through into action that he is stumped. Satan is trying to use your feelings to estrange us. I'm using it to strengthen your faith. My Presence is not a feeling. It is power. It is faithfulness."

Thank You, Father. I am especially thankful for Your Holy Spirit to keep my humanity under control. Tune my mind and heart to love and obey You, to remember Your care of me.

* *Living the Message*, Daily Reflections with Eugene Peterson, used with permission

June 6

Thank You, Lord

"Lord, thank You for inviting us to come in close to Your throne of grace, with confidence, so we may receive Your mercy and find help in time of need." (Hebrews 4:16)

There are so many needs in my life and in other's lives and in our country, that there's no way to cover them all in prayer. Thank You for knowing us individually through and through. Thank You for knowing our thoughts before we think them. (Psalm 139)

Thank You, You can supply all our needs from Your great store of riches in glory. (Philippians 4:19)

Thank You, as we seek Your will above all else, the things we need will be supplied. (Luke 12:31)

Thank You for telling us we must have faith in order to please You, and if we trust You to do what You have promised, it may be counted upon. You will bring it about. (Hebrews 11:1-6)

Thank You for Your long arm to reach and save no matter how low we have sunk or how far we have strayed. (Isaiah 59:1)

Thank You for satisfying the soul which longs for You, for filling the hungry soul with plenty. (Psalm 107:9)

Thank You for guarding over us and for neither sleeping or nodding off in a nap, for preserving us from the Evil One and keeping our souls in safety. (Psalm 121:3-7)

Thank You for being our Healer of body, mind and soul. It is by Your sacrifice that we are healed.   (Isaiah 53:12)

Thank You, Lord!

June 7

Our Restoring Lord

My family was out of town for several days. Each of the three said they would attend to certain tasks before they left, but not one remembered. Since I was having guests for lunch the next day, I did the chores myself. After ten hours I was still not through. My back hurt. I was tired, dirty and resentful. By evening I had worked up a good head of steam. Making a quick sandwich, I took it outside to watch the sunset and sympathize with myself. I fully intended to grumble to You, Lord, about "poor me." But the beauty of the garden, the late golden light through the trees jolted the ugliness out of me. In one big gasp I asked You to forgive me and to bless and protect my travelers. I told You I had missed You, Lord, during my resentment. I thanked You for painting Your glory across the sky in sunset colors. Your presence was all about me. Peace, delight and praise came like a benediction to my soul, and this little homemade hymn followed me into the house:

> When light begins to close her eyes
> and night falls like a veil,
> my heart begins to tune her praise
> in Your restoring presence.
>
> This off key day was in Your hand
> and now the night is Yours.
> My loved ones scattered about the land
> are kept in Your own way.
>
> Quiet joy and rest of soul settle in
> like birds at nest
> for Lord, Your forgiveness lifts my heart
> as day fades into night.

June 7

Lord, Your merciful forgiveness delights me. (Micah 7)

Your quietness and peace beyond human understanding enfold me, (Philippians 4, Psalm 23) bringing the joy of Your presence. (Psalm 21)
You lift my soul, on strong wings, from shadows to the light of Your love. (Isaiah 40)

Who else, Lord, would treat a grumpy, selfish woman the way You have lavished Your love on me tonight? No one else, Lord. No one but You!

June 8

Two Pictures

God gives two Old Testament pictures describing His Son in this world. In the first picture, the Father says of the Son, "This is My servant, My chosen One, My delight. My Spirit is in Him and He will bring justice to the world. He won't shout or make demands in the streets. He will not discard the bruised reed." (Isaiah 42:1-4)

From this last sentence we see a river bank covered with reeds. Children make whistles of the reeds. Often in the process they are bent or bruised and cannot be used. It doesn't matter to the children, for there's an endless supply on the bank. They simply throw the broken ones aside and cut undamaged ones.

A second picture arises from Isaiah's next sentence, "He doesn't snuff out the smoldering wick. He will unhesitatingly bring justice until it is established on earth." This picture is of a small clay lamp containing olive oil. When the oil is nearly gone the wick starts to smoke, burning the eyes and stinging the nose with its acrid odor.

God's Servant in Isaiah's story does not throw out the "damaged reeds or the unpleasant wicks." In today's society broken people are often considered throwaways, therefore Isaiah's sentence is in the negative form, "not discard, not snuff out." We don't need or want problems. But Jesus, God's Servant doesn't object to problems.

Lord, You are totally different from people and Satan. Satan, known as *the Accuser*, accuses us of our sins before You, Lord, and our consciences know the accusations are true. People can give us very little help with our broken places. We find no help from looking inside ourselves because society, Satan and our own consciences are in agreement. But in the midst of accusations against us, the Father says, "Look to My Son. He's not like that."

June 9

God's "New Thing" in Isaiah

Under the Old Covenant with Moses, people kept drifting from God, generation after generation, following false gods, adopting their "abominable practices." They sacrificed children to Moloch. Both men and women prostitutes waited at temples to help men "worship" in evil ways.

As evil peaked the nation's strength declined. Their own evil defeated and enslaved the people, carrying off the brightest leaving the poor, most uneducated to work the land.

For centuries prophets like Isaiah taught and preached God's Word. Some listened; some did not. Most prophets were thrown in dungeons or killed.

"God says, 'Listen, I'm doing a new thing! It's springing up. Do You see it coming? I'm making a new path through the wilderness. I'm creating streams through the desert.'" (Isaiah 43:19)

Throughout the Old Testament, Jehovah is uncovering His New Covenant of Grace. It's His plan of the ages, made before creation but new to mankind. When God's promised Servant comes, sacrificial lambs, the Old Covenant's *symbol* of truth, are to be set aside as the reality of the True Lamb of God appears.

God called Moses to lead captive Israel out of slavery in Egypt and into the Promised Land. This was not unlike God sending His Son in the first millennium to show us the way to God. True Believers, laymen as well as pastors, are to tell and show by their lives, the way out of slavery to sinful habits and attitudes, into the land of God's promises of hope, salvation and true freedom. This is truly a "New Thing!" It is God's New Covenant of Grace.

Note: This and five other passages dealing with covenants are notes I condensed and partially paraphrased decades ago from a book by Andrew Murray from my mother's library. Her library is scattered and I no longer have access to it or to the name of the book.

June 9

God's "New Thing" in Isaiah

Under the Old Covenant with Moses, people kept drifting from God, generation after generation, following false gods, adopting their "abominable practices." They sacrificed children to Moloch. Both men and women prostitutes waited at temples to help men "worship" in evil ways.

As evil peaked the nation's strength declined. Their own evil defeated and enslaved the people, carrying off the brightest leaving the poor, most uneducated to work the land.

For centuries prophets like Isaiah taught and preached God's Word. Some listened; some did not. Most prophets were thrown in dungeons or killed.

"God says, 'Listen, I'm doing a new thing! It's springing up. Do You see it coming? I'm making a new path through the wilder-ness. I'm creating streams through the desert.'" (Isaiah 43:19)

Throughout the Old Testament, Jehovah is uncovering His New Covenant of Grace. It's His plan of the ages, made before creation but new to mankind. When God's promised Servant comes, sacrificial lambs, the Old Covenant's *symbol* of truth, are to be set aside as the reality of the True Lamb of God appears.

God called Moses to lead captive Israel out of slavery in Egypt and into the Promised Land. This was not unlike God sending His Son in the first millennium to show us the way to God. True Believers, laymen as well as pastors, are to tell and show by their lives, the way out of slavery to sinful habits and attitudes, into the land of God's promises of hope, salvation and true freedom. This is truly a "New Thing!" It is God's New Covenant of Grace.

Note: This and five other passages dealing with covenants are notes I condensed and partially paraphrased decades ago from a book by Andrew Murray from my mother's library. Her library is scattered and I no longer have access to it or to the name of the book.

June 10

Watch It Unfold

God told His people He was going to do a new thing. It would be a new way through their impossible wilderness. He wanted them to be on the lookout for it. (Isaiah 43:19)

Isaiah could just as easily have written, "God's Purpose of the Ages is coming soon. When He comes He Himself will show us a new way through the barrenness of our inability. The new way will be under the guidance of His Suffering Servant."

In Old Testament times Jews believed the way to God was through obeying the laws of God. The first law is, "You must have no other gods before Me." (Exodus 20:3) Jesus translates this as "Love the Lord your God with all your heart, soul and mind … The second is like it. Love your neighbor as much as you love yourself." (Matthew 22:37 and 39)

All Ten Commandments sound reasonable, but the problem is we can't even keep the first two.

In His mercy, God doesn't leave us floundering in our helplessness. His plan, new to Old Testament Jews, had been on His drawing board since before creation. (I Peter 1:18-20)

God called Moses to take his people out of Egypt and back to Israel. It reminds me of Jesus' commitment to the Father's call to lead believing people out of slavery to sin and into God's Kingdom. The Way, ever since Jesus' death and resurrection would not be through priests and animal sacrifice but through the all sufficient sacrifice and resurrection God's True Lamb who takes away the sin of the world.

Old Testament Jews were told to watch for clues in Scripture of the Suffering Servant's coming in order to believe when He came. On this side of the cross we are told to watch for His return and be ready.

A few references pertaining to God's Servant: Genesis 3:5, Isaiah 7:14, 11:1-2, 42:1-4, 49:63, 52:13-53:12, Zechariah 9:9

June 11

Jehovah: I AM, God of the Covenant

All Hebrew names of God come from His works except *Jehovah*. It comes from the verb *havah*, to be, and the verb *chavah*, to live. Jehovah means the Being who IS life -- permanent, ever revealing, unchanging and altogether self-existent.

A Hebrew scholar writes: "*Jehovah* is a proper name denoting the person of God and Him only. A Hebrew may say the *Elohim*, the true God in opposition to false gods but he never says the *Jehovah*, for *Jehovah* is the name of the true God only. He may say my God or my *Elohim* but never my *Jehovah* for when he says my God he means *Jehovah*. He speaks of the *Elohim* of Israel, but never the *Jehovah* of Israel for there is no other *Jehovah*. He speaks of the living God but not of the living *Jehovah* for he cannot conceive of *Jehovah* as other than living."

The name was used early in Genesis (2:4) but its full significance was not revealed until Moses talked with God by the burning bush. Moses asked, "When I tell Israel, 'The *Elohim* of your ancestors has sent me to you,' they will ask, 'What's His name?' What shall I tell them?" (Exodus 3:13-15) God answered Moses, "I AM WHO I AM. Tell them I AM sent you." The origin and meaning of what God said here is the same as that of *Jehovah, the* One who always WAS, IS, and always WILL BE in personal, absolute existence.

Whenever God wanted to reveal Himself He used the name *Jehovah* because He is especially the God of revelation. Later He told Moses, "I am *Jehovah*, God of the covenant, who appeared to Abraham, Isaac and Jacob as *El Shaddai*. Even though I did not reveal My name *Jehovah* to them then, I entered into covenant with them promising to give the land of Canaan for their descendants." (Exodus 6:2-4)

June 11

Elohim is the name connected with creation and preservation of the world, but as *Jehovah* He is God of revelation and covenant. He gave Israel the revelation of Himself through Scripture, the Word, and later He sent the revelation of the Living Word, God Incarnate in Jesus Christ, the ever-existing One. He is the eternal I AM, the ever coming and becoming One who appears for our redemption.

June 12

Jehovah, Holiness and Love

We could assume that the mighty *Elohim*, who created the universe and promised to sustain it, had moral and spiritual attributes but the name *Jehovah* reveals it. The name *Jehovah* is used only after the general account of creation. As the account of Adam and Eve, and God's relationship with them begins, *Elohim* is called *Jehovah-Elohim*. (Genesis 2:4) It's as *Jehovah* that God put humanity under moral obligation and responsibility, "You shall. You shall not." When Satan spoke to Eve, he used only the name *Elohim, not Jehovah*. Satan must have hated the name, Jehovah. After Adam and Eve's disobedience they hid from the Lord. His holiness and their new sense of guilt frightened them. But God called them back to Himself. (Genesis 3:8-9)

Righteousness and holiness are two of God's great attributes. The name was considered so holy to ancient Israel, they didn't dare pronounce it for fear of profaning it. Even today the name *Jehovah* is not used in synagogues. They substitute the name *Adonai*, and because of this the original pronunciation of the name we call *Jehovah* has been lost.

God's first requirement of His people is, "You shall be holy as I, your *Elohim*, am holy." (Leviticus 9:2) "Holy, holy, holy is *Jehovah* of hosts." (Isaiah 6:3)

It is against Your righteousness that we sin, Lord God. Your holiness condemns us. But You, *Jehovah-Elohim*, are also love. You grieve and suffer for our sins. "I have loved you with an everlasting love." (Jeremiah 3:13) "In their distress He too was distressed." (Isaiah 63:9-10)

While God's righteousness condemns our unrighteousness, Jesus' sacrificial love redeems us and seeks to bring us back into fellowship with the holy God. Just as He called Adam and Eve back after they ran away, so Jesus call us. Then He teaches us to approach Him through a substitutionary sacrifice.

June 12

    Jehovah accepted Abel's offering of the sacrifice of an innocent life but He rejected Cain's because there was no sacrifice. The only sacrifice which will cover our sins is the death of the True Lamb of God. Jesus laid down His life so that we may be "holy as He is holy."

June 13

Part of a letter to a Dear One

"I get the idea, right or wrong, from your letter, that to you life is like an impossible box of puzzle-pieces with many missing, which you're trying to force into a comprehensive picture. There's a piece for the unknowable, holy God, "high and lifted up who inhabits eternity" (Isaiah 57:15) and one for unholy, uncomprehending man. There's a piece for man, originally "created in God's image." The problem with that third piece is man is *not* like God. Even those of us who want to be changed by Him and developed into His likeness, find to our dismay, we are still fallible, selfish humans, made of *humus,* soil of earth. We're still me-first, prideful people who fail to the point of being at odds with others, even those who want to be conformed to the likeness of Jesus. Most people don't know Him and don't want to. They think He's too blunt in telling them they are *sinners.* They don't like that word. They think God wants to spoil their fun and interfere with their goals.

"So we find ourselves in one "mell of a hess." We can't live up to His demands. He demands. We can't deliver. He made the "First Adam" perfect but we blew it through our God-elected representatives, Adam and Eve, receiving from them the virulent sin gene. But God, instead of lowering His standards, gave us The Ten Commandments saying, "Keep them!" But we can't, no matter how hard we try. They are beyond us. Doesn't seem fair does it?

"But that's the whole point, isn't it? He knows we can't obey, but He doesn't leave us floundering in this impossible dilemma. If He demands something of us which we don't have, He will supply it, if we truly seek Him. He made a way – the only way, through our wilderness and promises to walk it with us. He knows we are law breakers. He just wants us to admit it, to ask for help, to open our walnut-shell wills and hearts to Him for forgiveness and cleansing. As He breathed physical life into Adam, He wants to breathe His eternal Spirit of Life into those who ask Him. When this happens changes begin to take place.

"You told me years ago you knew there was no way a person could know God and it's impertinent for us to claim we can. I'm sure we can't know Him without His help. We can't, in our current state, know everything about Him. But we *can know what we need to know* for now. He is Spirit and man is unable to relate to spirit alone. So, God sent Jesus as the "Second Adam," His Son, exact in holiness, but in flesh and blood as we are, to show what holiness in a human being would be like, to tell us *if we want to know God, we must look to Jesus.* (John 1:1-18)

"Jesus, the pre-existing Christ, came to do more than let us know God. He came to deliberately step on the executioner's block and take our death penalty. After His resurrection and ascension, He, our eternal High Priest, (Hebrews 4:12-5:1-6), took the blood of His sacrifice into God's presence, and sent the Holy Spirit to earth to seek us out, to comfort, teach, and be the One who comes along side to assist us in our need. God the Spirit came to live in us so we can begin to take on the family likeness of our Father.

"I say in humble amazement, 'I know and trust God. I see His guidance throughout my life. He's the unchanging foundation of contentment, peace and trust under whatever pain, joy, doubt, or guilt comes my way. He's always been faithful to me even though I'm not always faithful to Him.'

"I love you, dear heart, and yearn for your peace to be 'the peace of God which passes all human understanding which will keep your heart and mind at peace in Christ Jesus.'" (Philippians 4:7)

June 14

Blessed Through Abraham

The Lord told Abraham: "All nations of Earth shall be blessed through you." (Genesis 12:3)

This prophecy of blessing for the nations has been, and is being fulfilled, for it is through Abraham that God sent His Son. We owe the Jews respect and appreciation because they were called to be the earthly conduit through which God's truth could flow out to all the world. Our only Savior came through the Jews. They preserved Scripture and the knowledge of God through millennia of fierce persecution.

Lord, in the beginning You revealed Yourself to the people as *Jehovah-Elohim*, God of the Covenant, choosing Israel, even before there was a nation of Israel or people called Hebrews. (Genesis 12:1)You led Abraham to the Land and promised it to his de- scendants forever. (Genesis 17:4-8) The covenant was renewed with Isaac and Jacob. (Genesis 21: 9-13, 22: 16-18, 25: 21-26)

Down through centuries Jews have miraculously been preserved as a people even though the Land has often been ravaged and its people driven away. Conquering nations have worked diligently at genocide. To date the highest score of a single attempt is 6 million during the Holocaust.

Nations try to foil God's plans for Israel but it can't be done. "He who sits in the heavens laughs at those who try." (Psalm 2) The latest rebirth of the nation was in 1948. Since then the flag of David continues to fly over the Land. A promised ingathering has been taking place since then. "I am with you. I'll bring your descendants from east and west. I will tell the north, 'Give them up!' and to the south, 'Do not stop them! Bring My sons and daughters from all across the Earth!" (Isaiah 43:5)

June 14

Jews have not only returned to their Land, they have done something no other people in history have done. They have revived their ancient language, after many dispersions over hundreds of centuries. This too was foretold by the prophet Zephaniah, "I will restore their pure language to My people, so they may call My name and serve Me with one heart and mind." (3:9)

"I will gather the remnants of Israel. I will bring them together as sheep in the fold, as a flock in their pasture." (Micah 2:12)

Lord Jesus, things look bad for them in this new century. After all they have been through they have not turned to You yet. It's true many individual Jews have accepted You as the promised Messiah but the nation as a whole has not. Lord, I wonder if this is the beginning of the final ingathering or must there be yet another dispersion?

Your will be done.

Future Plans
A paraphrase and condensation of Romans 11

"So," says Paul, "are you wondering if God has thrown Israel away because they rejected God? The answer is NO, definitely no.

"Remember what God told Elijah as he ran for his life from Ahab, King of Israel? Ahab had demanded that all his subjects accept Baal as their god. Elijah was dismayed because he thought he was the only believing Jew left in all of Israel. God told him there was a remnant of seven thousand Israelites who had not 'bowed the knee to Baal.' (I Kings 19)

"I myself am a Jew," said Paul, "a son of Abraham, a Christian, so I say, 'No, God has not rejected His people, He chose them in the first place.' God always has His remnant of the faithful.

"Israel is like an olive tree with many branches, whose root is holy. The branch of the unbelieving Jews was cut from the tree in order to give pagan Gentiles the opportunity of acceptance.

"So don't boast, Gentile Christians, because you, the wild olive branch, have been grafted into the Family Tree. Instead be fearful. If our kind but all seeing God did not spare the natural branches, He will not spare you if you follow their example of rejection. Just remember God is able to graft them in again to the tree from which they were cut.

"I want you to know that what Israel carefully looked for has not been found by the majority, but the *remnant* remains true. The understanding of the majority has been sealed until the complete number of Gentiles have come in then Israel will understand.

"It is written, 'The day is coming,' says the Lord, 'when I will make a New Covenant with Israel and Judah. It will not be like the Old Covenant I made with the patriarchs, which they broke. In this new contract I will engrave My Words on their hearts and they will *want* to love and obey Me. Then they will truly be My people and I will be their God. They will know Me, from the rulers to the street sweepers. I will forgive their sins, and will remember them no more.

"'I rule Heaven and Earth. Land and sea and all creation obey My laws. Seasons come and go at My command. Israel is Mine and will always be Mine. Only if all rules of nature, all My governing laws of science vanish from the universe will Israel cease to be My chosen nation,' says the Lord. (Jeremiah 31:31-36)

"Gentiles listen, the Jews are enemies of the Messiah for your benefit, but concerning election, they are loved because of the patriarchs. Just as you, who were once disobedient to God, have been granted mercy because of their disobedience, so they too, who are now disobedient, will be given mercy because of God's mercy to you. All humanity, by nature, is tied to disobedience and lawlessness so God may have mercy on them.

Doxology

"God's knowledge and wisdom are deeper
     than human minds can fathom!
Knowledge of Him is treasure beyond measure!
Who can understand the Lord's methods,
     for His ways are not our ways?
Who can ever find a way to repay Him
     for what we owe?
Everything comes from and through Him
     for all that exists belongs to Him.
To Him be all glory, honor, praise and worship!"
                                        Amen

June 16

While Giving Thanks

In early day I look to You,
    and thanks begin to rise.
Thanks for all you've done for me,
    for changes You have wrought.

While giving thanks in new born day,
    a subtle change takes place.
My thanks begin to bring me joy,
    to grow and then to glow.

They soon begin to ring with praise,
    clear as crystal bells.
The praises grow and chime and sing
    'til Jesus' joy brings strength
    for whatever day may bring.
                                        F.N.

June 17

El Shaddai,
One mighty to nourish, satisfy and sustain

Lord, You first showed Yourself as *El Shaddai* to
Abraham. He demonstrated his faith by obeying Your command
to move to a land You promised to give him. Then You told him
You would fill the Land with his progeny. He had no children at
the time of Your promise. (Genesis 15:1-6,18) His faith held for
years as You as-sured him of an heir. When it became humanly
impossible for Sarah to bear a child, Abraham took things into his
own hands, at Sarah's insistence. Sarah's slave, Hagar, gave birth
to Ishmael, the progen-itor of the Arab nations. The offspring of
the two sons of Abraham are still fighting as the Scripture says in
Genesis 16:11-12.

You made it clear that Ishmael was not the child of Your
promise and Abraham was to expect a son by Sarah. You tested
him for thirteen more years! Then as *Jehovah-Elohim*, the One
who continually reveals Himself, You revealed Yourself as *El
Shaddai*. "I am God Almighty, *El Shaddai*, live before Me without
blame." (Genesis 17:1-2)

The word for God here is *El* -- *El Shaddai*. The name
Elohim is largely derived from *El*: mighty, omnipotent. It's the
name connected with creation. (Psalms 77:14 and 68:35) Isaiah
used it for the omnipotent, incomprehensible God. But how do we
understand the part of the name called *Shaddai?*

El Shaddai is translated as Almighty, but it's derived from
shad which means the breast. Used with *El* it becomes the One
mighty to nourish, satisfy, to supply, One who pours out
sustenance and blessing, the bountiful God who blesses with
nourishment, strength, growth and satisfaction, the blessings of the
breast. (Isaiah 65:11-13)

June 18

Confident in You, Psalm 138

O Lord, thank You! I thank You from the depths
of my being. All the angel armies of Heaven
hear me singing Your praise.
I bow before You as thanksgiving pours from my soul.

Your faithfulness is a marvel, O God, and Your love
and mercy, my comfort and strength.
The sacred Word is Your promise vowed in Your
holy and unchangeable Name.
I bless that Name! When I called You, You answered
and revived me with Your assurance.

One day, when Earth's rulers understand who You are,
they too will praise You, Lord,
for Your greatness and glory.
They will know You are exalted in power and wisdom,
yet You still notice the humble.
It's the self important ones You hold at a distance.

Even though trouble surrounds me, I know You sustain me.
Lord, catch the enemies of my soul *
by their necks with Your left hand
and save me with Your strong right.

Lord God, You know everything about me,
both my faithfulness and unfaithfulness,
and I'm confident that You will complete
what You have begun in my life.

The merciful love You show me daily gives this certainty.
I understand too, through the long history of Your

June 18

      faithfulness to Israel, that Your love
        and mercy are eternal.
      So Lord, please, don't abandon me now
        for You created me.

*David, the writer of Psalm 138, had physical enemies. I don't. Mine are within me. The names of some of mine are Self-ishness, Laziness, Fear, Greed, Criticism, Worry and Doubt, Grumpiness, Phoniness and Faithlessness. Actually there are too many to list. Be my victory in this, Lord.

June 19

Forgive and Be Forgiven

There's a scary prayer which seriously incriminates us, yet we pray it often. Do we realize what we are asking of the God who answers prayer? It is from the Lord's Prayer (Luke 11:4): "Forgive our trespasses, O Lord, in *exactly the same way* we forgive others." Jesus also said, "... forgive and you will be forgiven." (Luke 6:37)

There's a story of a little girl who first heard a bagpipe. She told her daddy, "If he'd let go of it, it would stop screaming." Her words echo Luke's beliefs regarding forgiveness. Until we let go of our resentments and hurts they keep screaming inside of us, replaying the grudge, putting another log on the fire.

Father, You forgive us innumerable times for Christ's sake. Your Son is our Savior and example so let's not hold anyone a prisoner of unforgiveness, including ourselves, regardless of who is at fault.

Some believe certain forms of mental illness are brought on and maintained by those who carry the burden of unforgiveness. Lord, we know from Your Word that we must forgive if we want spiritual and mental health. It's as healthy for those being forgiven as it is for those doing the forgiving.

"If we walk in the light, as Jesus is in the light, we have fellowship one with another and the blood of Jesus Christ cleanses us from all sin." (I John 1:7 KJV, notice the present tense) Jesus' blood goes on cleansing us. *But there are conditions.*

We must *confess* our sins to God. We won't surprise Him by our confession. He knows our sin, but confessing it takes honesty and humility. When we "walk in His Light," we're not making excuses. We did wrong so we must forgive and confess to each other. St. James links this kind of confession to healing of mind, relationships, bodies, personalities and memories. *Think*ing forgiveness in our minds isn't enough, or even forgiving or being forgiven. We must repent, turn away and no longer do it. Our

June 19

changed attitudes and actions will show both God, and ourselves, that our forgiveness is real. (James 5:15-16)

Lord, You give us strong, healing promises which come with forgiveness. Here are a few examples out of many:

"Come, let's talk this over," says the Lord, "even if your sins are red as blood, they will be pure white. If they are brilliant crimson, they will be like newly washed wool. If you are willing and obedient, you will be well nourished. But if you are stubborn and rebellious you will be cut down." (Isaiah 1:18-19)

"If we say, 'I am not a sinner,' we are living a fantasy. But if we own up to our guilt, God, in His faithful justice, will forgive us and cleanse us from all sin." (I John 1:8-9)

"If you forgive those who sin against you, your Father in heaven will forgive you, but if you do not forgive others their sins, neither will your Father forgive you." (Matthew 6:14)

June 20

When We Plant Beans

"With the merciful You show Yourself merciful; with the upright You show Yourself as upright; with the pure You show Yourself pure; and with the obstinate You show Yourself to be obstinate." (Psalm 18:25-26)

These verses puzzle me, Lord. What do they mean? Surely our personal characteristics have no influence on Yours? You are changeless (Hebrews 13:8) and impartial. (Deuteronomy 10:17b). We can't thwart Your plans, for "No wisdom, no insight, no scheme can succeed against the Lord." (Proverbs 21:30)

Do they mean we tend, unless taught otherwise, to attribute our own traits to You? We mortals are prone to that in dealing with others. If we're cheaters or liars we may suspect others of the same schemes. If we're honest, we may judge other's standards by our own. But Lord, You're not like us.

Is it more like poetic justice on an enormous scale? Being minuscule dots in this great creation, we are too small in every way to realize what and how You do things. Maybe You allow our treatment of others to boomerang on us? You show the merciful Your great mercy. Those who steal or cheat find their self respect has disappeared. Murderers watch themselves become bitter, revengeful and hate filled. Our actions backfire on us. We reap what we sow.

Scripture illustrates this principle. In Esther 7 Haman was hung on the gallows he built for Mordecai. Jacob cheated his brother out of his birthright then his father-in-law cheated him out of the bride of his choice. (Genesis 29)

Isn't this an image of a natural law of harvest? When we sow beans we may fully expect to harvest beans.

June 21

Firm Ground in a Shaky World, Psalm 18

I love You, Lord. You are my solid ground,
  my Rock, and the strength of my soul.
You are my God, and protecting Shield. I trust You,
  my Deliverer and powerful salvation.
Your daily faithfulness has become my long view.

I have no adequate words to express my praise.
I was near death. The noose was about my neck.
Then, with all my might, I cried for Your help.

Your weapons are a marvel to me, Almighty God.
You used earth, sky and sea to blast me from their grip,
  then You reached and caught me
  before I crashed, setting me on firm ground.

When I saw I was broken, I brought my fragmented
  self to You. You mended the shattered
  places and grafted in the missing pieces.
But Lord, that's the way You are; You make us whole
  again and breathe Your Life into us.

Those who know You will be known by You.
With those who are merciful, You show
  Yourself to be merciful, with good people
  You are Righteous, with those who forgive,
  You are forgiving.

But You puzzle the wicked. They hope You aren't real
  because they cannot understand Your ways.
You are a mystery. They don't like what they see You do.
  It is beyond them.

June 21

But Lord, I like what You do. You turned on the Light
of Life within me and chased out the darkness.
It's by Your Light I have broken through
the darkness and leaped over my wall of fear.

I Bless Your Name, Lord! Is there any other like You?
No indeed! There is no one like You!
I bless, love and trust Your Holy Name!

June 22

Purpose of Prayer

"Jesus told them a parable of the unjust judge to explain that to pray is a necessity and we should never give it up." (Luke 18:1)

Praying consistently is often hard. All of us have experienced this difficulty. Some ask, "If God is good, and loving, and if He really knows what we need before we ask, why on earth doesn't He just give us what we want?"

Lord, do You give us needs simply so we'll come to You and ask Your help? Our most pressing, but often unrecognized need, may be just that. We have many wants and needs. If we're sick, we need healing or a job, if money is tight. But it's less common for us to understand the greatest, never ending need of the human soul is You, Yourself.

A little boy may "run away," but when shadows grow long and the cookies in his pocket are gone, he goes home. His mother is there. She feeds and bathes him, cuddles him and dries his tears. He needs all those comforts, that's true, but his greatest need at this time is to have his mother.

Lord, You supply us with *needs and with problems* so we will bring them to the One who can help. As we come to You for help, by our asking and by Your answering, communion (coming-to-one) begins. Our prayers are the beginning of communion with you. As we return with our other wants and needs, we begin to see that You are our greatest need. We need to know, trust and follow You.

Without needs many Christians would never pray. You grant some requests but that's not Your ultimate purpose. I believe Your main purpose is to gather Your children to Yourself in communion. You hold back so we will ask.

June 23

Inexpressibly Awesome

"Let Earth and Heaven, and all its creatures, stand in awe of our ineffable God; for He telegraphed His commands throughout space and they stand firm." (Psalm 33:8-9)

Lord, there is very little present day Americans consider awesome. Yet many young folks have latched onto the word *awesome* and have dropped the simple word *good* from their vocabularies. They say the movie was *awesome*, the hot dogs were *awesome*, the new car is *awesome*. Even a Christian youth may say God is *awesome*. (Right along with the hot dog?)

We know, Lord Jesus, that You are our Savior and true Friend but both old and young often abuse that benefit. Using the same adjective to describe a hot dog that we use to portray You is only a part of the problem. At times we don't show respect in our prayers. We rush into Your Presence and rattle off a list of requests. We sometimes treat Your forgiveness flippantly, reasoning: "The Bible says, right there in black and white, that He loves me enough to die for me, so I'm sure He'll forgive me if I go ahead and do this little off color thing -- just this once, of course!"

Dietrich Bonhoffer, the German theologian, executed for his faith by the Nazi regime, calls that *cheap grace*. Nothing God does or gives is cheap. Forgiving us cost Him a great deal and it costs us something too. The *something* it costs is love and obedience.

Lord, as Your absolute holiness begins to dawn on us, we are filled with awe, shock and fear as we compare it to our faithless unworthiness. We are overwhelmed with joy and humility that You, Lord Christ, have bridged the uncrossable gap between us with Your own life.

June 24

A Life Changing Vision

Isaiah, the prophet of redemption, lived in Judah during the reigns of Kings Uzziah through Hezekiah. He was given a vision of God which changed his life. Are visions and dreams different? Scripture doesn't tell us. Some say visions occur while one is awake and dreams come during sleep. (Isaiah 6:1-8)

Isaiah's vision filled him with wonder, and awe. "I saw Almighty God sitting on His throne; it was high and raised up. The train of His royal robe filled the Temple. Six-winged seraphim stood before the throne. Each seraph had six wings. Two covered their faces. A second pair covered their feet and they flew with the third pair. They called out to one another,

'Holy! Holy! Holy is Almighty God!
Heaven and Earth are full of His glory!'

"The foundations and door posts shook at the sound of their voices. A cloud of smoke filled the Temple and I cried out in fear, 'O God! I'm as good as dead because I am sinful! My very words are impure, not fit to speak. I live among people of uncleanness. I have seen the King of the Hosts of Heaven and the comparison has devastated me!'

"One of the seraphs flew to me with a glowing coal he had taken from the altar with tongs. He touched the coal to my lips and said: 'Look, I have touched your lips. Now they are clean and your sins are forgiven.'

"Then I overheard the Lord asking, "Whom can I send? Who will go for us? I answered Him immediately saying, 'I'm right here, Lord. Send me!'"

Isaiah was filled with penetrating awe. As he "saw" God, he overheard what He wanted. God wanted Isaiah!

Lord, am I so intent on my projects that I don't even *hear* Your search? Tune my "ears" to understand Your purposes for me.

June 25

Bread That Lives

Jesus said, "I am the Bread of Life. Whoever comes to Me will never be hungry and whoever believes in Me will never be thirsty." (John 6:35-40)

The people were amazed when You said that, Lord. You had just fed a huge crowd with bread and fish. Everything about Your action reminded them of manna God gave Moses' people in the wilderness. It was taught that when Messiah comes He will feed people manna. You told them by Your actions who You were.

You claimed to be Bread. That's food, Lord! Nourishment. Without physical nourishment life dies. You also said You were Life. It doesn't take a lot of discernment to realize Your meaning goes past "natural" bread and life. Both our bread and our earthly life are transitory things and You came here for *everlasting* purposes. Surely You meant real, eternal life with God is made possible only through the spiritual nourishment of Yourself. Wheat bread may satisfy the stomach but not the soul. There's a place, a deep, hungry place within us which keeps on gnawing and growling with dissatisfaction, like hunger pangs, until it has the Bread of Life. Your Bread has let Believers get off the endlessly turning treadmill of wanting, grasping and yet remaining unfilled. What a gift that is!

June 25

Perhaps it could be said this way. Ordinary bread is meant for eating, for taking into ourselves. As we chew and digest it, it becomes part of us as blood and brain cells, muscle, bone, vitality and strength. So it is with You, Lord Jesus. You are the life-giving Bread of the everlasting part of us. We take You into our lives, not through the mouth but through an open heart and mind. As we chew and meditate on You, You become a spiritual unity within us, in our thinking, being and living. You become our spiritual backbone which holds us up, and our muscle and strength by which we move and act.

So Father, as I feed daily on the Living Bread, may I always remember the price Your Son paid and be thankful. Help me to let Him be dominant in my thoughts, wants and actions.

June 26

Our Teaching Lord

Jesus said, "The Father will send the Holy Spirit in My Name, to be with you. He is the Comforter and He will teach you..." (John 14:26)

Lord, You are always ready to teach, guide and help us. But we easily forget our Teacher, the Spirit, is here, waiting to counsel us. You begin teaching us about Yourself when we are babies discovering the wonders of our beings and coming to know the love of parents. The natural world reflects much about You. As little ones we take delight in listening to the brook chuckle as it hurries over rock and sand, in watching clouds pile up in every imaginable shape, in seeing butterflies have lunch on the flowers we "helped" plant in the spring. We even enjoy tasting a bug or two while mother isn't looking but we soon decide her picnic is tastier.

Later, we begin to recognize Your bold signature written across Creation. Skies illustrate Your authorship. Earth proclaims it clearly. Night and day are pictures of Your power, precision and perfection. (Psalm 19)

But, dear Teacher, You don't stop teaching us after we discover You as Creator. Your revealing Word is close at hand for "whosoever will" and when we mix our faith with Your Word, You come to us Person to person. You come and say, "Let Me into your living. I made you and I want to bring love, forgiveness, peace, joy and hope into your life. Let Me in." (Hebrews 4:2, Revelation 3:20)

Understanding begins to dawn as we open the door of self to You. It's like sunrise and music! When we listen, things become new. Words of Scripture become the Living Word within us, and that Word is You! (John 1:1) Your Truth is alive in us, guiding, lighting our darkness with joy, hope and praise. You help us in difficulties, in planning, and You always comfort and lift us.

June 27

Surrounded by Enemies

Today I can sympathize with King David, as he tells of his enemies closing in on him, for some of mine have surrounded me. I recognize them because I've fought them before. Discouragement, Fear and Doubt, a deadly trio, circle me, waiting. Lord, Your arch enemy sees his opportunity, for he knows my vulnerability. He wants to plow up my soul with my own oxen (personality).

But Lord, You have provided what I need for this. Paul speaks of your provision as the armor of God. (Ephesians 6:10-18) He provides the helmet of salvation, the uniform of truth and the breastplate of Your righteousness. The boots are my preparation in the Gospel and the shield is faith in You. The only offensive weapon is the sword, the Word, the communicator of the mind of God. All this is given for protection against such enemies. I take up the sword, which cuts the false from the true, and the temporal from the eternal.

Your Word to me today is more beneficial than a doctor's prescription: "Let the mind of God be in you, for it's also in Jesus Christ, for God *is working in you...*" (Philippians 2:5, 2:13)

"Always rejoice in the Lord and don't be anxious over anything. Instead of worrying, pray and thank Him, telling Him your requests. Then peace, straight from God, will fill and guard over your heart and mind in Christ Jesus." (Philippians 4:4)

"Let your mind dwell on worthy things... If there is any good news or any lovely thing, if there is any virtue or anything worth praising, think about these things." (Philippians 4:6-8)

Thank You, Lord! I want to want what You want. Your Words have poured trust into my mind and taken the fight out of my enemies. You are absolutely worthy of the praise of my life.

June 28

Daily Choices

Moses said, "I set before you life and death, blessings and curses. Choose life, so you and your children may live, love the Lord God, hear and hold fast to Him ..." (Deuteronomy 30:19)

Joshua said, "Choose today whom you will serve." (24:15)

This is easy to say, Lord, because it sounds like a one time decision -- but it is not. It's a daily or hourly, and sometimes even a moment by moment decision, which must be made with the *will*, not simply with the lips. We may choose Your Way in the morning, and tell You of our choice, then due to some turn of events, we may find ourselves sprawled on our backs far from the King's Highway. The Way is mined with the dangers of selfishness, materialism and evil for the Enemy of our souls is at work.

When this happens, and it does, as all of us have experienced, it's not for us to lie there in despair crying and berating ourselves. We're to "get up and get going," realizing You have not abandoned us. The Apostle reminds us in 1 John 2:1, "When we sin we have a personal and powerful Defense Lawyer, before our Father, the Judge. He is Jesus Christ the Righteous."

So when we make the daily decision to go God's Way, what are we choosing? What are we asking? We ask for, accept, and believe in, Your forgiveness. We ask Your help to stay close to You, Lord. We ask You into our living, thinking and speech. "Let the words of my mouth and the meditation of my heart be acceptable to Thee, my strength and my redeemer." (Psalm 19:14 KJV)

I ask: To be willing to be changed into what You want me to be, to stay in close communication with You, through Your Word and prayer, to live in You, keep Your Word alive in me, to obey, and love You, to enjoy what You enjoy and dislike what You hate, to bless and praise You in everything.

June 29

The Still, Small Voice

Lord, walking closely (living) with You is never boring. It always involves surprises. It's through some of these surprises that You teach us about ourselves, about You, and our relationship. When we think we've come to know You so well we can walk with You without really watching or listening to You, we discover it doesn't work that way. If we turn down our hearing aid and plunge ahead with our plans, we find ourselves walking alone. We may see You up ahead or behind us a ways; perhaps You've even disappeared from our sight. Then it's not unusual for us to wonder what happened to our relationship.

You tell us, "I am the Good Shepherd and My sheep hear My voice." (John 19) But Lord, it's *so easy* to listen to other voices. They speak more loudly than You do. Some clamor, demand or nag. My experience of yesterday reminds me of Elijah. He had been about God's business, publicly showing up King Ahab and Queen Jezebel's god, Baal, as a fraud. The Queen was furious and sent soldiers after him with the promise of death. Elijah, filled with panic, fled the city, entered the dangerous wilderness and took refuge in one of its many caves where he dropped from exhaustion, hunger and mortal terror. God called him and told him to come out of the cave because He wanted to talk to him. When Elijah obeyed, all he could hear and see was the howling wind of hurricane force with sand and debris being hurled about. God was not in the wind. After the wind-storm there was an earthquake but God wasn't there. Then lightning slashed, igniting anything flammable. But God wasn't in the fire. After the fire came a still, small voice, just a gentle whisper. When Elijah heard it he covered his head. And God asked, "What are you doing here Elijah?" (I Kings 19) Elijah answered, "Lord, the Israelites have broken Your covenant and torn down Your altars. They've killed Your prophets. I'm the only one left and they want

June 29

to kill me!" God told Elijah to go back the way he came, for He had another task for him.

Like Peter who sank in the water because he looked at the waves instead of at Jesus, like Elijah who listened to the voice of fear rather than the voice of trust, like me barging ahead of the Good Shepherd, we all three lost sight of our Leader and suffered disappointing surprises.

Window with a View

Down among the trees and hills
    earth seems very large.
Sky and cliffs stretch up so high
    with valleys remote and deep.
But up here Lord, with a plane's eye view,
    I see with different eyes.
Bright clouds drop shadows on the sea
    and waves are merely ripples.
Mountains thrust upward but still can't
    reach the unattainable blue.
Down there a ship takes a luxurious
    trip with merriment, feasting and song.
Deep blue water, lacy white wake, clouds
    like glory in the sun.
From here the picture is all off kilter,
    how toy like it seems to be!
Beneath me is home, that minuscule globe,
    while above there's ceaseless space.
Endless space -- a mystery I can't fathom,
    but Your love reaching me,
holding me fast to Yourself, is the mightiest
    mystery of all, dear Lord.
You, Eternal, Infinite, spoke the Word
    and these worlds came to be.
Then Your love reached out through vast
    expanse and claimed this finite me! F.N.

July 1

Trees by the River, Psalm 1

David's Psalm shows the pattern for, and the vast difference between those who love God and those who don't.

God's people whom He blesses, don't follow illegal advice,
nor do they model their lives after unbelievers.
They don't hang around talking and laughing
with those who mock God.

Instead they take pleasure in His Word, drinking it in
until the Lord's Book becomes alive in their hearts.
They become like trees growing by a river
whose roots are nourished by the Living Water.
Their fruit matures; their leaves stay green and vibrant
because the Lord replenishes their souls.

Those without God are different. Their lives become dry,
empty like chaff -- blown about by every passing wind.
In God's court of judgment godless are defenseless.
They are even ill at ease in the company of the redeemed.

The Lord, our Protector, watches over the path of His people   but the way of the wicked becomes the route of terror.

Lord, I pray this for my family.
Plant each, like a tree, by Your
river of Living Water so they
may flourish for Your Kingdom.

Jehovah-nissi

After the battle with the Amalekites "Moses built an altar and called it *Jehovah-nissi*, the Lord is Our Banner." (Exodus 17:15)

Lord, even though You saved Israel from Pharaoh's armies, met all their needs, gave them food and water in the desert, they criticized Moses and lost faith in You. Again the Amalekites marched against them. Under Joshua's leadership, Israel's armies went to meet the enemy. Moses' role was not to fight but to pray. He climbed a hill, taking the staff he carried throughout their deliverance from Egypt. When he held up the staff in prayer, Israel dominated the battle. When he grew tired and lowered his arms, the Amalekites prevailed. Two of Moses' men stood beside him, holding up his hands with the staff of God lifted over the battle. So Joshua, whose name in Hebrew is *Y'eshua*, or Jesus in English, and Moses, with the rod of *Elohim* held high in his prayerful hands, gained victory under God's Banner.

Nissi translated here as a banner, flag or rallying point for armies. It may be an ensign, a staff or pole with a top to reflect light. In this instance it was Moses' staff, representing God's Presence.

Lord, Christians have battles to fight which non-believers don't have. You, *Jehovah-jireh*, provide us with armor to protect us. We notice (Ephesians 6:12) no armor is provided for our backs. We face the enemy, but never alone. If we stand alone we lose. You, *Jehovah-nissi*, are our Banner, our rallying point. "When the time is right, the Root of Jesse will stand as a banner for His people and the nations will rally to Him." (Isaiah 11:1-12)

Who is this *Root of Jesse*, this lifted Banner, but You, Lord Christ? You are God's mighty power for our redemption, our victory in the battle over sin and death. "If God is for us, who can be against us? (Romans 8:31-39)

July 3

Our Lord Our Banner, Psalm 60

David is in the midst of a fierce battle; the tide turns against
him. It is said his battles were a continuation of Joshua's commission from God to clear Israel's godless enemies from the land.

Lord, why have You turned from us? Are You angry?
I'm overwhelmed! Please help us!
Are we never to be made whole again?
Our defenses are beached, the Land is torn apart.
People are in terrible straits. This defeat makes us
     stagger and reel like drunks.
But Lord, You gave us a banner to be the rallying point
     for those who trust You.
You, Yourself are that Banner, *Jehovah-nissi!*
May Your people gather round You for deliverance.
     Rescue us, Lord, for we are Yours.
These battered cities of Israel are still Yours, Lord.
You know each by name. We will shout the victory
     over the Philistines. But who will lead us
     back to besieged Jerusalem?
It will have to be You, Lord! Even though You said "no"
     to our prayer today,
     won't You lead our armies again?
Help, Lord God. Human help is futile.
With You beside us, breathing courage
     into our quaking souls,
     we will be victorious.
It is You, true King and Protector of Israel,
     who will give us victory over our enemies.

July 4

Sweet Land of Liberty?

God says, "I know you inside and out...You're neither hot nor cold. It's better to be one or the other! You're stale. Stagnant. You anger me with your bragging and superiority." You may tell yourself, "No, I'm rich and respected. No one can contribute anything to me!" But actually, you're pitiful, blind, deaf and naked." (Revelation 3:15)

God have mercy on us, Your lukewarm people. You have been our Dwelling Place since we were a tiny colony struggling for survival in this land. You have been our hope, help, our only God.

Now we're transferring our trust and loyalty to a whole bevy of gods, an unholy trinity: Self, Materialism and Greed. We are losing our way in this jungle. Mouths spew out raw sewage. Movies, television and books feed us violence, hatred and bloodshed. Sex is rampant in all deviant forms. Adultery is in. Fidelity is out. Truth is important only if it's to our advantage.

We no longer say the "Barbarians are at the gate." They're *among us*. No longer do they look like thugs. They look like we do. They may be rich, poor, black or white, educated or illiterate. They may wear business suits, sequined gowns, baggy shirts, priestly collars or cowboy boots.

What will it take to wake us up? Must we continue to rot internally until we become so empty that we crumble? Lord, in Your mercy pour out Your Spirit of Truth upon us. Bring us to repentance and back to Yourself. Revive us. We're fainting, drying up. Dying. We've lost our saltiness and hidden our light. Lord, raise up Christian leaders of principle and courage who, like our early patriots, are willing to live for or die for Your truth. Save us.

"Long may our land be bright with freedom's holy light.
Protect us by Thy might, great God, our King!"

July 5

Our Instructing Lord

Isaiah says, "The Lord will guide you in the way and will satisfy your soul in times of drought. He will give you a healthy soul so you may flourish like a well-watered garden." (Isaiah 58:11)

God tells us: "I will instruct you ... but don't be like a stub-born mule." (Psalm 32:8-9)

The human mind asks: "How will You instruct me, Lord? When? Now or later? How will I know it's *You* guiding me?"

The Spirit replies: "Trust Me enough to put your weight on My promises. Even though you don't know everything about guidance, you know certain principles. Act on them. *Seek* My advice and I will guide you in what you don't know. I never guide contrary to My Word. I'm building My likeness into your understanding, so cooperate by working from what you know. I'll lead you step by step through shadowy areas. Temporal cares often press scriptural principles down into the subconscious mind. Keep them before you in your conscious, working mind.

"These are the steps you know to take:

(1) Pray. Prayer is conversation. You talk and listen. If you do all the talking how am I to speak to your soul? Be honest. Speak truth in prayer.

(2) Read and study My Word. Paul told Timothy: 'All Scripture is God-breathed. It's purpose is to teach, rebuke, correct and train in righteousness so God's people may be equipped for good work.' (II Timothy 3:16)

(3) Talk the situation over with a mature Christian. Consider and learn from events and circumstances of your own life."

Thank You, for reminding me to pray honestly, read thought-fully, seek Your guidance, then discuss it with mature Christian.

July 6

This Sleeping Nation

"Put off your old corrupted life and put on a fresh mental and spiritual attitude, created in God's image in true righteousness..." (Ephesians 4:22-24)

Almighty God, help! Wake us up. Our nation, even some churches, have gone to sleep. Help us rediscover Your terrible holiness. Holiness and purity are not qualities we humans come by naturally. We're geared to the Me-first syndrome, doing and planning self promotion. Too many of our prayers are like a grocery list of "gimmies," gimmy this and gimmy that.

It may be comforting to think of You, Lord, as our loyal Friend, but it is unacceptable and presumptuous to let our "friendship" overshadow the fact that You are *the High and Holy One who inhabits eternity."* (Isaiah 57:15) We presume on Your forgiveness when we tell ourselves that since You are so good and loving You will surely give us anything we ask for and forgive us if we go ahead and do this shady thing – just this one time, of course.

Here again is an example of what Bonhoffer, calls *cheap grace.* God's grace cost Jesus His life, and costs us what we're not always willing to pay: living God's way rather than our own.

We know You are not an indulgent old grandfather, Lord, who pets and pampers his children. Your concern is more for our spiritual development than for our comfort and happiness. When we come into Your Presence and recognize Your absolute holiness, we are filled with awe, shock, praise, humility and reverence. In our society today there is little reverence. We seem to either be unconcerned or totally ignorant of any such thing as God's holy Presence.

Forgive, teach our nation. Shake us awake, Father!

July 7

Jehovah-jireh, Our Lord Provides

This compound name takes much of its meaning from *Jehovah*: the eternal I AM, the self-existing One, God of revelation, God of moral and spiritual qualities, of righteousness, holiness, love and redemption, the One who makes covenant with His people. Many compound names of God couple the name *Jehovah* with an event which shows *Jehovah* meeting our human needs.

Jehovah-jireh is first used in Abraham's test in Genesis 22. As *Elohim*, Almighty God, You command Abraham to sacrifice his son, Isaac. Abraham believed Your promise that it would be through Isaac that his progeny would come. He knew if young Isaac were dead he could father no children. Faith won because You, Lord, had built and strengthened Abraham's faith over the years, enabling him to trust You for the *whole* promise.

On the climb up Mount Moriah Isaac asks, "Where's the lamb, Father?" Abraham's faith replies, "Son, God will *provide* the lamb." After Isaac is bound to the altar, Abraham raises the knife, and the angel stops him saying, "Don't hurt the boy. You have not withheld your only son from Me." Looking up Abraham sees a ram caught in the brambles. Surely he falls to his knees as "he calls the place *Jehovah-jireh,*" the Lord will Provide.

After Your *pre*vision, *pro*vision of what we will need follows. Yes, Lord, the things You see we need to complete Your purposes, You provide. You saw the challenge Your command would be for Abraham and You built in him the necessary faith to obey, then You provided the sacrifice.

Abraham and Isaac are a preview of You and Your Son making provision for our needs. "God loved the world so much that He gave His only Son." Abraham proved his faith in God's promise to give Israel to his progeny. He was willing to obey.

July 7

God did not demand that Abraham follow through with the sacrifice of his son, however God the Father did not hold back His Son, but freely gave *Him* in sacrifice for us. (John 3:16)

Millennia later John the Baptist answered Isaac's question of "Where's the lamb, Father?" As Jesus went to be baptized, John told the crowd, "Look! *Here* is the Lamb of God who takes away the sin of the world!" (John 1:29)

July 8

There is a Difference

"The Love Chapter," I Corinthians 13, has been around a long time. KJV of verse five reads this way: "Love does not behave in an unseemly manner." The NIV says, "Love is not rude."

Lord, excuse me for saying this, but this is confusing because both You and Paul seem to be downright rude at times. You often called people derogatory names, although the names fit. You called people sheep, wolves, dogs and foxes. You even called the Jewish religious leaders fools, hypocrites and vipers. Yet You loved them too.

A couple of years ago I read where a literal translation of the Greek, "love does not behave itself unseemly," could read, "love does not behave without a plan." That explanation helped. We are to love all people but there's a difference in the way we should respond to the terrorist and to his victims. If the shepherd treated the wolf and his dog the same way, soon he would lose his flock. Parents handle an obedient child differently than an unruly one. If a criminal attacks an innocent person, both of whom I may love in a Christian sense, I will try to protect the victim if possible, even to slamming the crook's head with a tire iron. I must consider their different purposes.

We don't have the same attitude toward those who adulterate Scripture to suit themselves as we do toward true Believers. We think differently about defenders of our country than those who blow up buildings. "Tolerance" is an *in word* today. Unfortunately it means *anything goes*. This is our society.

"Love does not behave unseemly." In his book *Reaching Toward the Heights*, Richard Wumbrand, from whom I learned this interpretation, points out that Christian love does not treat every person the same. Neither did Jesus!

July 9

God's Pattern for Love, a paraphrase of I Corinthians 13

If I influence people by my persuasive speech but don't love them, I'm noise without substance. If I'm wise, knowledgeable and have faith, but don't love, I am not equipped to deal with life. If I'm generous, willing to die for my faith, but don't love others, what have I gained? Nothing.

Love is willing to wait. It tries to help meet other's needs. It's not greedy or rude. Love isn't stingy, grouchy, moody or easily bruised. It's generous. It keeps no record of the wrongs of others, holds no grudges and is quick to forgive. It takes no pleasure in circumstances which embarrass or injure the reputation of others. It is just and truthful.

Love doesn't go to pieces in times of trouble but remains strong, resilient and encouraging. It outlasts failure, criticism, disappointment and pain. It's unsinkable, remaining afloat through storms of life. It believes God is in control and He moves in troubles and tragedies, causing the sum of them to equal blessings.

Our human knowledge is partial but God's plan for our life is whole. In eternity our fragmented knowledge will vanish as smoke in the wind, giving way to complete understanding of Truth.

We are like children who are limited in understanding. We strain to see through our dimness what God holds in store for us. It won't always be this way. When we see Him face to face, cataracts will fall from the eyes of our understanding, and we'll see, and know minute details, for we will see and know Him as He has always seen and known us.

Until then there are three lasting goals which we must move toward, faith, hope and love, but the greatest one is love.

Lord, may it be.

July 10

Summertime

It's summertime, Lord, a season you're making day by day.

An idyllic picture comes to mind of lazy, sunny afternoons, a hammock slung between two shade trees. Shoes off. A good book is lying open and face down across my waist as I watch wind push cloud pictures in the sky. A glass of iced tea waits nearby.

An old song says it's "Summertime, an' the livin' is easy..." but Lord, this summer doesn't appear to be either restful or easy. Even so, I'm resting in the hammock of Your love and forgiveness, living in consciousness of Your Presence.

David and Paul's instructions are wise and wonderful when responsibilities seem overwhelming, "Throw all your cares upon Him for you are dear to Him." (Psalm 55:2, I Peter 5:7)

July 10

Here they are, Father, my worries, inadequacies, habits, fears and problems. I'm giving them to You with thanksgiving and with the same confidence the person in my mental picture has as she leans back in the hammock, relaxed, unhurried and unworried, never wondering if the hammock's ropes will hold fast.

I can't see how everything is going to fit into the remainder of the summer, but this I know, Your Spirit is like a flashlight, illuminating the shadowed path at every step. Your Spirit and Your Word will point me in the right direction. "Your Word is a lamp for my feet and it lights up my path." (Psalm 119:105) Jesus said, "Don't be afraid, just believe." (Mark 5:36 and Hebrews 13:6) "The Lord is my helper; I will not be afraid."

Lord, I have two options, don't I? I can sweat, worry and be distraught, or as Your daughter, I can exercise my right to trust You with my future. I *choose* the latter.

July 11

Another Goodbye

Deep sloping woods, I shall miss you. All your moods and dress up outfits have spoken to my soul with the voice of God. Your leafy tunnels send out invitations to walk their lengths. The changing beauty of seasons lifts me out of my earth and time bound self giving a tiny glimpse of God's glory.

In Spring you put on a lacy mantilla, wearing it with graceful charm. As breezes stir, fragrance spills across the hills. Blossoms spring up like jack-in-the-boxes, splashing brown and green earth with color and hope. Spring never fails to bring restoration to both winter weary earth and the human soul.

In Summer your greenness is patterned in sunshine and shadow. Sweet bird song and the rustle of wee furry creatures dining on the Lord's bounty, bring quiet peace and restfulness.

Cool fire of Autumn's splendor wraps me in awe, nearly taking my breath away. The many seasonal changes which come from year to year often appear the same yet are stunningly different. The lift and thrill of God's beauty moves through me like adrenaline.

Blankets of muffling snow in Winter tune my ears to listen to silence. Skeleton trees, black by contrast, dance wildly to wind's harsh music. I shall miss the fires on fog thick nights, humming and crackling as flames leap against darkened stone. Gray curling smoke, like transparent velvet, carries an occasional lively spark up the chimney. But the time has come to say another goodbye before we leave you and move to a place where river and sea move side by side.

It will seem strange, for a while, without hills and woods, without vivid seasonal changes. But this is my Father's world and He will be there, leading the way. I'm not saying goodbye to Him. I'm only saying hello to Florida. He's already there.

July 12

A Task in Common

Lord, You have created countless people, each unique but with similarities. Christians have task in common. As students of the same divine Teacher we all have the same homework.

The majority of believers can't be in full time Christian work but we can all witness to Christ. In court cases it's those who know something of the case who are called as witnesses. Those who know You by experience, Lord, are to witness to others about You.

Opportunities arise to share what You mean in our lives. Our witness may be the first glimpse some ever have of You, so we need to be clear on our beliefs. Making an outline for ourselves, can help us be clear and to the point. It's helpful to *show* from Scripture what the Bible says about our beliefs. We all need to hear and see from the Bible that God loves us and has a plan for our lives. "God loved the people of this world so much He gave His only Son so any who believe in Him ... will have everlasting life." (John 3:16) Jesus spoke of God's plan: "I came to earth so you could have life and have it *more abundantly.*" (John 10:10) The Father says, "I have plans for you, not to hurt you, but to cause you to flourish." (Jeremiah 29:11)

Everyone is sinful, "*All* have sinned and fallen short of God's demands. (Romans 3:23) "The price of sin is death. But God's gift is eternal life because of Jesus Christ's sacrifice." (Romans 6:32)

God made *one* provision for sin, Jesus, death and resurrection. "God proved His love for us while we were still sinners Jesus died in our place." (Romans 5:8) "To all who believe, God gave the right to be His children...Their second birth is not by the decision of man but by God's great sacrifice." (John 1:12-13, 14:6)

July 13

Give and Take

Lord, You give us assignments when we become members of Your family. One of these is to sow the truth of Your salvation among others, like a home owner sows seed over his lawn in the fall.

This may be difficult. We aren't theologians. Anyway it's no time to preach, although preaching may be easier than tactfully controlling the tongue. Honest discussions of the difference Jesus has made in our life is more interesting and may raise their sights. It's good seed to sow over empty lives.

Having a give and take conversation doesn't mean either will have a change of mind, but it may start a new trend of thought. As we water the seed with prayer, we pray it will send down roots.

It's easy to come across as narrow-minded or argumentative. Keep us from that, Lord, and keep us also from the other extreme of softening the clear truth of who You are.

Our goal is to introduce people to the Living God or at least sow seeds of Truth. We can't reflect the One who "loved us and gave Himself for (*all* of) us," if we're argumentative or angry. These attitudes aren't like You, Lord.

I read a good tip somewhere years ago. If a person tells us he doesn't believe in God, we could ask, "What kind of God is it you don't believe in?" His concept is often twisted. With a chuckle, we may reply, "Well, we agree there, I don't believe in a God like that either." A touch of humor often smoothes any ruffled feathers resulting from disagreement.

If I'm too rude to listen graciously to others, why should they listen to me? Lord, I need help here. Help me listen without breaking in with a rebuttal when a person makes a point. Guide me into what needs to be heard. Also, Lord, protect my spiritual immune system so I don't catch the virus of unbelief.

July 14

Every Christian Can

As a new Christian my mother had never spoken to anyone about Christ. The thought terrified her, but she had promised God she would do so *that night* at the large Christian service. She had attended the instruction classes, memorized the verses which explain what Christ has done for us and how we may accept His Gift.

An elderly man came in and sat in the seat in front of her. She chose him to be *the one*! She had been advised to speak to a person similar to herself. But in her fear, she forgot all the instructions. He was a man, she was a woman. He was old, she was young. He looked to be a Jew, she was a very nervous Christian. After the service she asked, "Pardon me, Sir, but are you a Christian?" He turned and smiled, joy in his eyes and said, "Oh yes, for many years!" Her fear melted in relief as she asked, "Would – you tell me how it happened?"

He told my mother, "My father was a rabbi who came to America when I was a small boy. He saw all his children educated and established in business. He started me out with a well stocked grocery store. The day my store opened for business, a winsome six year old girl with wide blue eyes came in to buy a loaf of bread for her mother. As she took the bag she looked up and asked, 'Mr. Erlich, do you love Jesus?' Surprised and a bit amused, I replied, 'No, I do not believe in Jesus.' Without a word she left. "The next day she returned on another errand. Again she turned serious eyes to mine as she asked, 'Do you love Jesus today?' When I smiled and shook my head she turned and left. The next day she was back, and the next, and the following day always asking, 'Do you love Jesus yet?' She came daily; sometimes for no other reason than to ask her question. I always answered negatively, sometimes impatiently. Never once did she reply but at times the innocent eyes looked long, and wistfully into the eyes of this strange man who did not love her Jesus. At times I felt uncomfortable under her wondering scrutiny.

"One day she came in when I was in an irritable mood. As I heard the inevitable question I said 'Now Mary, I'm tired of this! You ask me every day if I love your Jesus, and every time I've told you I do NOT love Him. Don't ask me again!' The little one did not reply, although she searched my face for a moment, then dropping to her knees by a box, she bowed her head and prayed, 'Lord, let Mr. Erlich love You. *Please* Lord, let Mr. Erlich love You!

"Such a simple, short prayer from a child's heart! and yet at that moment my eyes were opened. Somehow I *knew* Mary's Jesus was none other than the Messiah my people had expected for centuries. I couldn't speak. My eyes were filled with tears. I saw the child leaving and hurried after her. 'Mary,' I said, 'I do love your Jesus now. From now on He is my Jesus too.'

"I locked the store and went home with the child. I told her mother, 'You have been a customer of mine many months yet you have never spoken to me of your Savior. Your little girl has never failed to ask me if I love Him. I've come to tell you that it has been shown to me that her Jesus is my Messiah and I'm giving my heart and life to Him.'"

Mr. Erlich paused a moment and then said to my mother, "You Gentiles don't know what it costs a Jew to be a Christian. It cost me my mother and father, siblings, my home and inheritance. When I told my family I was a believer in Christ, they used every means to turn me back to Judaism. When they realized I could not be moved, I became as one dead to them. But as much as I have lost, I have gained much more, for I have gained Christ. I have great joy because He has used me to bring fifty two Jews to Him and to educate several young men, both Jews and Gentiles for the ministry."

July 14

Mr. Erlich was a Christian minister who learned first hand from a six year old that any true Believer in Christ Jesus can be a witness to Him. So did my mother.

July 15

Look Above the Storm, Psalm 29

David's country is swept by war. He seems to be watching
a storm rage about him as he writes this prayer. Remembering
God's power calms Him. The storm is frightening but he is
reveling in God's rule over all things, both in war and hurricanes.

All you strong sons and daughters of earth,
    give thanks to God.
Great Praise is due Him, so worship Him
    in the beauty of holiness.

His voice thunders across the waters.
His voice rages over the sea. Hear His power
    in the crashing waves?
God's voice will be heard by everyone.

Yes, Lord, Your voice sweeps the Land.
A howling storm splinters cedars of Lebanon,
    shaking them so they skip like lambs.
Lightning rips the clouds, hurling fire to earth
    in jagged brilliance.

Your voice explodes across the desert,
    flattening the wilderness.
Your decree brings life or death deep in the forests.
People in the Temple quake at Your power.
Yes, Lord, You reign above this deluge of trouble,
    for You are King of all kings forever.
You will bring Your people the needed strength,
    and You will, one day, bring peace.

July 16

Our Enabling Lord, The Holy Spirit

".... the Father, who knows all hearts, also knows the mind of the Holy Spirit because the Spirit intercedes with the Father on our behalf." (Romans 8: 27)

Holy Spirit of God, You are the One who brings us to the Father, through the Son, in the first place. You are our Helper, Comforter and Enabler. Webster defines the word *enable* as "to authorize, empower, commission, to render able, often by giving power, strength or competence." You help us to know God and to live the Christian life.

You help us to win over temptation. You enable us to endure. I appreciate an illustration I read long ago concerning Your work. When we lift an object two forces are working on it. Gravity pulls it down and our hand holds it up. The law of sin and death is likened to the law of gravity, pulling us down. But the law of the Spirit is like the strength of our hand, holding the object up, overruling gravity's downward pull.

When we give You, the Holy Spirit, control of our lives, You begin to shape in us the characteristics Jesus manifested during His earth life. This happens, without strain, just as apples begin to form on a healthy apple tree planted in good soil and given water, nourishment and light. Christians, like apple trees, are expected to bear fruit.

"Fruits of the Spirit are love, joy, peace, patience, faithfulness, gentleness and self-control...We live by the Spirit's guidance, so let's keep in step with Him." (Galatians 5: 22-23, 25)

As we turn from ourselves, toward You, You touch our understanding, and there we are, face to face with You! We realize God is our living Lord, a personal presence, with nothing separating us. *This* was Jesus' prayer for us at Gethsemane.

July 17

New Covenant in Jeremiah

The Lord said, "The time is coming when I will make a New Covenant with My people. It will not be like the covenant I made with ancient Israel as I led them out of Egypt. They broke that contract. This time I will write My law on their hearts and mind. (Jeremiah 31:31-34)

Concerning God's old covenant with Israel He told them, "If you obey Me and keep your part in the covenant then you will be My treasure, chosen from all the nations." (Exodus 19:5) But they, like we today, had no power in themselves to obey. Their nature was also carnal and selfish. The first covenant made no provision for human innate inability to obey. The covenant, as with the Law of Moses, showed them their total helplessness in living up to God's requirements.

What Scripture calls God's New Covenant is described and woven throughout Scripture. It is first promised in Genesis 3:15 as coming through the seed of the woman. This covenant, also called *God's promise, plan or purpose*, is signed in blood at the death and resurrection of Messiah-Jesus. Through it we may know what God is like. Through it we have the option of forgiveness, joy and salvation. It is the new Exodus, where Jesus, the new Moses, will lead His people out of the land of slavery to sin and into a new relationship with God not only of power but of grace.

In the New Covenant God provides a way for people to be acceptable to Him. God Himself will write His law on hearts and minds "not in ink but with the Spirit of the Living God." The Spirit and the Word will fill and strengthen the powers of the inner life.

The weakness of humanity as seen in the first covenant is in sharp contrast to God's New Covenant, as Christ our Passover Lamb is sacrificed for us, bringing God's power into our human weakness. The human impossibility of our lasting faithfulness is overcome by the power of the "Helper coming alongside us," imbuing us with sincere obedience. This describes the Christian who believes God's word and claims His promise: "They shall not depart from Me." The degree to which we experience God's keeping power is always in proportion to our faith: "According to your faith it will be given to you."

The New Testament promise is that through God's New Covenant the Holy Spirit will renew the hearts of His earnest ones and will show them His power to keep them.

July 18

To Know God

Moses asked God to teach him how to know and please Him. He met and talked with God but he wanted to know Him better.

There are different ways of knowing: (1) to be aware of, (2) to know of, to have heard about or read about, (3) to know by experience.

Moses wanted God to change him. So do earnest Christians today. The big question is "How?"

In his book *Knowing God*, J. I. Packer tells us in order to know God we must listen to His Word for He speaks to us through it. As we listen, the Holy Spirit makes it personally applicable to our situations. We can see His characteristics of power, mercy, forgiveness and sacrificial love through His Word. As we come to know Him by obeying and accepting His invitations, we discover they are real invitations. "All you weary ones come to Me and I will give you rest." (Matthew 11:28-30) "Come with confidence in His promise to His throne of grace, so you may receive mercy and grace to help in your need." (Hebrews 4:16)

As we begin to take in His love and forgiveness, we start experiencing the joy and confidence He offers us. His faithfulness brings us into trusting fellowship with Him. God's creation in Christians neither ends with our physical birth nor with our new birth. It's a continuous process which works in us individually as we remain open to Him in obedience. He's not through with us for we are not yet what we will be.

"If anyone is in Christ, he is a new breed of human. Old habits, patterns and goals have passed away and everything has become new." (II Corinthians 5:17)

To know Him this way we must come to Him as a little child to its father. Forget about impressing others and let Him be free to create.

July 19

He Lets Us Know Him

There's no way we can know God on our own. False teaching and propaganda about God are pouring upon earth. Satan, "the father of lies," is seeing to it. False cults proliferate. Half-truths are taught, only the parts that don't remind us of our selfishness and disobedience are tolerated. Churches today are revising Scripture to fit their desired life styles.

If it's true that the world is drenched in lies, where do we go for the truth, the whole truth? We go to the Scripture, the Word of God. We go to Messiah-Jesus who the Bible says is the Living Word of God, the exact image of God the Father.

"Before creation began, the Word existed with God. In fact the Word *was* God. He, the Word, was with God from the beginning. Every created thing was made by Him. Life was in Him and that Life was the Light that showed people the way to God. His Light (truth) shines in the darkness of spiritual ignorance of this world. Even though the world doesn't recognize the Light, earth's darkness has never been able to extinguish it. The Word came here in human flesh and lived among us. We saw the glory of the only begotten Son of God who came from God. He showed us what God is like, showed us His grace, glory and truth.

"It's from His grace that we have all received blessings without number. He is God's Word, God's Purpose. God's mercy and truth have come to us through Jesus Christ. No one has ever seen God but we have seen the Son who is the three dimensional, free standing image of the Father. It is through the Son that we may know the Father." (John 1:1-18, Colossians 1:15-20)

To know Him, we like Moses must ask Him to teach us His ways. Scripture is His textbook, teaching of Jesus, God's exact likeness. He is God in flesh and blood. Jesus told Philip, "If you have seen Me you have seen the Father." (John 14:9)

July 20

Truth in a Mixed Up World?

With all the confusion in the world today, mistaken concepts and deliberate deception, how can we find Truth? If we find it, will we recognize it?

We still can't measure how far it is to the "ends" of space. We don't know how to make snowflakes and pile them up in great silent heaps. There is too much out there to know all the truths of science.

Theories concerning science alone change constantly. Con-cepts once considered absolute fact, have been discarded. There's an old Jewish saying, "Man thinks and God laughs." New theories rise and fall like tides. One huge scramble of theories, which has become a joke, is which foods benefit the human body and which harm it.

If we ever hope to separate truth from the heap of discarded theories on religion, morals and politics, the criteria by which we judge must be true. If our criteria are wrong our conclusions will be also. Scripture is the true standard by which we must be guided.

There's a huge difference between something that's true for the moment and the *truth*. It may be true that that you have the flu but next week it may not be so. Scripture gives a definition of *the truth* as everlasting in its changelessness. Jesus says He is the Way, the Truth and the Life. No Believer will wake up to discover Scriptural Truth is no longer true, although for generations certain groups have tried desperately to change God's truth. Their current effort is "Revisionism" where parts of the Bible they don't like are being called irrelevant to modern times. This is considered new and progressive but actually it's as old as Scripture itself. Jesus told the Jews who professed Him as the Messiah, "If you live by My teaching, you are truly my disciples. You will know the truth and the truth will set you free. (John 8:31-32)

July 21

Faith and Fear at Work, Psalm 27

The Lord is clear light to me; He is the salvation of my soul
    and the strength of my life. Why should I be afraid?
When evil people try to devour my reputation, they stumble
    and fall. If they surround me, I need not fear.
Even if war comes, my confidence is in the Lord.
The main thing I ask of God is to always be
    continually in His Presence,
    praising and learning from Him.

In times of trouble He will keep my soul in the secret place
    of His Presence.
He will set my feet on bedrock, not quicksand.
He lifts me up so I may see beyond my enemies
    and into the faithfulness of God.

Joy fills me and overflows in songs of praise.
    So hear me, Lord, when I ask for Your help.
Faith and fear are both at work in me. You have told
    me to seek Your face in prayer.
My heart replies: "Yes, Lord, I seek Your face."

I realize at times earthly parents desert their children,
    but You, Lord, never do that.
You are everlastingly my faithful Father.
Keep teaching and helping me, Lord, for not all
    my people love me. Their false accusations
    and cruelty would have caused me to give up
    unless I believed I would live to see
Your goodness in this life. I hold onto my courage,
    knowing You will help me.
So, Lord, I set aside fear, take up faith and wait.

Temptation / Inspiration

The inner voices of temptation and inspiration we "hear" seem to come from natural thoughts, but do they?

As Jesus grew up He knew He was "different." Mary did too. His conception and birth, the prophecies of Simeon and Anna concerning the baby, proved to Mary that Jesus was to have a role in God's eternal plan. We don't know whether Mary shared this with Jesus or kept it locked in her heart. But we do know at His baptism the Father put His seal of approval on the Son, commissioning Him as the *Servant of God*.

After the baptism "the Spirit drove Jesus to the wilderness" to fast, pray and wrestle with what it meant to be the Father's unique Son and how He was to proceed.

Both Satan and God send messages to the human mind. The devil's thoughts come easily and naturally to us. Jesus knew He had certain talents. Should He use them to draw people to Himself in order to teach them about God? Satan tempted Him through hunger.

Satan threw the next temptations at Jesus under the guise of a good way of showing the Father to the people. He was suggesting that Jesus show off His own power, which could open the way for Him to present the Father's glory and power.

With failure of these efforts, Satan quoted Scripture to Jesus. His words filled Jesus' mind: "Look! I can't lose! Angels will catch Me if I stumble. Think of the influence I would have if I jumped from this pinnacle and landed unhurt. It would be a miracle!"

Jesus didn't let the tempting thought linger in His mind or search for a guiltless way to use them. He chose to free the world from Satan's power by denying him access to Himself. He used Scripture against him. (Matthew 4:1-11)

Had Jesus yielded to the temptation of glorifying Himself rather than the Father, where would we mortals be?

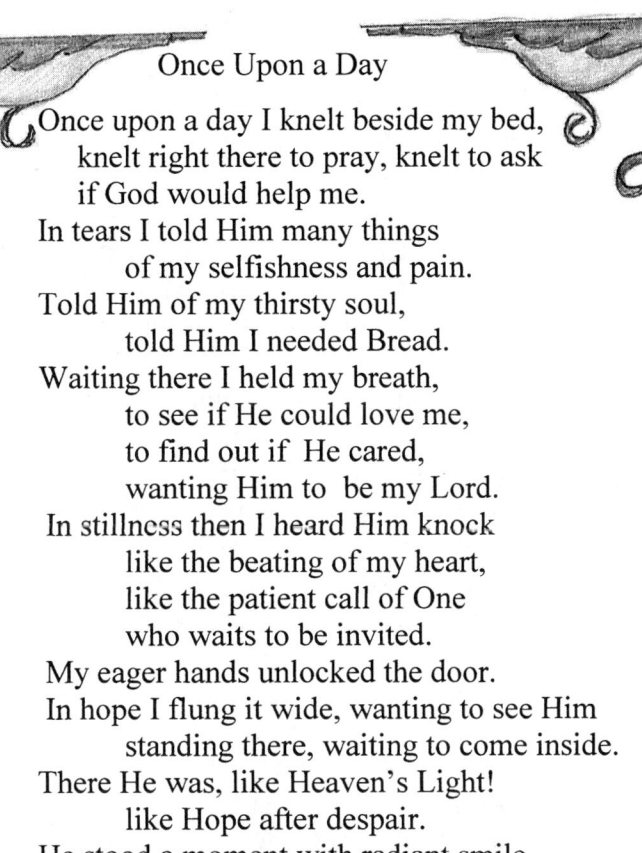

Once Upon a Day

Once upon a day I knelt beside my bed,
    knelt right there to pray, knelt to ask
    if God would help me.
In tears I told Him many things
    of my selfishness and pain.
Told Him of my thirsty soul,
        told Him I needed Bread.
Waiting there I held my breath,
        to see if He could love me,
        to find out if He cared,
        wanting Him to be my Lord.
In stillness then I heard Him knock
        like the beating of my heart,
        like the patient call of One
        who waits to be invited.
My eager hands unlocked the door.
In hope I flung it wide, wanting to see Him
        standing there, waiting to come inside.
There He was, like Heaven's Light!
        like Hope after despair.
He stood a moment with radiant smile,
        stood and then came in.
Life walked in that far off day
        with Light like dawn of morning.
He wrapped me in eternal Love
        and said forgiveness was free.
He took me up in creative hands,
        began to press out a shape.
Clay begins to change its form
        reflecting the One who knocked.   F.N.

Eat the Words

Jeremiah said, "When Your words came to me, *I ate them*; they are my joy and delight, for I carry Your Name, O Lord." (15:16)

"Don't only listen to the Word. Obey it! If a person listens but does not heed, he's like someone who looks at his face in a mirror, then turns away and promptly forgets what he looks like." (James 1:22-23)

Lord, You speak to us to guide us toward Yourself, to redirect our lives and to reshape our character into Your likeness. For this to happen we must do more than read Your Word. Jeremiah says he *eats* Your Word with alert mind and heart. He puts it into himself. It is as we "eat" Your Word, take it deeply into ourselves, chewing on its meaning, swallowing and digesting it, that it speaks to us, uniting with our character, transforming and shaping us.

The world constantly presses in on us on every side, with customs and events, trying to squeeze us into its mold. But You, Lord, have a different plan for us. If we are to stand against the world's erosion of faith and standards, we must take Your Word as our guide and let You reshape our minds and hearts from the inside.

Daniel, as a young man, was taken hostage into Babylon after Jerusalem's defeat. He was threatened and pressured fiercely to give up his faith in Jehovah. He clung desperately to You, Lord, and poured out his soul in prayer. "How can a young man keep his life clean in times like these? The only way is by being obedient to You, Lord God. I'm earnestly seeking You. Hold me steady. Melt my heart, and my pride. Don't let me take a wrong path. I'm eager to understand Your ways; so I'm memorizing Your Word, storing it away in my heart so I won't sin against You.

July 24

"Teach me, Lord, and I won't neglect the lessons; instead I will rejoice." (Psalm 119:9-16)

Lord, help me "eat" Your Word. May it be a light on my path, guiding me, and my daily nourishment strengthening me.

July 25

It is Reliable

"Scripture is God-breathed. It teaches truth and corrects wrong beliefs. It shows us how to prepare to live the Christian life." (II Timothy 3:16)

Today enemies of Scripture do endless research to cast doubt on Scripture even though at least 5000 Greek manuscripts of Scripture exist today from the second century AD and several parts from the first. Doctrines necessary to salvation do not differ.

Luke is noted for his accuracy of history, politics, customs, geography and technology of Jesus' times. Since his details are accurate, it's reasonable to accept his accuracy in other events.

Rabbis of the first century encouraged pupils to memorize the material because scrolls were rare. Rabbi Jesus was no exception. His disciples listened in order share it correctly with others.

Today, disbelief, ridicule, hatred of Scripture, or anything Christian, is growing. In the past politics, sex or religion were taboo at dinner parties, now people yell at one another over politics. Speakers tell dirty jokes and audiences laugh. Only Christianity is taboo. Prayer is outlawed in public. The only acceptable use of Jesus' Name is as a curse.

There is so much evidence of the Bible's accuracy if it were any other book it would have been accepted. The only explanation for this prejudice against Christianity is the feverish activity of the devil described so well in C.S. Lewis's book *The Screwtape Letters.*

God the Father, ruler of time and eternity, laughs at the absurdity of people, created by God, striving to exclude Him from His world. (Psalm 2:1-3)

Voltaire, writer and critic of Scripture, predicted in the 1800's that in a hundred years Bibles would only be found in museums. But the house in which he wrote these words became a Bible Society printing company producing thousands of Bibles!

July 26

Hold Tight to the Truth

Part of Jesus' prayer in the Garden was for *us*, "Make *them* holy by Your Truth. Your Word is the Truth." (John 17:17)

St. Paul loved young Timothy like a son and took him on missionary journeys to train him as a church leader. In a letter he advised his young friend, "Keep and practice what I've taught you as the pattern of sound teaching. Guard the truth carefully and trust Jesus Christ with what has been entrusted to you. Stay true to God through His Word with the Holy Spirit's help." (II Timothy 1:13-14)

We've met people who repent and turn to God with great joy. But something goes wrong and they soon give up. Their roots are shallow, as in the parable of the Sower, when the hot sun of difficulties bombards them, they wilt and drop away. What happened was they neglected God's Word and prayer. Jesus tells us, "I am the Way, Truth and Life." We communicate with Him, the Truth and the Life, through prayer, and He communicates with us through His Written Word and the Holy Spirit to nourish our souls. C. S. Lewis says Jesus and His Word are the only fuel the human spirit was made to run on, the only food our souls can digest. The fast food of instant gratification, so readily available today, does not, cannot, nourish our souls.

The same drying up which happens to a person who neglects the Word of Truth can happen to churches. If pastors and teachers don't teach and guard the gift of the Spirit through continued communication with the Lord, false doctrines begin to seep in, almost unnoticed at first, resulting in trouble.

Individuals and churches which base their lives on obedience to the Scripture will have the joy of seeing God's power at work in their lives.

July 27

Power to Change

Luke praises the people of Berea because they were hungry for God's Word and they studied Scripture carefully to make sure Paul was teaching the truth. (Acts 17:11-12)

The Bible has power to change lives and nations. It has many writers but the same Holy Spirit inspired them all. It took millennia to write. With all its differences, it tells *"one story* about *one God* and His *one* plan" to rescue creation. It's God's personal letter to each person. It fits all needs. It influences the lives of those who study it. Since its thrust is spiritual, we need to ask the Holy Spirit to help us understand it. It's our responsibility to participate in our own spiritual growth and understanding. We are told to *work out* what God has worked *in* us. (Philippians 2:12-13) He provides salvation by His death and resurrection and gives us the Holy Spirit. We are to carefully work out, with His help, the practical application of our salvation in our habits, living and thinking.

The Bereans set a praiseworthy example for any who want a life changing faith. They *wanted to learn* and were *obedient* to what they learned. They spent time in God's Presence, with His Word and in prayer. They fed on Him and His Word daily in their hearts.

Our daily meals act as a parable of our spiritual needs. We eat every day. But what we ate yesterday or last week isn't enough for today's needs. Jesus and His Word are the nourishment our souls need to be healthy. He says, "I am the Bread that lives and I give that Life to you." He comes to us fresh every morning and new every evening. Without Him as our daily diet, our souls become emaciated, shriveled, too weak for the battle raging for our souls.

July 28

"You Don't Know Scripture"

A group of lawyers, loyal to Herod gathered about Jesus. They were loyal to Herod. They plotted questions designed to confuse Him, but He was not to be confused. He said, "Your questions are in error because you don't know Scripture or the power of God." (Matthew 22:29)

That may be the center of many problems in both churches and individuals today. We draw wrong conclusions for we don't know Scripture or the power of God. Too many Christians today, even active church members, don't have a comprehensive Bible knowledge. They know it only superficially.

Christians should all be students of Scripture. There are many resources for Bible study which will be a great blessing if we use them regularly. It is suggested we begin with a good translation of the original and a modern paraphrase. References, footnotes, and commentaries are a help. But the best help comes from asking the Lord's help in understanding. That's the first step, for He *wants* us to understand His Word. Pray for guidance in reading then do some research on it.

The Bible is too deep to begin to understand in only a thirty minute sermon on Sunday. Some things Jesus said sound strange to those unfamiliar with Scripture, such as, *I am the bread of life, eat Me. I am the living water, drink Me.* He tells us He is a Shepherd, a door, and a light of the world.

The size and scope of the Word of God and what we are told to do with it, reminds me of a child's riddle, "How does one eat an elephant?" The answer of how to understand the Bible is the same: "One bite at a time." We begin to take in His magnificent Word and make it an actual part of us. We go back to school, become students of the Holy Spirit. We chew one bite at a time, digesting it, incorporating it into our core of being.

July 29

A Beautiful Thing

O Lord God, it's beautiful to sing praise to You, the Most High God, to celebrate Your love each morning and rejoice in Your Presence each night!" (Psalm 91:1)

Today You are to me: Wonderful
Counselor, Guide
The Mighty God
The Prince of Peace
Healer, Protector
Victor over life and death
My Shepherd, Comforter
Righteousness,
Forgiveness
Emmanuel, God with us
Creator and Re-creator

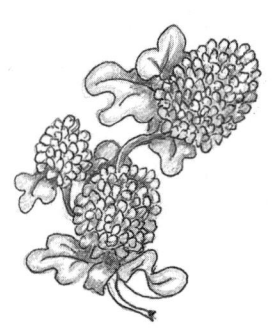

Today I thank You for: Increased strength and joy
in today's opportunities
Unfolding seasons
My precious family
Glorious dawns and sunsets
Enemies within myself defeated.

Today I praise You for promises that believers may

Flourish, stay green and fresh
Still bear fruit even in old age
Have hope, love and faith,
Know the Living Word (Jesus)
Trust in God's promises
Welcome the Holy Spirit into our days.

July 30

Resentment: a Prison of Unforgiveness

How does one forgive a person who is no longer living? I can't give an answer. I just know I did, and it worked. This must be one of those impossible things which God makes possible.

As a teenager, I found my responses to my parent's wishes changing. Resentment of my strict father was mixing its ugliness with my love for and dependence on him. He and Mother were determined that I should grow to be a circumspect and Christian young woman. I was quite sure that would be exceedingly dull.

They lived an exemplary life before me of loving and obeying God, of helping others physically, financially and spiritually. We attended church morning and evening on Sundays and Wednesday night church supper and Bible study. Every night, with the exception of Wednesday, we six gathered in the living room for Bible reading and prayer on our knees. The phone often rang in the hall. Almost as often as it rang I heard Annie May say, "She cain't come to de phone rat now. Deys havin' de Bible readin'." Her words caused me to cringe with embarrassment.

I realized I must carefully plot ways of earning more freedom and a later curfew. The standard teenage complaint, "But Daddy, everyone else does it," availed nothing. I must use stealth and deception to get the better of the dear old Scot. My three older siblings assured me that I had it easy, for their struggles had softened him up for me.

When I was seventeen, Mother told me she prayed for me daily. My reply was, "I wish you wouldn't. Of all the things in life I could be, I'd never choose to be a Christian!"

Two years later, alone in my college room, and on my knees, I turned my life over to Christ. Many life changes came quickly and joyfully. But there was still much to learn and unlearn. I've come to see that spiritual transformation is a lifetime pursuit. The Lord is still making changes in me this very day.

I went to college, married and had two children. All that time I was learning, giving over to God and soaking up His Spirit. I taught adult Bible studies in churches and homes. But from time to time I realized vestiges of old resentments of my father lingered in my mind. They attacked when hands were busy but mind was free, like while ironing or sewing. My mind replayed the rebellions and resentments. My heart called out to God, "Lord, this is not right. It must stop. Help me! I took advantage of my father's love and I can't even ask him to forgive me -- because he's dead! I can't tell him I forgive him for hurting me. Please, Lord, I don't want either of us to remain locked in the prison of my unforgiveness. Please take this ugliness from my heart. Nail it to Your cross and let it die with Your death, that I may rise up free of this burden. Will You tell Daddy for me?"

Lord, I never heard of anyone praying such a prayer. But You answered mine. It's a burden no longer. It does not gnaw on my conscience anymore. Whenever I think of why I had to pray that prayer I'm flooded with thanksgiving for Your magnificent mercy.

July 31

Our Transforming Lord

"When we are in Christ we become a new creation. Old ways are gone. All things become new."(II Corinthians 5:17)

There's no miracle more astonishing than when You, Lord, remake a person. No one is too bad for Your love and no one is too hopeless for Your power. Peter is a good example of a man trans-formed by Your power. We all like Peter. We can affiliate with his blunders. He was brash and impetuous, tripping over his ego. When You needed him he denied even knowing You. At Pentecost You filled him with Your Spirit and Simon the fisherman became Peter, the rock upon whose confession You built Your Church.

Then there is John. He and James were sons of Zebedee, the fisherman. Because of their loud voices and fiery tempers You, nicknamed them, with a smile, "the sons of thunder." (Mark 3:17)

There must have been a particular winsome quality about the thundering young John for he is called "the disciple whom Jesus loved." You loved them all Lord, even Judas who never gave You his heart. But John always seemed special to You. He was the youngest disciple, probably in his mid-teens when You called him and James. John, like Peter, was changed by You, not to be like Peter, but to be *totally John* in whom the Spirit of God lived. The loud, angry "son of thunder" was remade into the Apostle of Love. (I John)

Saul. There seemed to be nothing gradual about *his* trans-formation. He was riding toward Damascus on a mission of terror against the Christians, "breathing out threats and slaughter" when You knocked him off his horse and called him by name. "Saul, Saul, why are you persecuting Me?" The result astonished both his friends and his foes. Saul, the proud Pharisee, terrorist of Christians, became Paul, the servant, the "bond slave of Jesus

July 31

Christ" as he called himself. (Acts 9)

Under Your care and teaching Peter became a loyal, courageous man of insight and eloquence. John's temperament was made new. Paul's life mission did an about face.

How about me, Lord? What do You want to change in me?

August 1

Good Morning, Lord

Good morning, Lord! Earth still sleeps;
      there's neither sound nor light.
Silent trees stand resting.
May Jesus Christ be praised!

I'm lethargic, drugged with sleep,
      thoughts just barely stirring.
May Jesus Christ be praised!

Coffee pot chuckles and birds wake up
      as morning looks
      in the window at me.
May Jesus Christ be praised!

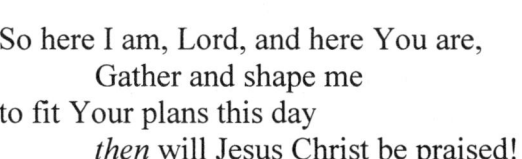

I asked You, Father, to wake me early
      so we might have our visit.
May Jesus Christ be praised!

So here I am, Lord, and here You are,
      Gather and shape me
      to fit Your plans this day
      then will Jesus Christ be praised!

F.N.

August 2

Every Eye Shall See Him

Jesus, in Your parable of the lost coin, You picture the Holy Spirit as a woman sweeping her house searching for her lost coin. (Luke 15:8-10) We know, Lord, You prefer finding lost people to judging them, for Scripture warns us in Psalm 2:10-12, "Listen, while Time exists. Make a hundred and eighty degree turn. Kneel before Messiah Jesus. Exalt His Name! Your very lives depend on it! God's anger is lethal but His blessing is Life, abundant and eternal."

Lord, we long for Your return. We look for it. We yearn to see You face to face without the obscuring fog of humanity misting our vision. We want to know You as You know us.

When the time is right You will be back to reclaim Your Kingdom. Those who are disloyal to You will be exiled. They won't wonder why because to their dismay, they will recognize You. "Every eye will see the King and they will look on Him whom they have pierced and mourn for Him as one mourns for his only son." (Psalm 22:16, Zechariah 12:10, Revelation 1:7 NKJV)

You are now "preparing a place for us." (John 14:2) In the meantime, we have the Holy Spirit as Your representative on earth and our comforting Helper and Teacher. When everything is ready You will come for us, not as God's Suffering Servant, as in Your first coming but as the great Potentate of Time and Eternity, accompanied by uncountable hosts of Heaven.

We're not puppets. We have a choice to serve You or ourselves but we don't have eternity to decide. When You return all eyes will see You, either as blessed Savior or fearsome Judge.

August 3

Jehovah-rohi, the Lord My Shepherd

Psalm 23 draws a picture of the name *Jehovah-rohi*, which means the Lord is my Shepherd. It's a name that comforts a little child, frightened of the dark, or a sick person knowing death is near.

David may have written the psalm as the young shepherd of his father's sheep, or as the old King of Israel who trusted You all his troubled life. He remembered You never left him. He believed Your twin blessings of goodness and mercy would follow him to life's end.

Rohi means to feed, lead and pasture as a shepherd does. It's also used metaphorically in relationship between a king and his people. The tribes of Israel said to David, "...even when Saul was our king, you were the one who led us, for the Lord told you, 'you shall shepherd My people and care for them.'" (II Samuel 5:2)

The ancient Jews thought of You, Lord, as frightening and unapproachable. You demanded too much of them. But Your Name, as revealed in Psalm 23, *Shepherd*, holds only tenderness and care. "*Jehovah-Elohim* will come in power and He will feed His people like a shepherd. He will carry the lambs on His shoulder. He will gently lead those who are with young." (Isaiah 40:10-11)

Jehovah-rohi, our Shepherd, is none other than *Jehovah-Jesus* of the New Testament. He never changes! (John 10:1-18) You actively seek Your lost sheep Lord, "I Myself will seek them, keep them safe and feed them with good pasture. I will gather the lost ones, bind up the broken ones and strengthen the weak." (Ezekiel 34:11-16)

August 3

Lord, You know us as a shepherd knows his sheep, every need, every peculiarity and weakness. You lead us to fresh meadows and clear waters, guiding us over life's rough places and through dark valleys. Your guidance is always in the direction of our Final Home where we may "live in the House of the Lord forever."

August 4

Look to the Shepherd, Psalm 23

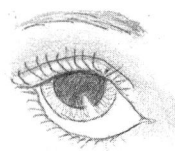

The thought of God as his Shepherd lit up David's soul as he sang,

"Lord, You are my Shepherd. You care for my every need.
You lead me to grassy meadows where I may feed
on your bounty.
You heal my tattered soul and body as I rest by quiet pools.
by quiet pools.
When my strength is restored, we journey on together
for You are *Jehovah-rohi.* *

Even as the path bends back to the Valley of Fear,
I am not afraid because You,
Jehovah-shamma,* are there with me.
Your directing staff and protecting club comfort me,
keeping enemies of my soul at bay.
You feed and nourish me, even as red-eyed predators
lurk nearby, salivating.
The healing oil of Your Presence cures my wounds
and blessings overflow my cup.

Your twin encouragements, Goodness and Mercy
follow me each day of my life.
After our journey, I will be with You in Your Kingdom
of Many Mansions for all eternity.

Jehovah-rohi means God is my Shepherd, *Jehovah-shamma*
means God who is there. Both are Hebrew names of God.

August 5

Jehovah-tsidkenu, the Lord Our Righteousness, I

The era of the judges ended. Centuries passed. Kings lived and died, conquerors ebbed and flowed, the kingdom was divided. People and rulers forgot God and slid into total corruption. The prophet Jeremiah warned them of Your coming judgment, Lord. Babylon was to be Your instrument to wake them up. Their captivity by Babylon didn't cancel Your promise to raise up a "Righteous Branch" from David's line who would be called *Jehovah-tsidkenu* God our Righteousness. (Jeremiah 23:5, 6) It was through Him people would be redeemed and made righteous.

Tsidkenu means righteous and straight. Straight with others. Straight with You, Lord, giving You worship and love, offering You the sacrifice You desire. "The sacrifices of God are broken pride, a teachable spirit and a melted heart. That's when we are ready to love and worship God." (Psalm 51) It's clear Lord, You are demanding something we do not have. But we *must* have it. It is You, righteous God, who provides *Your own* righteousness for us.

But how can we cover our unrighteousness with Your righteousness? Old Testament people understood offending Your righteousness carries the death penalty which must be paid. Lord, You decreed a substitute, a lamb without blemish, could be offered in trust with thanksgiving. That's the basis on which You could see the guilty person as innocent and the innocent lamb as guilty. (Isaiah 61:10, Romans 4:7)

The innocent lamb of the Old Testament is a vivid picture of Jesus, our sin bearer, wounded, bruised and sacrificed in our place. (Isaiah 53) In Your eyes, Eternal Father, I take on, put over myself, the True Lamb's righteousness and Jesus takes my guilt on Himself to the cross. That transaction is made and sealed when I believe it, repent and ask You to live in and through my life, actions, plans and attitudes!

August 6

Jehovah-tsidkenu, the Lord Our Righteousness, II

The people of Israel were taught they had no hope of becoming righteous in themselves. They were to put their hope in God who revealed Himself as "the Lord Our Righteousness," our *only* righteousness. They understood the punishment for their wrongdoing did not in itself cleanse the sinner but the innocence of the sacrificial sufferer was credited to the account of the sinner. They were acquitted of being unrighteous, and also of the guilt.

What a marvelous picture of Your grace, Lord!
"Abram believed God and He credited it to him for righteousness." (Genesis 15:6)
"You, Lord, forgave the iniquity of Your people and covered all their sins." (Psalm 85:2)
"I delight in the Lord; my soul rejoices in my God. For He has clothed me with garments of salvation and covered me in the robe of His righteousness." (Isaiah 61:10)
Lord, Your provision for our necessary righteousness is seen in clear focus in Jesus Christ, *Jehovah-Tsidkenu*. The character, work and suffering of God's Righteous Servant is wrapped over us as a covering robe of perfect and acceptable righteousness. As You look at Your reborn ones, You see Your Only Begotten Son. "For He (the Father) has made Him (the Son) to be sin for us even though Jesus never sinned, so we could be made the righteousness of God through the Son." (II Corinthians 5:21)
The name, *Jehovah-tsidkenu*, shows how You, Lord God, accomplished Your incomparable plan for our redemption, and the quality of Your love and acceptance of us. We're made clean by the substitute sacrifice of the True Lamb of God.
Jehovah-tsidkenu -- what a blessed name!

August 7

Needed: A New Attitude

Lord, I haven't been keen about meeting with You these last few mornings. Even today I'm slow in coming to You. But I've missed that sense of eager anticipation which so energizes these hours. What's wrong with me? St. Paul says in his letter to the Romans that nothing in all creation can separate us from Your Love. That means Your Love is still there. It must be I am the one who wandered off.

You are fully aware of all my thoughts and attitudes whether I tell You or not. So, Lord, I may as well confess. I desperately need a new attitude. I'm so blessed. I have everything I need, everything possible to help me. Yet I can feel as impatient as a spoiled child who doesn't get what it wants. I'm weary with recuperation. It's been slow, restrictive, lonely and painful. *I've let it be that way!*

I don't respect my attitude, Lord, or my hesitancy to seek Your help sooner. I need You. My heart aches. I'm pressed down and dark inside. I need Your gracious Spirit and Your transforming Presence. Forgive me, Father. I'm sorry. I grab Your shining promise: "If we confess our sin, He is faithful and just to forgive our sins and to cleanse us from all unrighteousness." (I John 1:9 KJV)

I need a new attitude. In Your strong Name, I send this one away. At Creation You "breathed into man the breath of life." (Genesis 2:7) Breathe into me now, Lord. I'm waiting, uncovered, before You. I breathe out the "carbon monoxide" of my disgruntled and impatient spirit and breathe in the recognition of Your pure Presence in me. I breathe out and breathe in. Empty me of this ugly attitude. Fill me with Your Spirit. I breathe out hardness of heart, breathe in tenderness toward You in grateful praise. Out me, in You, Lord. Out doubt, in trust. Out tension, in peace.

August 7

David's prayer in Psalm 51 is mine today. "Create a clean heart in me, O God, and renew my spirit. Don't take Your Holy Spirit from me. Don't deprive me of the joy of Your Presence, rather plant within me a deep rooted spirit of obedience and praise." (Verses 10-12)

NOTE: It was because of boredom and discouragement with the long years of recuperation that I prayed this prayer. Then the God of all glory and merciful Love bent down and nudged me to paraphrase the hundred and fifty psalms.

What a transformation! As I took on the Psalm project, boredom vanished. Interest and vitality rushed in. Dark shadows of "what-ifs" fled away before Your Light. Pain melted in the regenerating heat of praise. Sorrow didn't have a chance against "the joy of the Lord!' Thank You!

August 8

Definition of a Fool

A *fool*, in the biblical sense, is one lacking in judgment and common powers of understanding, one who spends time on trifles, who is morally deficient or harmlessly deranged. "The fool has decided in his heart that there is no God." (Psalm 14:1)

"The fool's mouth brings him trouble. His soul is maimed by his own words. His mouth builds a trap in which he himself is caught. Gossip, spoken or heard, is like a morsel of spoiled food. If swallowed, it goes into the deepest part of the personality causing spiritual ulcers." (Proverbs 18:7-8)

"To answer before listening is both contemptuous and stupid. It drags embarrassment in its wake." (Proverbs 18:13)

"As a log thrown on glowing embers rekindles a fire, so a quarrelsome person throws gasoline on the flames." (Proverbs 26:21)
"A fool immediately broadcasts his fury while a wise person quietly considers all angles." (Proverbs 29:11)

"Watch out for those who continually speak without thinking. There is more hope for the simple-minded than for them." (Proverbs 29:20)

Teach me, Lord, to set a guard over my words and thoughts.
Amen

August 9

God's X-ray, Psalm 139

O Lord, You X-ray me and see all my secrets;
    my habits and whims are an open book to You.
When I wake up each morning You know my words
    before I speak them.
Quick and fleeting though some thoughts may be,
    not one escapes Your understanding.

Wherever I go You accompany me; You even stop
    with me when I must rest.
Your unseen Presence surrounds me, covering,
    following, and preceding me.
Lord God, Your fingers are on my pulse,
    knowing the condition
    of my body, soul and imagination.
This is a fact, yet I still can't grasp it completely.
    It is higher than my mind can reach.

May I never hide from You, Lord? Is there no place
    I may go to escape Your Presence?
If my path leads to joy, You are there in my joy.
When I am crushed by misery or fear, there You are.
If I could ride the sunrise to the depths of space,
You would be there with Your hand on my shoulder.

Whether darkness covers me or light illuminates me,
    You always see me just as I am.
The blackest dark is no hiding place. Darkness and
    daylight are alike to You.
While I was in the womb, Your protection held me
    there as You knitted me together,
    cell by cell, gene by gene.

August 9

I marvel at the intricate interaction of my construction.
It is truly past human understanding.

Lord, Your thoughts concerning me are numberless
as grains of sand on the shore!
Each morning upon awakening I realize anew
that You are here with me.
So, Lord God, keep me, I pray from the stinginess
of a praiseless heart, for that is unspoken blasphemy.
And Father, steer me away from those who are set
against You.
Continue to search me and know me. Show me where
hidden sin lies within me.
Then, Lord, lead me along the path to wholeness.

Centuries ago David learned even though God knew him inside and out but He loved him anyway.

To the well known children's song, *Jesus Loves Me This I Know*, add the line *Jesus Knows Me This I Love* and we have an eternal truth in a nutshell.

August 10

Stunned By His Mercy

Great conferences, national and international, in elegant places, were a consistent part of my schedule as my husband began his move up the corporate ladder. I was happy for him but I dreaded them. He knew everyone. Everyone knew him. But by comparison, in my newness, I knew practically no one.

During a conference in San Diego at the Del Coronado Hotel I was dressing for a huge cocktail party and dinner. Bill had gone down to speak to someone. I grumbled, "I don't like this, Lord. I feel out of place, so unprotected. Do something. Help me!" Out of the blue, the old song *Rock of Ages* flooded my mind. Your message came to me as words spoken into my mind, "Yes, 'hide' your old self in Me. I'll go with you." Startled, I asked, "Would You *really*, Lord? I didn't know You went to cocktail parties." Your reply, "Don't you remember I went to a wedding party in Cana? I had a good time. I'll be with you, Little One, right by your shoulder. Let's go!"

As I walked into the swarming sea of people my courage began to fail. Turning my head toward my right shoulder, I thought, "Help!" His wordless reply was, "Look at those people standing near the wall. What do you see?" In amazement I thought, "Why Lord! They seem to feel as strange and insecure as I do."

As I looked about I saw the 'important people' were clustered about my husband to catch the eye of the boss. And of course he was eager to hear their story and congratulate them on their successful work.

So, my 'mission field' was the newcomers. I made my way to young couples to welcome them. Each couple assured me they were 'having fun' but several admitted they were out of their comfort zone. To be approached by the 'first lady' seemed to lend them confidence, especially when I owned up to the fact that I knew exactly how they felt! After a few minutes of conversation, I would pull in another couple who looked a bit lost. It warmed me to leave them happily chatting with new acquaintances.

That night was a turning point for me, mentally, socially and spiritually. It was as though the Lord gave me a new mission beyond my family and church. My mission field was to minister to new, successful business people. This gave me a new realization of God's interest in and love for me as an individual. Surprising opportunities to share God's love grew from that long ago evening. Once again I was stunned by His mercy. Just imagine, the Lord of all glory having compassion on a small, selfish and discontented woman who was thinking, not of her husband, not of others, and not even of her merciful Lord and Savior, but only of her own stingy, up tight self. *Imagine!*

August 11

From Blessing to Blessing

That is not the end of the story. It's the beginning. God's blessings aren't static. They have a way of moving, a way of opening closed doors and flowing out to others.

Opportunities I never dreamed of presented themselves because this uncomfortable young woman hollered to God for help and then stumbled along toward obedience. Opportunities came, which went beneath party masks, down to real people. At first it seemed remarkable that through this new approach, with Jesus 'by my shoulder,' several people opened the door to deeper conversation. Only later did it dawn on me that people really have a hunger for what's real and true, and even if we don't always know where to find it, the Lord has His ways of getting the attention of the seeker.

I learned some truths about God that night. He's actually there with us wherever we are, whether we realize it or not, ready to listen, comfort, strengthen, answer, prepare or enable. All we need to do is ask, then obey.

At these conferences, groups would meet on free mornings, some to play tennis or bridge, some to sight see, shop or sun by the pool. God planted a question in my mind which would not be set aside. *Why not have a gathering of Christians?* I took this to be what it was, the Lord's suggestion. We could share our faith, count our blessings and encourage each other with prayer. When I mentioned this to a Christian friend she encouraged me to follow through with the idea. At the next conference we invited three Christian women to come for prayer, fellowship and a continental breakfast in the suite. Seven came.

Our numbers grew from year to year, opening lives of some to a brand new concept of God's love and encouraging others along the way. At the last conference before my husband retired we had forty women, filling the large living room and dining room of the suite. Some sat on the floor. My talk was of the Prodigal Son, picturing God the Father watching from the window of His Omniscience for the return of His much loved son from the Far Country. Many eyes were bright with tears. Our wonderful tenor, Steve Rogero, agreed to be the only man in the group in order to sing *I Cannot Tell, But This I Know*. There was even a grand piano in the suite! That was just one more over-and- above gift from our generous and surprising Father.

After all these years I still hear from some of the women involved in those Care and Prayer groups. It reminds me, Lord, no request is too small for Your love or too large for Your power.

August 12

I Cannot Tell ... But This I Know
(to be sung to the tune of Londonderry Air, *O Danny Boy*)

I cannot tell why He, whom angels worship,
Should set His love upon the sons of Earth,
Or why, as Shepherd, He should seek the wanderers,
To bring them back, they know not how or when.

But this I know, that He was born of Mary,
When Bethlehem's manger was His only home,
And that He lived at Nazareth and labored,
And so the Savior, Savior of the world is come.

I cannot tell how silently He suffered,
As with His peace He graced this place of tears,
Or how His heart upon the cross was broken,
The crown of pain to three and thirty years.

But this I know, He heals the broken-hearted,
And stays our sin, and calms our lurking fear,
And lifts the burden from the heavy laden,
For this the Savior, Savior of the world is here.

I cannot tell how He will win the nations;
How He will claim His earthly heritage;
How satisfy the needs and aspirations of
East and West, of sinner and of sage.

But this I know, all flesh shall see His glory,
And He shall reap the harvest He has sown.
And some glad day His sun shall rise in splendor,
When He, the Savior, Savior of the world is known.

August 12

I cannot tell how all the lands shall worship
When, at His bidding, every storm is stilled,
Or who can say how great the jubilation
When all the hearts of men with love are filled.

But this I know, the skies will thrill with rapture,
And myriad, myriad human voices sing,
And Earth to Heaven and Heaven to Earth will answer;
At last the Savior, Savior of the world is King!

Words by William Young Fullerton, 1857-1932
Page 809 of the original Methodist Hymn Book
Page 149 of Redemption Hymnal.
Sung by Steve Rogero at Prayer and Share group Bermuda

August 13

That They Might Know You

Father, You by whom all things exist, must grieve for Your world with its billions of people who never recognize You. You grieve too for those who call themselves by Your Name yet only have a veneer of Christianity.

Each day we hear of more needy people who ask for prayer. We can't pray for everyone but we can pray for those we know and love. Neither can we judge those we wonder about. Only You, Father, know their hearts. Your Word gives strong clues of who trusts You and who does not. "You can identify Believers by how they live just as surely as you can tell a tree by the kind of fruit it produces." (Matthew 7:16-21)

Lord, You know all the people I lift to You in prayer. You know those who are missing the boat. Please, use every circumstance of their lives to draw them to You. We are free to ask this because You gave Your life for each of us, but in order to have the eternal benefits of Your sacrifice, each must personally receive Your gift. We ask for the salvation of others because without it they perish. "There is salvation in no other Name. Yours is the only Name in Heaven or on Earth which can save us." (Acts 4:12, John 3:16)

Thank You, Lord, for seeking us. Pursue us because You love us. Thank You that "If we confess our sins, You are faithful and just to forgive our sins and wash us from all sin." (I John 1:9) Bring us into Your forever family. Bless us with understanding so we may know You as our only perfect and adequate substitute. Fill our lives with the joy and peace of Your Salvation. Prepare us to serve You. All praise and thanks to You, *Abba*, Father.

August 14

Lord of the Second Chance
parable of the barren fig tree, Luke 13: 6-9

Lord, You told the story like this: "A man plants a fig tree in his vineyard. When it's time for the tree to produce figs, he goes out to check on it. Finding no fruit he tells his gardener, 'This tree's useless, cut it down. It takes up space, giving us nothing in return.'

"The gardener replies, 'Sir, I'd like to give it one more year. I'll loosen the soil and fertilize it. Perhaps next year it will have a crop. If not, then let's cut it down.'"

It usually takes three years for a fig tree to produce fruit, but if there is no fruit by then there probably never will be. Here's a story of a fruitless tree given a second chance. That's Your way too, Lord. You give us opportunity after opportunity to open our lives to You and be fruitful. Believers throughout the centuries have jumped at Your gracious "second chances," then testified to Your mercy and forgiveness in giving them another opportunity.

For three years the tree took in nourishment, water and sunlight but it didn't do what it was created to do, produce figs. Nothing thrives if it only takes. If we refuse Your many opportunities for grace, all Your nudges and challenges, the day of our final chance will come. And when it does it's not that You have shut us out, but that by our deliberate choices of "till later," we have closed the door. We've turned the lock on the inside and shut You out.

Thank You, Lord, for this parable. It is short but it's strong encouragement, especially when we take a wrong turn. It tells us of Your desire to give all of us slow growing "fig trees" another opportunity to produce the expected fruit in our lives. You are truly our Lord of the second chance. Your grace shines through every line of the story. Even its warning shows Your loving concern for us.

August 15

A Prayer for Dear Ones

This and the next several entries are prayers from my
prayer diary concerning different needs. They are not used often,
but if my spirit is pressed low, they may serve as a springboard of
wonder into the Presence of God. The simple act of remembering
who He is and what He does for us will often inspire a dragging
Christian to begin the flow of prayer, like priming a pump starts
the flow of water.

Father, thank You. You are the source of all good, of
wisdom, love and mercy. You are knowledge and power beyond
human conception. You are the only way to salvation and Your
very own righteousness is the unique robe with which You cover
my spiritual nakedness.

Because of Your ability and desire to impart these blessings
to Your people, I ask an outpouring of Your Spirit upon these I
hold dear, especially _____ and _____. Fill them with Yourself
and with a continual appetite for Your truth. You Yourself are our
Peace, *Jehovah- shalom*, our Joy, Strength and Unity. You are our
Protection, Comfort, Faith and Praise. *Jehovah-rophe*, You are
our God who heals, You are our health of mind, body and spirit.
Jehovah-jireh, You are our Provider. And, God of Eternity, You
are the One who is with us, right here, right now. Our God whose
Name is *Emmanuel.*

Where we lack knowledge, teach and guide. Be in us as a
Spring of Living Water welling up to abundant Life and Salvation.
I ask this for those You have given me to live with and love, for
my self and Your people everywhere. Plant us as trees near a
river. Incline our hearts toward You and use our circumstances to
lift, renew and shape us in Your image. In the strong Name of
Jesus we pray. Amen

August 16

For the Church Universal

Father, we Your people may come to You boldly because You have invited us to come in the Name of Jesus, our great and eternal High Priest. Lord, we lift the Church, Your body on Earth, to You for help. It's infected with the virus of unbelief. We have thrown out the reality of absolute truth. Personal pleasure and advancement are our gods. Tolerance of everything, right or wrong, is considered a virtue. We accommodate evil on every side. Whatever we want is OK. Enlarged pride is considered a trait to be nurtured.

Christians are being persecuted for their faith, some by ridicule, or job discrimination. In some countries faith draws a prison sentence or physical abuse, even death. Comfort and protect those in such circumstances. Give them courage, the sense of Your Presence, endurance and loyalty.

Rescue us, Lord, let Your people, pastors and priests be open to You and honest with us and others. Be our wisdom, our discernment. Restore to us the joy of our salvation that we may truly be people of the Book, people of praise and trust. Go before us as Shepherd of our souls to alert us to traps and snares ahead which would distract us from Your purpose. Send Your angels to protect us from the Enemy's attacks and prod us away from laziness. May neither attachments nor personal situations deter us from Your plans for us.

Open our eyes so we may see that we were made for You and Your Kingdom. Teach us that the unsatisfied longing within us is the desire for You rather than the allurements of this world. Heal our wanton self-centeredness. Create in us pure hearts and renew a right spirit within us, O Lord. In the Name of Jesus. Amen.

August 17

Let the Little Children

Lord God, thank You for loving children and wanting them know You. Breathe Truth into their understanding until Christ is formed in them. May they start an awakening in the souls of adults in this misguided world.

Father, incline the hearts and minds of children toward You in trust. May their ears grab up Your Good News. Encourage parents and teachers to let the little ones come to You and not deny them by failing to teach the Truth.

Protect them from ignorance and indifference. Send angels to guard their fragile lives and minds, their habits, bodies and personalities. Keep them, Almighty God, from the wiles of the Evil One. Protect them from people under Satan's control. Lead these lambs, Lord, in the paths of righteousness.

Lord, when the disciples were bickering over who would be greatest in Your Kingdom, You picked up a little one, hugged it, and told what You think of earthly greatness.

"Listen carefully," You said, "unless you are willing to become humble like this child, you won't enter the Kingdom of Heaven. The humble are elevated in the Kingdom. If you welcome a child in My name, you welcome Me. If you cause a child to lose his faith it would be better if you were drowned in the sea, so teachers and professors beware! Many of you are wreaking havoc with our youth. Never belittle or injure one of these children, for their angels in Heaven have instant access to My Father."
(Matthew 18: 1-5, 10-11)

August 18

For Protection

Holy Father, thank You for Your protection. We need You constantly, without You we would be devoured from within and without.

I lift those who are particularly vulnerable at this time. My prayer is based on Your Word and I ask that You hear and send help. I realize You know and love them. I'm asking these blessings for _____ today with thanks and praise.

Thank You, Lord, You surround Your people like mountains surround Jerusalem. (Psalm 125:2)

You preserve us from evil, keeping our souls safe. You watch over our coming in and going out. (Psalm 121:7-8)

You give Your angels charge over us, to guard us. They lift us up lest we trip on a stone and fall. (Psalm 91:11-12)

You won't let us fall, for in guarding us You are always alert, neither taking naps nor going to sleep. (Psalm 121:3-4)

You rescue us from hidden traps of evil's contagion; You cover us, offering us refuge. Your faithfulness is our shield and wall of defense. (Psalm 91:3-4)

Those who obey You live securely. They are safe from the tense dread of evil. (Proverbs 2:33)

You bring gladness to those who take refuge in You. So let all who love Your Name be joyful. With love and praise, Amen

August 19

For Relationships

Father, I praise You for being *Jehovah-shalom*, God who is our Peace, who breaks down barriers of irritation and dislike which we erect between ourselves and others. You can make us one in the Spirit.

Especially I ask You to take _____ and _____ up in Your hands. May they give up their resentment and fretfulness with each other and forgive. Teach them to store Your Word in mind and heart so they may not sin against You or others. (Psalm 119:11) Reunite and rebuild their love for each other and may their forgiveness be like a healing salve.

My prayer is the same as Paul's, that Christ "will give them wisdom to understand who Christ is, and all He has done for them. May their hearts be flooded with light so they see something of the future He has called them to share." (Ephesians 1:17-18)

I thank You Father that with Christ's strength they may let anger and cruel words be put away. May they be kind and considerate of each other, forgiving the same way You forgive us for Christ's sake. (Ephesians 4:31-32) What a burden is lifted as resentment is given up!

"Lord, may they (we) never let a day end in anger with the other. If we do, we give Satan a foothold in the relationship. Instead may they (we) bear with one another in love." (Ephesians 4:26-27)

Reunite them and rebuild their mutual forgiveness, their love of God and each other, so love and forgiveness becomes the eternal adhesive binding heart to heart and life to life.

With thanks and great expectations in Jesus' Name   Amen

August 20

Faith of an Old Man, Psalm 71

Hear me, Lord, for You are my refuge of steadiness. I keep
returning to You because You are where I live. You are my
address, my home. Rescue me, Lord God, my enemies are many.

You brought me through birth so I could know and follow You.
   You have always been my confidence.
I've surprised many by following Your ways. You have been my
   refuge and joy all my life. My strength is failing
   and my enemies watch me, like hawks, whispering,
"God won't protect him anymore. He's old and useless.
Let's grab him now that there's no one to help him!"
Lord, I won't give up hope, for I'm remembering how
   You rescued me more times than I can count.
You have guided me from birth, Lord, don't put me on the shelf
   now that my strength is gone and my hair is white.
I want to finish the assignment You've given me of proclaiming
   Your righteousness.
 I want this current generation and those yet to come,
   to know Your Truth and revere You.
O God, Your creative power embraces us.
   It inhabits endless space and covers earth.
   Your works are mighty and unexplainable.
Who is like You, Lord? No one! No one is like You!
You have let me see bitter trouble in my life.
   It has dogged my footsteps like shadows on a sunny day.
Back stabbers knock me down, but You lift me up,
   bringing confidence this time will be no different.
Even though I'm gasping, fainting, You will raise me up.
I will joyfully sing of Your deliverance, with lyre and harp
   for accompaniment.
Song pours from my heart, rejoicing in Your magnificent rescue
   of this soul You have redeemed!

August 21

An Old Man Remembers

The old man of Psalm 71 is looking back over his life. His strong memory is of God's constant faithfulness to him. He tells God, "You are my refuge and my unshakable Rock ... You, Lord, are where I live, my address. You are my home."

He tells God his needs, troubles and fears. He prays, "Lord, my strength is failing and my enemies know it. They watch me like hawks, whispering, 'He's old and helpless. Let's snatch his goods while there's no one to help him!'"

Old people are vulnerable. They know it. In retirement the prominence of their position is greatly diminished. Income is down, prices are up. Strength wanes, friends and family members die. Memory fades. The old man feels helpless, but he knows the One whose love never changes will help him. "Don't leave me, Lord!" he calls. "Don't retire me to a corner shelf because I'm old and weak."

In Hebrew Scriptures, he uses the name *Elohim* in his prayer, remembering that it means God, *Creator and Sustainer.* The Name reminds him of God's power to keep His creation. He thinks of the many times *Elohim* has helped and sustained him in disaster.

Remembering God's help in the past encourages him, as it does us today. He tells God, and himself, "I won't give up hope. I'll continue to trust and praise You. You've never let me down so why should I think You will fail me now?" He believes he can trust God no matter what life hands him. Experience tells Him God is too wise to make mistakes and too powerful to have His plans thwarted. He *commits* himself to trust and praise.

Lord God, some of us will grow old, but You will never turn away from Your own people, whether we're young, middle aged or old and weak. We may put our trust in the only reliable source of eternal safety. That's You, Father. That's You!

August 22

The Psalmist Sings of God, Psalm 96

Sing! Sing a new song of joy to our Lord! Circle Earth
    with His praise! Bless His Holy Name.
Tell someone every day that He saves!
Tell of His wonderful works. Tell it to the neighbors!
    Tell it to the nations!

The Lord is above all powers. Respect Him above all
    "gods" for He only is God.
Our Lord made the brilliant splendor of the heavens.
    Majesty and strength surround Him.

Let all families of earth honor Him with grateful
        hearts, bringing Him the offering of godly lives.
Tell all governors He is King above all kings.
He is Creator, Owner, Sustainer of earth.
He will never change. He will judge the people with justice.

So, heavens rejoice! Earth be glad! The sea roars
        its approval of His tides.
Fields unfurl their brightest blossoms and breezes
        waft their fragrance over all.
Trees of the forest clap their hands in adulation
        and bow their leafy limbs to Him.

All created things obey His purposes for them.
He is coming! He is coming in majesty
        and blazing glory to judge the earth
        in equity and faithfulness.

August 22

Now Let Me Sing to You

Now, Lord, let me sing a song to You,
    a song of love and praise.
I know Your Name, I see Your hand
    in all the eye takes in.

While day is early, sweet and new,
    I turn first thing to You.
Your blessings fall like freshening dew
    upon my thirsty heart.

I drink in Your mercy, feast on Your truth.
The more I eat, the more I drink, the deeper,
    the higher grows my praise
    till I'm afloat in You.
                    F.N.

August 23

Both Savior and Judge

How do we see You, Lord God? Is the picture in our mind focused on the stern Judge who watches for infringements of "the rules," or do we see You more clearly as our loving God, who paid the price of our sin? We know Your commandments don't save us because we can't keep them. Being good, even doing good, does not do it, for we're never good *enough*. Ever since Satan tempted humanity in the Garden we've had real trouble.

We are helpless to make ourselves acceptable in Your sight but You had a plan of rescue. A ransom, *in kind*, would be paid -- human life for human life. Not any human life would do. If the life of the one to be sacrificed were not sinless, that sinner must first pay his own debt before he pays for another. The perfect life is only found in Christ Jesus. Remember the first Passover before leaving Egypt, the land of slavery? (Exodus 12:5-7) The Lord told Moses to sacrifice a lamb, not just any lamb, but a *perfect lamb* with no defect, like a torn ear or a lame leg. The people were to take the lamb's blood and put it over their doors so the Angel of Death would *pass over,* or skip, the marked house. This was to prefigure the coming of the true Lamb of God, sacrificed for us.

Lord God, You love us before You judge us. It's Your right to judge us harshly. We know before anything else Lord, You are our Savior. You save us by forgiving and changing us. And You could do that only by making Your sinless Son, the perfect Passover Lamb.

You pay our ransom, redeem our lives, mend our broken places, heal our sick souls and cover our shameful nakedness with the robe of the Son's righteousness. Your sacrifice was once for all time and all people. Our mother or father's faith cannot save us. It must be individually our own. Each of us must personally reach out and accept Your offer. Words are not adequate to thank You, Lord.

August 24

How Very Like You, Lord

On a trip to the Middle East we visited Philippi in Macedonia where on a Saturday morning centuries ago Paul met Lydia of Thyatira. The purpose of Paul's travels was to plant Christian churches in the important cities of commerce. His pattern in each city was to use the local synagogue as his pulpit. Since Philippi was a rough Roman outpost and the Jewish population was too small to have a synagogue, the devout few met each Sabbath at the river for prayer. Paul, Silas, Luke and Timothy joined the group there and began to tell the Good News of Jesus, the Messiah. Lydia, a wealthy woman, whose business was selling purple cloth to the upper class and royalty was there with her family.

For a Pharisee to teach women was against all traditional rules of behavior but Paul had greater things on his mind than political correctness. God's purposes were on his mind and God's love was in his heart. He followed Jesus' example and treated women as graciously as he treated men. Paul wrote "In Christ Jesus we are all equal, there is neither Jew nor Gentile, slave nor free, male nor female, for we are one people in Him." (Galatians 3:28)

Lydia was a Gentile but she may have heard something of Jesus, the "One True God" who had somehow become our Sin bearer. Since she was unbaptized it's unlikely that she had any real understanding of Him. Perhaps she wanted to hear more.

How very like You, Lord, to bring together the man who wanted to share the Bread of Life and the woman who was searching for, hungering for the Living Bread. As Lydia listened, what little she had heard before as rumor began to fall into place like pieces in a puzzle. The Lord opened her heart to respond to Paul's message. She was convinced by the evidence, not by pressure and not by intimidation.

August 24

After being baptized she wanted to learn more about the faith that had been born in her that day. She invited the four evangelists, two Jews, two Gentiles, to stay at her house. Once again, Paul and Silas set aside the strict Jewish tradition of shunning "unclean Gentiles" for a much greater cause, God's redeeming love for all people. Lydia and her family were now blood brothers and sisters with the evangelists, not by parental blood of earthly families but by the eternal and transforming blood of Jesus. (Acts16:11-16)

August 25

Longing for the Temple, Psalm 84

Lord, ruler of heaven's hosts, how beautiful is Your Temple!
I long to be there in Your courtyard again.
My soul and voice are hungry to sing praises in Your Presence,
    my Living God.
It is joy beyond expression to be there. Even birds of the air
    seek to build their nests in Your courtyard.
They lay their young next to Your altar, O God.

Those who know You as their strength have joy for when
    they must walk through the Valley of Sorrows,
Your strength fills the Valley with clear pools and blessings
    fall upon them as gentle spring rains.
Lord, our Defender, our Fortress and Shield, look on David,
    our king, with mercy and protection.

One day in Your Temple is better than a lifetime outside.
I'd rather be there, even standing on the threshold,
    than to live in the luxurious homes of lawbreakers,
    for You are like the sun in the sky, O Lord.
You give light and warmth, grace and glory to those who follow
    Your path. You withhold no good thing from them.
O Lord of Heaven's hosts, all who trust You are blessed,
    and blessed, and blessed.

Note: Written by a descendant of Korah. They were Levites and gatekeepers of the Temple. (I Chronicles 9:19) During the reign of Hezekiah, Assyrians had threatened the land and then retreated. Perhaps this Levite's scheduled time of service in the Temple had come round again. He loved the Temple, had missed it during his time off. He longed to be within its gates again.

August 26

Lord, Teach Me to Wait

Today I walked along the edge of the Atlantic Ocean with You, Lord, as my companion. I recognized anew how dramatically sea and sky "declare the glory of God." I was weary, inside and out, tired of waiting, tired of praying for an unresponsive loved one. I was discouraged and asked, "How long, O Lord?"

Thoughts darted through my mind like wee sandpipers hunting breakfast. The sea reminded me of life, a challenge to the adventurer, a threat to the timid soul. Magnificent whatever its mood. I'm a mix of these: adventurer, mouse and awed observer.

It was mainly the shore, with its litter of shells, some whole but most fragmented, which kept edging into my mind. The shells were empty, washed by the sea, sterilized inside and out by the gritty cleansers of salt and sand.

I felt the emptiness of the shells. Within myself I was tattered and scrubbed by the agitation of impatience, faded by the heat and glare of unanswered questions. Self pity had seeped in as sea water fills depressions in the sand. I stood there on the shore, wrapped in sunshine and breeze, conscious of my need; conscious of Your strong, loving Presence.

Then the song began. It filled my emptiness, cooled my fever, and lifted my fainting spirit with hope and trust. The song was Isaiah's: "They that wait upon the Lord will renew their strength; they will rise up on eagle's wings; they will run and not be weary; they will walk and not faint." (Isaiah 40:31)

No eagles were there, but sea birds were numerous, soaring upward on strong wings. On the walk back to the condo my mind's eye "saw" my precious one complete in You, Lord, "ransomed, healed, restored, forgiven." Your Spirit took my discouragement and replaced it with praise, peace, prayer and purpose.

Teach me. Teach me to wait, Lord. I'm willing.

What do You Seek?

Some Christian groups say, "Don't seek an experience... seek God." Well, of course, Lord! It's You we seek, but as we seek and find You, we are led through an "experience." I can't imagine a Christian seeking to know You for the "experience" any more than I can imagine marrying my husband for the "experience." I had reasons for marrying him, but that was not one of them. I loved him. He loved me; we *liked* each other. We had similar goals, morals and Christian beliefs. We wanted to have babies together and enjoy each other's companionship, grow old and wait for Heaven together. We talked of all these things, yet we never said, "I married you for the experience." In looking back over our marriage, we both marvel at the *experience* it has been. How can a life changing event *not* be an experience?

When I called out to You, Lord, I recognized Your mercy, love and forgiveness as a magnet. As we began to communicate You warmed my heart, showed me how much I needed You. An invi-tation came addressed to me. It was clear: "FJN, come to Me and I'll give you rest. Take Me into your life, be nourished with fresh Bread of My Presence. Your soul need never be dry or undernourished again." My reply was also an invitation, "Yes, Lord, come into my life. We'll walk Your Way together."

This event, the new birth, is like a good marriage in a way. You tell us, "I will give you a new name, a new legal status, a new address. I'll move your citizenship to the Kingdom of Light. I'll never leave you for all Eternity."

What an *experience* it is to walk life's road with You Lord! It's the joy of being together, of knowing the relationship is permanent. It is the comfortable, strong realization that no tragedy, no disappointment, no "better opportunity" can separate me from You. I am Yours and You are mine. Forever.

August 28

Lord, Keep Me Salty

Jesus said, "You are the salt of the Earth. But if you lose your flavor, you lose your worth." (Matthew 5:13) Lord, salt seems such an earthy illustration to use for children of the King. But then, what could be earthier than earthlings?

As we look at the uses of salt we see your point, Lord, in using it as a simile. It flavors many foods. I cannot imagine a crisp, cold salad without a sprinkle of salt.

Just as salt enhances our food, so You, Lord, enhance our lives by bringing flavor, completeness and interest. Your Spirit becomes our zest and treasure as You continue to permeate our living. As we become salty Christians we may bring the flavor of Heaven to our community. Salt is a preserver. It curbs bacterial growth and prevents putrefaction. This is what we are here for, to be the preservative of Your Truth and Light in this confused world. Without it, society would rot. So would we. We Believers need to be a cleansing force, helping to wipe out the highly contagious infection of sin in our world.

Lord, You call us the *salt of the Earth*, the flavor of Life eternal, the preservative of Your Truth in the world and in the church. Your Truth is the only effective antiseptic for this disease-breeding world.

Lord God, keep me and all Your people, salty!

August 29

Read the Small Print, We Have Benefits

Jesus says, "This isn't the whole contract. Read the small print, then come live in full relationship with Me. Ask My Father and He will give you the Holy Spirit. You'll be like a branch of a sturdy grapevine. Stay firmly connected to Me, as the branch is attached to the vine, and what I am will begin to flow out to you." (John 14-15)

As a branch draws nourishment from its root, so Believers are invited to participate in Your abundant life, Lord. You begin to shape us, not by the world's pattern, but to Your own likeness. As we live in You and draw in Your likeness, You fulfill Your promise that our lives will bear fruit, abundant, lasting and obvious.

"The fruit of the Spirit is love, joy, peace, patience, kindness, goodness, faithfulness, gentleness and self-control." (Galatians 5:22)

There are Christians whose lives seem barren and dry. No one wants to live a fruitless life. You don't want that for us either, Lord. Fruits of the Spirit are ours legally, provided by You but we must claim them.

Victory over our spiritual enemies is ours too. Our enemies may be outside circumstances, or an old habit which claimed us years ago. It can be an attitude of resentment, selfishness, criticism, or a dirty mouth. We can obey You, Lord, and win out or we can ignore You and the enemy wins. As we seek Your will, as we find and obey You, each victory becomes a concrete experience. As we add event after event of Your work in us, there's soon no denying that You, our Infinite God, live in our finite selves.

Taking God into the deepest parts of our living assures us of more than "salvation-by-the-skin-of-our-teeth." We have daily comfort, guidance and peace. Hope, faith, joy and love are there for us, even in pain and trouble.

August 30

Dark Clouds

Clouds darken each life as surely as they form in summer skies. Trouble threatens to scramble our well planned lives.

Much is said in Scripture concerning trouble in human life. Experience tells us we bring much of it upon ourselves by unwise words, foolish decisions or undisciplined actions. (Matthew 6:34, John 16:33)

When our wrong actions bring pain or trouble, You want us to know and correct it, Lord. The author of Hebrews says, "Don't scorn the Lord's correction or grow discouraged when He rebukes you. For God trains and disciplines His children as earthly fathers correct the children they love. No discipline is pleasant, but in looking back we see the result of His careful training in our lives." (Hebrews 12:5-11)

> Have you watched a summer's day
> darken as clouds tumble over the sky?
> Have you listened to the stillness as earth
> holds her breath before the storm breaks?
> Have you smelled those first drops
> on the crumbly dry soil leaving
> splotches of wetness?
> Have you wondered why rain must come
> ruining carefully laid plans?
> Have you noticed what happens to grass
> and forest when they accept the rain?
> Does grass refuse refreshing showers,
> or do forests hold back new growth?
> F.N.

Lord, teach me to accept disappointment or correction in a creative, positive way from Your loving hand.

August 31

Calamity to Those Who Call Evil Good

This is an abbreviated version of the prayer of the Rev. Joe Wright at the opening session of the Kansas Senate. It was e-mailed to thousands.

"Heavenly Father, we come before You today to ask forgiveness and to seek Your direction and guidance. We know Your Word says, 'Woe to those who call evil good' but that's exactly what we have done. We have lost our spiritual equilibrium and reversed our values.

We confess that we have ridiculed the absolute truth of Your Word and called it pluralism,

We have worshipped other gods and called it multiculturalism,

We have endorsed perversion and called it alternative life style,

We have exploited the poor and called it the lottery,

We have rewarded laziness and called it welfare,

We have killed unborn children and called it choice,

We have shot abortionists and called it justice,

We have neglected to discipline our children and called it building self-esteem,

We have abused power and called it politics,

We have coveted our neighbor's possessions and called it ambition,

We have polluted the air with profanity and called it freedom,

We have ridiculed the time-honored values of our forefathers and called it enlightenment.

August 31

Search us, O God, and know our hearts today; cleanse us from every sin and set us free. Guide and bless those men and women who have been sent to direct us to the center of Your will. We ask this in the Name of Your Son, our Savior. Amen"

Response to this was immediate. Several legislators walked out in protest. In six weeks, Central Christian Church, where Rev. Wright is pastor, logged more than 5,000 phone calls with forty- seven of them responding negatively. The church has received international requests for copies from India, Africa and Korea. Paul Harvey aired the prayer on *The Rest of the Story* on radio and received a larger response to this program than any other he had aired.

"If you don't stand for something, you will fall for everything,"

September's Song

Let heavens rejoice and earth be glad,
    let dawning laugh with joy!
May day break forth in endless praise
    and darkness shine as light.
For God's own world is singing His song;
    listen to earth's hymn of delight!

It's a song of growth, of rhythm and change,
    drenched in the fragrance of fall!
It rises with heat, descends with rain,
    sweeps us with windy wings.
Earth's sights are a paean of praise to God,
    each ocean, each forest, each leaf.

O, that *we* would praise You so,
    with hearts to understand
    the meaning of transforming Love!
Lives would be mended, families made new,
    dark cities would ring with song.

Lord, kindle Your flame in floundering souls,
    so Light drives away the dark.
Call us by name. Ignite our hearts
    to step out and follow You.
Flood us in godly light to glow
    like this September's day.
                F.N.

September 2

Jehovah-rophe, Our God Who Heals

Another Hebrew name of God is *Jehovah-rophe*. *Jehovah*, which means I AM, combined with *rophe*, means to restore, heal, cure. It can be interpreted as I AM always the God who heals, not only physically but morally and spiritually.

Moses cried out to *Jehovah-rophe* to heal his sister, Miriam when she was stricken with leprosy. God did. (Numbers 12:13)

The psalmist praised God sayings, "My soul, thank God, who forgives your sins and heals your diseases." (Psalm 103:2-3)

We know the need for physical healing. There's an even greater need for moral and spiritual healing. Often we are more concerned with physical than moral healing. This isn't new. In about 700 B.C. Isaiah described Israel's spiritual condition: "Your head is covered with wounds and your entire heart is infected. From your feet to the top of your head you are covered with infection, open sores, bruises, boils and blisters. They are not disinfected, bandaged or eased by medication." (Isaiah 1:6)

Things haven't changed much. The media reflects society as an "open, running sore." We desperately need You, *Jehovah-rophe*, our Healer, individually and worldwide. Israel was told the remedy but they wouldn't have You. They went on refusing You "until there was no remedy." (II Chronicles 36:16)

Jehovah-rophe who heals in the Old Testament is *Jehovah-Jesus* who heals in the New. Lord, Your earth ministry began and ended with healing, physical and spiritual. Your first public readings at synagogue were a reading from Isaiah describing Yourself: "The Lord's Spirit is on Me. He appointed Me to preach God's good news, mend broken hearts, set prisoners free, to give sight to the blind." (Isaiah 61, Luke 4:18)

Your role has not changed. You are still our changeless God. (Hebrews 13:8)

September 3

Heal Me, Lord

Jeremiah prays, "If You heal me, Lord, I will be healed. If You save me, I'll be saved. Only You can do this and I praise You." God's reply, "I will heal your wounds." (Jeremiah 17:14, 30:17)

Lord God, You made us to have a loving relationship with You, with our spiritual family the Church, and with our personal families. St. Paul gives a wise formula for harmony and love. He tells family members, "Wives support your husbands by following their wishes in ways which honor the Lord. Husbands love your wives as you love yourself. Don't take advantage of them. Children, obey your parents. It pleases God when you do this. And parents, don't be too hard on your children or you could break their spirits." (Colossians 3:18-21)

In today's world it doesn't always work this way. Human personalities can be damaged by lack of love. Wounded ones often wear masks so others won't see their pain. Some hide themselves in a wise-cracker's mask, or a pious façade, others choose to be a know-it-all, or the tough guy with no emotions.

But Father, You can heal our false lives. It begins when we unlock ourselves and ask You in. (Ephesians 3:16-19) Of course, You know our hiding places, but we still need to tell You. Telling You runs out the ogres locked inside. As we give You our secrets, You turn on the Light of Your Presence and help clean out accumulated trash. Healing continues as we share and worship with other Believers. Then we can begin to be ourselves and let others be themselves.

From personal experience we know we hurt each other and others hurt us. Therefore we must forgive them, as well as ourselves. It's only through the indwelling Holy Spirit and through other imperfect but open Christians that You, Lord, begin to heal our inner wounds and soften the marred scar tissue surrounding them.

September 4

The "No God" Theory, Psalm 53

The foolish man convinces himself that God
    doesn't exist. Why is he so eager to spread
    this opinion? Is it because he knows
    if God *is* real, he's a dead man?
He may rationalize that his "no God" theory
    excuses his actions, relieving him
    of responsibility to change his ways.

God sees all this. He is looking for people
    who understand and seek Him.
He doesn't find many who take in His message.
Corruption, greed and the "me first" policy
    have taken control of the human heart.

How can it be that God finds so few who obey Him?
Can't we add two and two and still come up with four?
They belittle or corrupt the people of God and refuse
    to let their own hearts be challenged by Truth.

Terror and realization that God means what He says
    will come upon them when they least expect it.
Then unbelievers who fight against the God of all Truth
    will be scattered like straw across a field.

Lord, it's a grief to contemplate. Won't You please
    come NOW with salvation and restore Your
    people?
Only Your Presence can make us truly glad again.

September 5

Caught Between Absolutes

"While we were too weak
and stubborn to realize our need,
Christ came to earth to take our
place in death." (Romans 5:6)

Scripture is clear about Your
life's purpose on earth, Lord. We are
helpless to save ourselves. It's because of our very helplessness, You
came to offer Your holy life for our
unholy ones. You took our death
sentence on Yourself. This truth must
be carefully considered and either
accepted or rejected.

Life is too precious to give it up unnecessarily. To give our
life for another person there must be absolutely no other way for
that person's life to be saved. St. Paul sees us as caught in an
escape proof trap with no way out except through You. That one
way is to have You, innocent of any sin, take our death penalty
upon Yourself.

Sin isn't a word we hear much today. We don't like it. It
sounds too harsh. Therefore, we rename it, substituting words like
mistake, goof-up, wrong choice. But with all our cover ups, sin
remains strongly invasive. The Westminster Catechism answers
the question of what sin is this way: "Sin is any lack of conformity
to, or transgression of the Law of God."

Here we are, caught and held fast between two absolute
truths: God's demands and our inability to fulfill them. We *must*
find a substitute or we must be perfect in our love for God. This is
God's first law. The second is, 'Love your neighbor as much as

September 5

you love yourself. Mold your lives around these two and all others will fall into place.'" (Matthew 22:37-40)

Who can obey this? I want to, but my demanding *self* is always there, ready to elbow God and neighbors aside. Paul agrees, "All people sin and fall short of the glory of God. (Romans 3:23)

Even though we're trapped with the problem of God's demands and our inability to meet them, there is Good News. The love of God and our response to it can unlock our prison door. You, Lord, will come to us in our dilemma just when we need You most. Your love comes to us as an invitation, the ungodly, the disobedient, the imperfect, and says, "Anyone who is thirsty for the Water of Life, come to Me; anyone hungry for the Bread that Lives, come. You don't need money to eat, drink and be satisfied here. Accept My invitation and come to Me and your soul shall live." (Isaiah 55:1-3)

Thank You, Lord, for Your divine mercy.

September 6

What God Could Have Said

"God could have said to us, 'I've noticed that you often
appreciate many of My gifts, but I've also noticed that you have
hardly thought about what it means to *Me* to give them. I've had a
grand time making up gifts for you! Tens of thousands of them!
For example, I settled a long time ago on five senses to give you.
Thought it over quite a bit and five seemed to be enough for a
lifetime of interest and still not a number to overwhelm you. I
have some really fine new ones, which you've never once thought
of, waiting for you in Heaven.

"I had the delight of giving you many things for each sense
to discover:

Leaves that praise Me in rich hued colors as they die.
My own special blend of sky blue and spruce green
   still there, whenever you look up, after
   the psalm of leaves is ended.

Brooks I designed to gurgle and ocean waves
   to crash, the purr I put into kittens,
   every human voice an original design
   and some which spill over in music.

The juice in peaches, an apple's crunch,
   vanilla beans and watermelon.
The perfume that roses wear, the hard-sell
   way a roasting turkey advertises
   itself. Good leather. Black dirt.
Oh, those were all fun to give you!

September 6

The plus of a hot bath, the response of a
loved one's lips, wind in your face,
or just scratching an itch.
Every one of these and millions more
was a deliberate, loving gift from
Me to you.
Is there anything you'd like to give Me?"

Used with permission of Dr. Roy R. Riviere, 1974,
from North Avenue Presbyterian church bulletin,
Atlanta, GA

September 7

Adonai in the Old Testament, God is Lord

In the Old Testament the Hebrew name for God, *Adonai,* is translated in our Bible as *Lord.* It is almost always in the plural possessive, meaning my Lords' which, like the name Elohim, gives the concept of the Trinity. The singular form of the word is *adon,* used for a man, meaning a master, sir, owner or lord. Only when referring to God is it plural. In Psalm 110 "The Lord (*Adonai*) said to my Lord (*Adoni*)" ... or "Jehovah (Father and Spirit) said, My Lord Christ, (singular) sit here at My right hand until I put Your enemies under Your feet." In Matthew 22:41-45 Jesus refers this passage to Himself. When David is speaking of one person of the Trinity, the Messiah, he uses the singular *Adoni* not the plural *Adonai.*

Adonai is first used by Abram in Genesis 15:2 after he rescued Lot and defeated the four kings. Abram was lord (*adon*) of a large clan yet Abram, by addressing God as *Adonai-Jehovah,* acknowledged Him as the Master over all masters with complete right to all he was and had.

Moses knew Him as his Master with the right to his life and service, but he tried to plead off: "My *Adonai,* I'm a poor speaker; send someone else." But when God calls us to a task, He provides the equipment to complete it. (Genesis 3:11-13) At Joshua's defeat, he asked *Adonai* for guidance. (Joshua 7) When God called Gideon to save Israel, Gideon asked, "My *Adonai,* how can I save Israel?" (Judges 6:11-16)

Isaiah's life as a prophet began with a vision of God as *Adonai* on His throne, exalted above all earthly rulers, King of all kings, Lord of all lords, Owner of earth and creation. (Isaiah 6)

Prophets, priests and kings realized God's rights to command, use or dispose of them as He willed, for He was Lord, Master, Owner of their lives. His position has not changed.

September 8

Adonai in the New Testament

Since God is "the same yesterday, today and tomorrow," (Hebrews 13:8) it should not surprise us that *Adonai*, the changeless One, is also in the New Testament. The name is used for men of importance, who oversee others, as well as for Jesus Himself, as the second Person of the Trinity.

God the Father, the Son and the Holy Spirit is one Lord, our Owner and Master. He made us, sustains us and bought us back from the Law of Sin and Death at great price to Himself. Because of this we honor and glorify Him in our bodies, souls, and in our living. Paul writes, "Brothers and sisters, because of what we know of God's mercy, let me encourage you to give your bodies as a living sacrifice, one that is holy and acceptable to Him. This is true spiritual worship. Don't follow the world's pattern but let God transform you by remaking your mind." (Romans 12:1-2)

As our *Adonai* God protects, equips and sustains His people. He told Abraham, "I am your shield." (Psalm 28:7) Paul wrote, "The Lord stood beside me and gave me His strength." (Acts 23:11) The disciples who called Jesus Master, Teacher and Lord were transformed in mind and desire so through them God the Holy Spirit, might turn the world upside down.

Jesus, the Lord, our *Adonai,* is revealed in Isaiah as the Servant of God. "Look at My Servant," says the Father, "He is the One I have elected. I uphold Him and take delight in Him. I have put My Spirit in Him, He will not fail, for I will keep Him." (42:1-6) Satan has tried to derail those who serve Him but *Adonai-Jesus*, the perfect Servant of God, has brought liberty, joy and righteousness to His servants. "Those who are called to live their lives in Christ, even though they are servants, in Christ they are Adonais' freemen." (I Corinthians 7: 22)

September 9

Creator, Sustainer, Owner, Psalm 24

You made the whole earth, Lord, and everything in it.
You raised it up from the waters and laced it
    through with rivers.
What power You manifest in Creation!

Who among us can ascend to You, Jehovah? Who is able
    to stand up in the Holy Place of Your Presence?
It will certainly not be men who deceive
    nor scheming women.
It will be those whose intentions are clean
    and those whose actions match Your plans.
These will be blessed by You with the gift of salvation.
    These are the God seekers.

So Jerusalem! Open up!
Throw your City gates wide so the King
    of Glory will come through.

And who is this King of Glory?
He is the Lord, Jehovah the Mighty!
He is the Lord, undefeated in battle!
So Jerusalem! Open your gates!
Throw your doors of the City wide
    so the King of Glory may come through.

And who is this King of Glory?
    He is Jehovah, owner of this Earth!
He is Jehovah, Commander of Heaven's hosts.
    HE is the King of Glory!

September 10

Our Searching Lord

Jesus asks the crowd, "If you had a flock of a hundred sheep and one was lost, wouldn't you leave the others and search for the lost one until you found it?" (Luke 15: 4)

The story of the lost sheep gives a glimpse of God the Son as the Great Shepherd of our souls who knowing one of His flock is missing leaves the joy and comfort of Heaven and comes to earth to seek, find and bring it back.

We can almost see the shepherd of Jesus' story searching for the sheep, sweating from exertion and danger, scraped by rocks of the mountain, cut by brambles. Finally he presses back a prickly bush with his staff. There it is, tattered and fearful, caught fast in the thorny branches! He squats down, untangles its wool from the impeding shrubbery and gathers it up. Joy sounds in his voice as he speaks gentle words of assurance, "There you are, Small One! Come on, don't be afraid. I'm here. Let's go home!"

Upon his arrival at home with his precious burden, he calls friends together and says, "Celebrate with me! I've found my missing sheep!" By way of explanation of the shepherd's joy, Jesus tells the crowd, "It's the same here as in Heaven. When one sinner repents, the numberless hosts of Heaven celebrate with great joy!"

We recognize You, Lord Jesus, in the lines of these parables. You are the One who makes our return possible. You are the Word of the Father. (John 1:1) You are the call of the Father's love which we hear from the Far Country where we have wandered. We hear Your voice of love, Father, urging us homeward.

Father, may I bring You, and all heaven, joy rather than sorrow. Amen

September 11

Our Seeking Lord

Jesus asks, "If a woman loses one of her silver coins, wouldn't she stop what she was doing, light the lamp and turn the house upside down until she finds it?" (Luke 15:8-10)

In this second story of God as our Seeker, the valuable coin could have been from the woman's dowry or her day's wage. Losing it could mean there would be no food on the table. She stops what she is doing and begins the search, sparing no time or energy in order to find the coin.

Most of the simple homes at that time had hard packed earth floors over which straw was scattered. Windows were few and small so natural light was dim. What a job it would be for her to sweep out every nook and cranny looking for a dime sized coin in a rubble of straw in semidarkness!

Lord, aren't You using this simple parable of the seeking woman to represent the action of the Holy Spirit in our lives? He is the blessed Seeker who sifts through the debris of our lives looking for us. *We* are His treasures, His valuable silver coins!

Like the woman in Your story, Lord, the Holy Spirit must turn on a light, the powerful light of His love. He sees us by the light of His love. It's by His light, the Light of the world, that we may come to see *God.* Without His enlightenment, we can never realize God as our Seeker, searching us out and finding His own.

Lord Jesus, Your cross, the price of our ransom, is present in these parables. Our praises rise to You as we recognize Your merciful forgiveness and blessings pouring down on Your lost lambs, Your wandering sons, daughters and Your valuable lost coins.

September 12

Our Magnetic Lord

"While the son was still a good distance away, his father saw him coming and was filled with longing love for him." (Luke 15: 20)

The son is impatient with the restrictions and traditions of home. He wants "freedom," so he asks for his inheritance early and leaves home to explore the pleasures of the Far Country, away from his father's supervision and care. He lives as he pleases, satisfying his every whim, wasting his father's gifts. Soon "he begins to be in need."

The father, realizing this would happen waits with hope. One day he sees his son in the distance, coming home. He sees him at that distance simply because he is watching for him. While tending his land, his eyes are constantly drawn to the horizon. When he sees his son, he runs to him, hugs and kisses him. He RUNS! He *runs* to show his welcome and his joy. He cannot wait to embrace and forgive him.

Heavenly Father, Your love is like that. It's a giant magnet, so powerful it can draw Your estranged or discontented children back from the Far Country of disobedience or doubt, pride or misery to You.

The tough but tender love You have for us keeps You at the window of Your omniscience waiting and watching for us to turn back, for our hearts to reach toward You and call, "Abba, help!"

Father, thank You for Your strong, persistent, magnetic love which keeps drawing this vagabond's heart back to You.

September 13

Climbing Rainbows

George Matheson, a Scottish minister and writer, was losing his eyesight. The trauma and depression were followed by doubt. He began to doubt that God was with him and feared that he had been left to live the rest of his life in darkness, and alone.

On a black, rain swept night he went for a walk. He had no destination but was desperate at the thought of being separated from God. During that cold, bitter walk he wrestled with himself and with God, crying out to Him for help, and for faith.

When he returned home he fell, soaked and chilled, to his knees before God. In a matter of minutes his last poem, before he became totally blind, flowed from his Spirit saturated heart. Today we sing his poem as the hymn *O Love That Wilt Not Let Me Go*.

Before the Church would publish the poem they insisted he make changes. He had written, *I climb the rainbow in the rain and know the promise is not vain that morn shall tearless be.* Church elders said rainbows could not be climbed. Matheson's meaning was that we *climb to faith,* using every muscle, just as the mountain climber struggles for each step upward, in order to make God's promises a reality in his life. They had him change *climb* to *trace.* The preposition was changed from *in* to *through.* But he said he was literally *in* a storm of fear and doubt, not *through* it. He pointed out when he returned from his walk he *knew*, not *felt*, that the rainbow of God's promises were true and eternal, God would always be with him. He *knew* God's promises were sturdy enough for people of faith to stand on, putting the whole weight of life and future on the absolute trustworthiness of God's promises.

I vote *yes* with the Reverend Matheson's meaning of *climbing* the rainbows of God's promises. Our gaining of any goal doesn't happen without effort. Regaining the heights of trust, even in his blindness, was a struggle with both himself and with God.

September 14

Love That Won't Let Go

O Love that wilt not let me go,
I rest my weary soul in Thee;
I give Thee back the life I owe,
  that in Thine ocean depths
  its flow may richer, fuller be.

O Light that followest all my way,
  I yield my flick'ring torch to Thee;
My heart restores its borrowed ray,
  that in Thy sunshine's blaze its day
  may brighter, fairer be.

O joy that seekest me through pain,
  I cannot close my heart to Thee;
I trace* the rainbow through the rain,
  and feel * the promise is not vain
  that morn shall tearless be.

O cross that liftest up my head,
  I dare not ask to fly from Thee:
I lay in dust life's glory dead,
  and from the ground there blossoms red
  life that shall endless be.
     Amen

* climb
* know
George Matheson, 1882, Presbyterian, Episcopal and Baptist Hymnal

September 15

Jehovah-M'Kaddesh, I

Lord, it's beautiful to see how You reveal Yourself through Your names as the spiritual needs of Your people arise. Sin appears in Genesis and You reveal Yourself as *Jehovah-jireh*, our God who provides the sacrifice for sin. (Genesis 22) In Exodus You show Yourself as *Jehovah-rophe*, our God who Heals, healing in the time of dangerous wilderness living. In the war with the Amalekites You are there as *Jehovah-nissi*, the rallying Banner of Your people, taking them to victory as prayer is offered. (Exodus 17) In Leviticus, the book for holy living and worship, You show Yourself as *Jehovah-M'Kaddesh*, our God who sanctifies and makes us holy in every day living, not just on the Sabbath.

To sanctify is to set aside for a special purpose, to dedicate, to consecrate to a cause. Lord, You consecrated the Sabbath as a special, holy day, a day of worship and rest. The first born son was dedicated to Your service. The word *sanctify* applies to places also. The Temple, Mt. Zion are set aside for God's purposes. Jerusalem is called the Holy City.

Lord, You never force us but when we are willing You begin to create holiness in us. You give us free will in choosing whom we will follow. We may choose You and holiness or we may slip silently, almost unknowingly, into self serving. If You are our choice we must set a guard over our hearts and thoughts.

"Consecrate yourselves to be holy, for I am the Lord your God. Keep My decrees and follow them for I am *Jehovah-M'kaddesh*, God who makes you holy." (Leviticus 20:7-8)

September 15

Jehovah, the Holy One, is over and apart from His creation. "This is what the Lord says, 'Israel's King and Redeemer, the Lord Almighty, I am the first and the last; apart from Me there is no God.'" (Isaiah 44:6)

O Lord, God of all holiness, I want to want Your best. Create in me a willing heart to consecrate and dedicate myself to You.

September 16

Jehovah-M'Kaddesh, II

Lord, how do we apply this godly holiness to ourselves today? It's certainly no one time event. It takes a lifetime of daily choices. Only with Your indwelling Spirit of Holiness living in us can the process begin and continue.

Holiness may be Your most basic attribute. Your awesome holiness and Your plan to create it in us must be the reason for Your revelation of the meanings of the Hebrew names. You meet every spiritual need in order that we may set ourselves apart to be only Yours. It's not unlike a good marriage. Both husband and wife set themselves apart from others to belong totally to each other. Without dedication a marriage can't amount to much, neither can our life with You, Lord. It's in name only.

St. John says, "God is love." He is emphasizing the quality of love. He is referring to redeeming, purposeful, sacrificial love. Your love and purpose for us are inseparable. They are both magnificent. Your purpose is to bring us into the holy Presence of God and create holiness in us.

Isaiah's life changing vision of the burning holiness of God (6:1-5) made him a great prophet. It gave him a new realization of absolute holiness of God. "Holy, holy, holy is Jehovah, the Almighty. The whole earth is filled with His glory." From the time of the vision onward, Isaiah referred to Jehovah as the Holy One of Israel. Lord Jesus, You set Yourself apart as the only begotten Son of the Father, the perfect reflection of Him. "The Son is the radiance of God's glory, the exact image of the invisible God." (Hebrews 1:3)

Christians are "chosen by God to be a royal priesthood, a holy nation of believers." (I Peter 1:15-16 and 2:9-10) We are called to be like small pocket mirrors reflecting the image of Your holiness, love and forgiveness in this sin battered world.

September 17

Three Way Love

I. *The Father's Love*

The Father's Love! No words can tell,
    no tongue describe its worth.
It lived before all Time began,
    remains when Time is gone.
The Father's Love! The mind can't grasp
    its height, its depth or bredth.
He spoke, and man became a living soul
    to multiply and spread.
He offered Love, unbound and free,
    for human kind to see.
But man was blind through unbelief.
    He didn't understand.
The love of God broke through the wall
    of darkened human hearts.
He put on the robe of human flesh;
    His Love sent Jesus here.

II. *Christ's Gift*

The Father's Love, who can know it
    in all its gracious care?
God is Spirit; we cannot not grasp
    the concept of Spirit alone.
So Jesus came, humble in birth,
    in order that we might see
Spirit and Flesh in dimensional form,
    pressed out and standing free.
He trod the path our feet should go,
    He demonstrated and explained.
He walked straight into death's dark jaws,
    walked through, then out again.
God's Love brought Him to us.

September 17

His Love took Him back, our Prophet
and Priest and King.
As He entered anew into Heaven's realm
His Love sent the Spirit of Power.

III. *The Spirit's Search*
Seven fold Spirit, what love You show
as You baptize with fire!
Jesus is returning, but You walk now
among the halls of earth,
Seeking temples not built by hands
but living bodies of flesh.
Your Love calls out to hungry hearts,
"I've come to join your life!"
So Spirit, come! My temple is crude.
Some walls are buckled and cracked.
Damp, shadowy places need Your Light
to banish their moldy growth.
Rebuild, transform me with Your Plan
and pour Your Love through me.
Amen
F.N.

September 18

I Want Your Heart, Psalm 50

God will come, in fullness of time, and summon people
    from east and west, north and south.
He will come from Zion's brilliant light.
    He will call and not be silent.
All Heaven and earth will gather
    to judge the Land and its People.

In omniscience He will call, "Gather My godly ones
    to Me, those who have kept covenant with Me."
He will judge with justice and truth. Heaven and earth
    will see His powerful wisdom displayed.
He tells us, "Listen, My people! You sacrifice to Me
    regularly, but there is something
    You do not realize.
"It is not animal's blood I want from you.
All animals are Mine, whether from field or forest.
All cattle that dot the thousand hills are Mine.
No, I don't need your animal sacrifices.

"What I require of you is you, yourself
    with a truly thankful heart.
Offer Me your living heart. I want your trust,
    and obedience in both easy and troubled times.

"I do not tolerate unbelievers speaking of My Covenant
    as if it referred to themselves.
My promises are not for them. They have no inheritance
    from Me because they disregard My Words.

"Some among you associate with evil, with cheaters,
    hypocrites and adulterers.

September 18

Some slander your own brothers,
deception is your delight.

"I do see. Do you think I'm blind, like you?
You deceive no one but yourselves.
Your character is known and you will
be drenched in shame
and self incrimination.

"Listen, you who claim to be My equal.
Listen, lest You suffer the agony of the self damned.
It is those who offer the sacrifice of a thankful
and contrite heart,
those who keep their feet on My path
who will know the joy of eternal salvation."

September 19

New Covenant in Ezekiel

"I will wash you clean from your sin and slavery to idols. I'll take away your rock-like heart and give you a heart of flesh and give you My Spirit. My Spirit will empower you to follow and obey Me. You will live in the Land I gave your ancestors. You will be My people and I will be your God." (Ezekiel 36:25-27)

As in Jeremiah, God is promising a thorough cleansing of heart, mind and life so His followers will be enabled by the Holy Spirit to keep His ways. Here again we see the contrast between the old and the new covenants.

Paul said, "...where sin abounds, grace is super abundant." Why can't Believers experience this? Because it's neither believed nor taught. We don't *expect* it to be fulfilled. Courage shrivels where sin stands tall. Timidity doesn't appease evil. It gives it growing room. The promise is there, however, clearly stated by Paul. (Romans 6:14)

Paul explains, "The power of the life giving Spirit of God is mine because of the completed work of Messiah-Jesus, who freed His people from the law of sin and death. Since the law had no power to save us, God the Father sent God the Son, in the flesh, to carry our sin to the cross. By doing this He broke the fierce grip of sin for those who live by the Spirit." (Romans 8:1-4)

Paul says he once was under the law of sin and death but now that Jesus has fulfilled the requirement of the law of Life for him and for all who live by the Spirit, the old covenant no longer applies and they are brought under the new.

It's the rare Christian who attains this, even though there is only one requirement, faith in Almighty God. Isn't it astonishing that He has made these promises dependent on *our faith* in Him?

Father, I do believe, *but help my unbelief.*

September 20

The Gospel Is Good News

"Jesus walked to all the towns and villages in the area, teaching the Good News of God's Kingdom. Wherever He went He healed the people's diseases." (Matthew 9: 35)

Lord Jesus, the Good News You preached is the startlingly Good News that You rule over us, forgiving, guiding, keeping, saving and protecting us from fear of the problems we must face in this world. It tells us who You are. Without the Gospel we have no idea that You love and forgive us. Some religions have fierce gods, who frighten their people into searching for ways to pacify them. Today many believe if there is a God at all He is a divine clock winder, winding up the world then leaving us to choke and die alone. Some think there is no god except those we put on a pedestal and worship, like money, power, pleasure, drugs, sex or power.

The Good News is about You, Lord. There wouldn't be any good news to write without Your birth, life, death and resurrection.

Your News is that You love and ransom us because You want to adopt us as Your sons and daughters to live with You forever. To those who personally know this truth and strength, it's absolutely earth's best news. It's Good News that all who want to may have You as their Savior. It's good for me. It's good for you.

Mark 13:10 tells us this news is so good that "the Gospel must be told to all the nations of earth" before time ends. But this brings a question to mind, *What about those who have never had a chance to hear it? Will they be saved?*

That's a question only You can answer, Lord. But Charles Spurgeon, a notable pastor of old, had a good answer. He said we were asking the wrong question. We should ask whether we, who have the Gospel, but fail to share it with those who don't have it, will be saved.

September 21

The Word Made Flesh

We don't know the ages of Matthew, Mark and Luke when they wrote their gospels but it is believed that John was a very old man when he wrote his Gospel, the Letters and the Revelation. He had moved to Ephesus, a great, wealthy city, steeped in Greek philosophy, culture and religion, where he became the leader in the flourishing Christian Church. During these years, the church elders, and the Holy Spirit, urged him to write the story of Jesus. The earlier gospels were already in existence. John presents the Savior in a way the new Greek Christians could understand. Jesus' actions and teachings and John's detailed knowledge of the Old Testament were stored deep within his mind and heart since before the crucifixion and resurrection. With the resulting perspective of years of God's work in him, and the Spirit's constant help, John was able to explain the *meaning* of Messiah's actions and teachings, rather than just the facts of the other gospels.

John gives us a glimpse of what God the Son did in eternity before the Incarnation. He says, "Before anything else existed, there was Christ, the Word, with God. He has always been alive and is Himself God. He created everything there is, nothing exists that He did not make. Eternal life is in Him, and this life gives light to all mankind. His life is the light that shines through the darkness -- and the darkness can never extinguish it." (John1:1-5, The Living Bible) The Holy Spirit was there at creation although John does not mention Him. But Genesis does. In the first chapter we see, "In the beginning God created the heavens and earth, which were empty and formless. Darkness covered the deep but the *Spirit of God* was brooding over the waters." (Genesis 1:1-2)

John's words, "Every created thing was made through Him (the Word), nothing was made without Him," are echoed by Paul in Colossians 1:16, "All things in heaven and earth were created by and for Him, what we see and what we can't see like invisible powers and authorities, laws of nature, science and behavior. Everything that is, was created by Him. He was there before creation began and it is He who holds it all together by the power of His Word." *All things*, from galaxies to snowflakes, from atoms to oceans.

David brings us personally to this great creative, preexisting power when he says, "You Lord, always see the real me, just as I am. The darkest dark can't hide me. Darkness and daylight both exist by Your command, so either way, we are continually in Your spotlight. Even while I was in the womb, Your protection knitted me together, cell by cell and gene by gene." (Psalm 139:13-16)

At His Incarnation, God the Son was born, human like us, in flesh, blood and emotions; the Son of Man through Mary, the Son of God through the Holy Spirit.

At His ascension He didn't drop His humanity. He took it with Him as He returned to the Father. Despite His power, His wisdom, purity and splendor, He is still the *Son of Man!* This realization never ceases to jolt me from complacency and remind me that HE wants ME to know Him personally, as the Purpose and Plan of God, as the Living Word, as real and eternal Life, as true Light.

September 22

Ignite Our Hearts

Lord, it's very early and I'm too groggy to pray. It's still dark outside as if morning and I have the same problem waking up. I'll just sit here quietly with You a while and watch You paint this new morning.

Timid, grey light is changing more rapidly than my pen can move. It reminds me of a film showing a flower change from bud to full blossom in a moment of time.

Coral, gold, pink and crimson flame out, staining the clouds with fire. And yes, Lord, Your "strong man," the sun, is there at the starting line and he's off like a shot running the race of day. (Psalm 19)

Color and light fall like music on the dark waters. River and sky, antiphonal choirs, take their parts. Sky sings with dawning brilliance and river repeats it, wrapping the land in glory and praise.

Sea birds, seeking breakfast, join the pageant. Their white breasts and dark tipped wings are brushed with sunrise colors as God's light ignites them.

I'm awake now, Lord, for who could stay sleepy in such a scene?

Ignite the hearts of Your people around the world, that we may reflect You to others as the broad St. Johns River reflects the sky.

September 23

God's Purpose Incarnate

Lord Jesus, You, Yourself, are God's purpose for human redemption. John the Apostle writes, "Christ the Word became incarnate in human flesh and lived in our midst. We have seen and touched Him. His glory amazed us. It was the glory of the Only Begotten Son, reflecting the likeness of His Father's grace and truth." (John 1:14)

Even though Your life, death and resurrection occurred millennia ago, it's more current than today's headlines. Its power to change lives never diminishes – nor does it cease to bring wonder and praise to my heart. St. John wanted people of every century to realize that You are God's vivid and eternal Purpose for every individual.

Relatively few people read the Scripture today. Words from true pastors often fall on unheeding ears. Our days are clogged with words and images. We are drowning in a tidal wave of horror stories from TV, newspapers, smut, brainwashing advertisements and gossip. Talking is easy, but living what we believe is another matter. The saying, "Christians may be the only Scripture many people read" is old but true. Lord, by asking the Holy Spirit to help us reflect You, the Living Word, to others with love, unselfishness and forgiveness, we illustrate Your power to mend lives.

Actions may speak louder than words, but the right words at the right time have great strength. Help the actions and words of Your people be compatible, Lord, for unless we say with our mouths, "Christ in me is my hope of glory," the reason for our lifestyle may not be plain to some. Declaring our faith verbally clears up any possible misconceptions. We make it plain it is *You,* Lord Christ living in Your people and not a "natural goodness" of character or upbringing. Saying and doing must agree in order to have a meaningful witness to Your powerful love and healing.

September 23

My husband and I often borrow David's words from Psalm 19:14 as part of our morning prayers, "Let the words of my mouth and the meditation of my heart be acceptable in Thy sight, O Lord, my strength and my redeemer." (KJV) Don't words, attitudes, plans and actions originate in the "heart?" *

*The biblical meaning of the word *heart* is the "center of unspoken thoughts and emotions."

September 24

Jehovah-Shalom, God is Our Peace

Lord, more than two hundred years had passed since You revealed Yourself as *Jehovah M'Kaddesh*. Israel had been conquered and the twelve tribes divided. People had forgotten You. There was no unity, no belief in absolute truths. Everyone did what was right in their own eyes. They had fallen into the trap of greed, illicit and distorted sex and idolatry.

Gideon was a young Israelite during terrible oppression by the Midianites. Those few who remembered their father's God called out for help. When the angel of the Lord appeared to Gideon with a message of deliverance, he was terrified. He, Gideon, was to lead the attack! But the angel said, "Peace! Don't be afraid!" At first he was hesitant but as his faith rose, fear subsided and he accepted the challenge. He built an altar in confident anticipation and called it *Jehovah-Shalom* (God is our Peace) in accordance with the angel's first word to him.

Shalom can mean peace, or wholeness, in trust and harmony with God, contentment and satisfaction in life. We know that peace is to be a quality of Your reign, Jesus, for You will rule as Prince of Peace in the City of Peace. (Isaiah 9:6)

Jehovah, who creates, owns, nourishes, provides, heals and purifies us IS our Peace. *Jehovah-Shalom* is best seen in the New Testament in *Jehovah-Jesus* who is the completion of our peace. Lord, You accomplished this peace for us through Your death and resurrection. (Romans 5:1) "God's peace is beyond human understanding; it has the power to keep your hearts and minds calm and on target through Jesus Christ." (Philippians 4:7) Paul also makes it clear that our peace is in proportion to our trust in, and obedience to You, Lord Christ.

September 25

In the Quiet of Evening

I walked and talked through the coolness tonight
    with God the Almighty King.
I poured out praise in my weariness, He filled me
    with joy and strength.
I heard His words when day was done,
    His music lifted my soul.

There's nothing more blessed than an evening walk
    with the powerful Lord of all --
unless, perhaps, it's our morning visit
    while day is tender-soft.
Or might it be in afternoon as heat
    and pressures rise?

But I need not choose between the hours,
    for my time is in His hand.
If it's early, I'd choose day's dawning.
    If noon, then that's my choice.

But when dusk descends and day's deeds are done,
    I seek His companionship then,
    to praise and listen, in the quiet of evening,
    to Jesus my Omnipotent Lord.
                                        F.N.

September 26

Fill Us Up, Lord

Father, by the time I asked You to fill me with Your Holy Spirit, I had known You as Savior for years. I knew You were with me. You helped and taught me, but to know You as God who transforms, as constant Companion and Indweller, was something I neither understood nor truly wanted. I was content to hold Your hand and the world's at the same time but this left me vaguely discontented.

I wonder why I took so long and why more Christians are not filled with Your Spirit. Perhaps we are too concerned with trivia or the term *Holy Spirit* remains a mystery. We know something of God the Father, and God the Son, but God the Holy Spirit? Does He remain unknown to us because of our unwillingness to forgive a long held grudge, or perhaps we are not eager to grow up in faith?

Years ago I read an article in which a glove was used to illustrate the difference the Holy Spirit makes in a life. It went something like this: A glove has no strength in itself. It must be filled with a hand before it can do anything. If I slip my hand part way into the glove, it can do a little, but not much. Only when I put my hand fully into the glove is it empowered to pick up the car keys and turn on the ignition. The glove is like life, in a way. When a life isn't filled with the Holy Spirit of God, it has very little power. But when the life is yielded to God as Lord and master, it has power.

Since we *are* like wandering sheep who stray off the Shepherd's path at times, we can easily see being filled with the Spirit is not a one time event. We need to ask for refilling each morning. We must ask for refilling whenever we mosey over into the world's meadow and begin savoring its grass.

The best way to be filled is to ask Him to fill us and forgive us, to feed on the Word, and trust in the truth of His promises.

September 26

This doesn't make us trouble free but it certainly brings His Power into our living. God is willing to give us the free gift of the Spirit when we ask Him. Jesus said, "If you parents want to give gifts to your children, don't you realize your divine Father, wants even more to give the Holy Spirit *to those who ask Him?"* (Luke 11:13)

Father, we know You don't give us Your Spirit only to benefit us as individual Christians, but to make each one of us a stronger, better witness to the Lord Jesus, thereby bringing others into Your Forever Family and enriching them. Thank You.

September 27

Autumn's Golden Touch

Cool crisp days of Fall's first month,
    sun that spotlights freshness
Leaves choreographed to the Maker's tune
    dance to the rhythm of change.

Silky waters, reflecting forests,
    sky as clear as tumblers.
Trees and shrubs and brawny poplar
    brighten their glow
with Autumn's golden touch.

Crimson, blue, gold and winey-red,
    my mind recalls it well;
Earth's colors combine in brilliant praise as
    seasons broadcast His glory.

F.N.

Lord, today I need a heart which reflects Your touch just as Your natural world reflects Your glory. May You be exalted in my attitudes and actions with the family and others. Work in, around and through our lives and prepare each of us to serve You.

I ask, too, for spiritual and physical stamina for the work of today. May I not hinder the rule of Your peace in my heart and mind. It's in Your holy and strong Name, Father, that I exhale my flurry and inhale Your quiet peace and assurance. Thank You.

September 28

Wilderness Temptation

"... take up the sword of the Spirit which is the Word of God ..."
(Ephesians 6:17)

That's just what You did, Lord Jesus, after Your baptism.
You took up the sword as Satan came after You. How like Your
ancient adversary to attack You while You were weak from hunger
after weeks in the desert! Satan used a three pronged attack on
Your body, mind and spirit.

He knew You were hungry and shaky from lack of food so
he tempted You to misuse God's power for Your own comfort.
Satan said, "You could turn these stones into bread." You faced
him squarely and used the effective weapon of the Word of Your
Father: "Man does not live only by bread but by every word of
God." (Deuteronomy 8:3)

Next the devil quoted Scripture to You this time, "Doesn't
the Book say, 'God's angels will hold You up, in case You stumble
over a rock?' So, if You really are God's Son, jump from this
highest point of the Temple. *Then* people will believe You really
are special." You came back with Sword, "Do not tempt the Lord
God." (Deuteronomy 6:16)

Once again he tried his skill at temptation, this time
appealing to the human desire for power. He stretched out the
panorama of earth's kingdoms before You and said, "If You will
worship me, I will give all these to You." Satan underscored his
reputation as the "father of lies" right here, because none of God's
creation was his to give. You said, "Get away from me, Satan! It
is written, 'Worship and serve only the Lord God.'"

Lord, You filled the dangerous vacuum between Yourself
and Satan with the Word and Presence of God. Whenever we find
ourselves struggling with temptation, we would do well to do as
You did, put the Almighty and His Word trustingly between Your-

selves and the Evil One. Only the Spirit of Truth enables us to keep a realistic view of the One whose authority, righteousness and power is total, above all "principalities and powers, all the forces of darkness." In short, we pray and remember Scripture in the face of temptation.

"Greater is He who is within me than he (Satan) who roams the world." (I John 4:4) I often quote this when I sense Satan's lure. These words are not a magic incantation, but they have power, the power of God's eternal truth. It's a reminder of who God is. It is a manifestation of trust in the Strong One who is always able.

September 29

Death is the Equalizer, Psalm 49

Hear this truth. It's for all people, rich and poor.
I'm going to sing you a story, a true one.
Things aren't always as they seem. Trouble surrounds us all,
　　but that's no reason to be afraid. It's foolish to think
　　riches can stave off trouble. They can't.
Wealth can deceive us, giving a false sense of security.

All of earth's riches cannot ransom one person from the
　　penalty of sin. An estate of multiple millions does not
　　compare to God's forgiveness. There's not enough
　　money on earth to buy back one precious soul
　　from eternal death.

Each of us, rich, poor, wise or noble, must die.
　　All creatures do. Nothing, neither wealth, power,
　　nor wisdom can give us an edge over death.
No one comes out of life alive. Death is the equalizer.
Power and prestige can only be enjoyed during
　　life's tiny breath of time.
If a great city is named after you, when you die you're
　　only a name carved in stone.
Others inherit your entire estate.

Death walks through life holding the hand of each person.
It finally leads each to the grave with empty pockets.
No worldly honors follow us there. But as for me,
I have a Redeemer. He alone has the power over death.
He keeps my soul safe on earth, and when the time is right,
He will receive me into His holy house forever,
　　very much alive!

September 30

Our Creating Lord

"In the beginning God created...." Lord, You have been Creator from eternity. No one can tell us when You began Your creation, or how You did it. But St. John tells of the Living Word of God, Christ Jesus, who made everything that has ever been made.

You created things we cannot see, like souls, angels, wind, gravity, love and thoughts. You put longings within us which are meant to draw us closer to You and to others. Many of Your created things are wonderfully visible to us, sunsets, rivers, seasons and people. We know of some of the forces You built into creation which cause things to change, to maintain, to reproduce, grow and finally fade away.

You made me. In fact, You are *still* making me, changing a bit here, a bit there. You're warming me up, stretching my heart, creating a new shape for my soul. You and I both know, Lord Jesus, there's no power within me to make those changes by myself. But Your Written Word tells us You want and expect us to become more and more like You.

"From the beginning God knew who would come to Him and He decided they should come to resemble His Son for His Son was the firstborn in His Forever Family of many sons and daughters." (Romans 8:29)

Lord, if You want that, I want it too but *You* must do it within me. Therefore I come to You, the Creating Lord, just as King David did about three thousand years ago. From my heart I pray his words, "Create a clean heart in me, O God, and renew a right attitude within me. Don't close me out of Your Presence or take Your Holy Spirit away from me. Give me the joy of Your Salvation and support me daily with Your Spirit. Lord, open my heart so with my mouth, I will praise You." (Psalm 51) Amen.

October 1

October's Glory

While driving from Summit to Princeton, I couldn't help it, I simply *had* to write. The glory of October intoxicated me. I was drunk on color in motion, blown by wind, sweeping earth and sky. Driving with one hand, writing with the other, I scrawled impressions while my eyes devoured afternoon's glowing scenes. Only after reaching my destination did it occur to me to thank God for keeping me safe during that foolish but delightful adventure.

Cornfields rustle, pale and crisp, a drawing card
for crows wheeling against blue.
Landed, as bits of midnight, they strut
their iridescent blackness.

Wind snatches color from ground and trees,
twirling leaves across the roadway.
Undulating willows, in gold hula skirts,
dance to the river's song.

October 1

Coppery pumpkins resting like fat eunuchs
    amid the clutter,
while sun gilded squirrels become ornaments
on fence and limb.

Such unique beauty for eye, ear and soul,
    and yet so fleeting!
October's fiery blaze fades too soon, extinguished
    by winter's silent white.

F.N.

October 2

Black Moments

The Christian life brings great joy and enthusiasm, but dismay and pain can still edge their way in. We know from experience what David meant as he describes his restless nights and tear drenched pillow. Our plans don't work out, relationships can splinter. Failure dismays us, discouragement eats up our joy.

Both Jesus and Job commented on troubles. Jesus said, "Just so you won't be shocked, let Me prepare you for the fact that the world is full of trouble; it can be a valley of tears. But take courage, I have overcome the world." (John 16:33) Job didn't mince words either. He said, "Everyone on earth is born to trouble as surely as sparks fly up from a fire." (Job 5:7)

A black moment came for me with the realization that if I didn't want to be an invalid I must have a third hip replacement. This would be the fifth operation in five years. The dark question, "How long, O Lord?" brought doubt. Fear nipped at my peace. Maybe God wasn't *really* with me?

I knew Jesus as the Good Shepherd who seeks, comforts and leads His own, but at this moment my mind was disputing my heart's memory of the many times He had come to me as Heart Mender. Occasionally He came immediately. Sometimes He didn't. Was He letting me wrestle with doubt for awhile so I might see for myself whom I could really trust?

After stewing for some time, I asked, rather woodenly, "Lord, restore to me the joy and trust of my salvation and renew a right spirit within me." But it was not until I began to paraphrase the Psalms that I sensed a flicker of light and hope. I lived in them and they came alive in me, bringing joy in God as well as repentance for my lack of endurance and ungrateful attitude. The Psalm's words of prophets, priests and kings of old, chased away my gloom. Discouragement was exiled and pain was conquered by the blessings of His Presence.

October 2

The words of David Watson, an Anglican priest, reminded me, "There's no telling what God can do with a broken heart, provided He has all the pieces."

Living in the Psalms those months glued heart and soul together again! As the concepts took root inside, fear and doubt were elbowed out, leaving room for God's Presence, peace and joy.

Truly, Lord, there are no Words like Yours!

October 3

Endurance

"You need patience so after you have done God's will you will receive what He has promised." (Hebrews 10:36)

The dictionary defines *patience* as "endurance and perseverance," among other things. For *endurance* it lists "continuance, durability, patience, permanence, perseverance and strength." Earl Palmer told us at a C. S. Lewis conference at Oxford University that the Greek word for all the above was *hupomeno*, meaning "hang in there." St. Paul used the term often in corresponding with young Timothy as he began his Christian ministry in a pagan society. *Hupomeno*. It has a nice ring to it, now that I know what it means.

The Old Testament account of Abraham comes to mind as we consider these qualities. While he was outside his tent marveling at the beauty of the brilliant night sky, God said to him, "See the stars, Abraham? Can you count them? One day your descendants will be as numerous as they are." Abraham and Sarah were old and they had no children. Many years passed and there was no child. There was no sign that God had ever made that promise. Could they have misunderstood?

We, like Abraham, are "right now" people. Why do You test us this way, Lord? Are you giving us opportunity to strengthen our faith? Perhaps endurance does for faith what exercise does for muscles. The Bible speaks of "the fullness of time" by which it means when everything is ready from all angles. You want us to wait, with patience, for Your time, not expecting You to meet *our* time frame. You want us to hold on to Your promises through good times and bad, even through what seems to be unanswered prayer. It's only in this way that we can see what kind of Believers we really are. Do we believe You are here, through thick or thin, or do we just *think* we believe?

October 3

Lord, I know You never act without a reason. Help me to hold to Your Word and to persevere with trusting patience, until You bring me out of doubt and back into the light of trust. Amen

October 4

Jehovah-Shammah, Our God Who Is There

When the name *Jehovah-Shammah* was revealed to the prophet Ezekiel, Israel was at an all time low. Ezekiel was a captive with Israel in Babylon between 593 and 571 B.C. He had prophesied the destruction of the Temple in Jerusalem because of Israel's total indifference to the Lord. When news reached the exiles in Babylon that the Temple had indeed been destroyed, the Lord gave Ezekiel *another* message. This message was one of hope. Restoration was implied in the new name He was giving their homeland, *Jehovah- Shammah*, Our God Who Is There. The Chaldeans destroyed the Temple, but God would build it once again and He would be there to occupy it.

Lord, You promised Your Presence with Israel from its beginning. You were with Moses in the burning bush. "...I will send My angel before you to lead you to the land I've prepared for you." (Exodus 23:20) The pillar of cloud by day and fire by night led them from Egypt. The *Shekinah, *** in the Tabernacle and later in the Temple were manifestations of Your Presence. Each manifestation was a picture, or preview, of the reality which was to come, and it was limited to Israel. In the New Testament Your Presence is clearer. It's more spiritual and more personal because it is presented in the person of Jesus. Jesus, in the Old Testament, is presented as the *Angel of the Lord*, the *Angel of His Presence* and the *Angel of the Covenant*. Isaiah calls Him *Emmanuel*, meaning God With Us. He is the Presence of Jehovah, *Jehovah-Shammah*, God Who Is There.

Lord, You are with believers today. Paul writes of us: "You are the temple of the Living God, for God says, 'I will live in them and be among them. I will be their God and they will be My people.'" (II Corinthians 6:16)

October 4

Like Israel of old, the true church today is called the dwelling place of God, for *Jehovah-Shammah* is there. *Lord Jesus,* before You ascended to the Father, You left us with the future promise that You will come back when everything is ready and take Your people to Your Father's house. This future House is often depicted as a city, The New Jerusalem, Your eternal dwelling place and our true residence. (Revelation 21:1-4)

Note: * *Shekinah,* the radiance, glory, or presence of God, dwelling in the midst of His people is used to signify God Himself.
This information is from *The New Bible Dictionary*

October 5

Shadow Angel

Father, a new morning has dawned, brilliant and beautiful. As best I know how, I put myself in Your hands with joy and thanks. Help me Lord, for that's where I want to stay – in Your hands.

Last night I was in a valley, dark, scary and unpredictable. Where was my faith? Was it discouragement of starting recuperation from the third hip replacement? What if this one didn't work? Perhaps my soul was crying for reassurance, no matter what happened. As I lay there, sleepless, asking for help, I rolled over, looked at the clock and saw there were still several hours till dawn.

Lights from the building filtered through the shutters, creating patterns on the ceiling. And there on the ceiling was a startling shadow in the shape of an angel with wings spread over my bed. For a while I watched the shadow above me as fretfulness began to seep out and assurance of Your care filled me.

I knew perfectly well what made the shadow. It was the lamp beside the window interrupting the passage of light coming up through the window. It was not the shadow of an angel for angels are spiritual beings and neither cast shadows nor interrupt light. But it might as well have been an angel for it brought me the restoring remembrance, the promise from the Psalms, "The angel of the Lord encamps around those who revere Him and He delivers them." And, "He will command His angels concerning you to guard you in all your ways. They will hold you up lest you stumble over a stone." (Psalms 34 and 91)

My soul became as content as a well fed baby. Lord, You reminded me that You are there as *Jehovah-Shammah*, loving and caring for me, and Your servants, the angels, are swifter than light in doing Your will. I knew, no matter what happened, there was no need to fear the future for You are already there.

The shadow of the angel never reappeared, though nothing in the room has changed. I believe that You, Lord God, sent that shadow, or illusion of the shadow, to comfort me. Thank You.

October 6

Even Man's Wrath

"Even the wrath of man will praise You." (Psalm 76:10, and Genesis 46-50)

Joseph, the youngest of many brothers, shared his persistent dreams with his family. He told them one day they would all bow down to him. This only made his brothers angrier. They wanted to rid themselves of him for He was their father's undisguised favourite.

One day the opportunity presented itself for the brothers to dispose of Joseph. They were out tending sheep when Joseph came bringing their lunch from home. They seized him, tore off his robe and threw him into a pit. When a caravan of traders heading for Egypt passed by, they pulled him out of the pit and sold him as a slave, for twenty pieces of silver.

The Lord was with Joseph and he brought prosperity to the house of his owner until his master's wife accused him unjustly of sexual harassment and he was thrown into jail. He asked, "Why Lord? First my brothers and now my master's wife hate me without cause. If my life's this bad at seventeen, what will it be in ten years? What's happening?"

Meanwhile, Pharaoh was having troubling dreams. He had heard rumors of a certain prisoner, Joseph, who could interpret dreams. The prisoner was called before Pharaoh. Joseph, relying on God, told Pharaoh there would be seven years of plentiful harvest followed by seven years of severe famine. Because of his God given wisdom, Joseph found himself in charge of all the food supplies in Egypt.

The famine reached Israel. Jacob sent his sons to Egypt to purchase grain. There they met their now grown and politically powerful brother, looking for all the world like a royal Egyptian. Although they didn't recognize him, Joseph knew them.

October 6

As in Joseph's boyhood dreams, the brothers bowed before him as they asked to buy food. Joseph questioned them harshly about their background. During their conversation, Joseph learned the answer to his *why questions* of so many years ago. He realized God had called him for a purpose. God had taken him from his home in Israel and planted him in Egypt in order to save his family from starvation. He could no longer hold back his tears. He cried, "'I am your brother, Joseph, whom you sold into Egypt! Don't be afraid, for God sent me here to save your lives and preserve our people. Brothers, *you may have meant it for evil but God meant it for good* in order to save our family.' And with many joyful tears he hugged and kissed them." (Genesis 46-50)

Today we have God's promise. "God weaves all events together for good in the lives of those who love Him and are ready to fulfill His purposes." (Romans 8) Joseph followed God in trust, and as history shows, he was indeed used for God's purpose.

We see the promise at work in Paul's life. He was called to preach. But soon he was put in prison. He could no longer preach, but he could write. From prison he wrote, "Christian friends, I want you to know that everything which has happened to me has helped spread God's truth." (Philippians 1) If Paul had not been imprisoned by Rome, we would not have his influential letters today.

Lord, help all of us to remember if we love You and answer Your call to obedience, You will not waste *any* experience of our lives but will use it for good in our lives. Help us and give us trusting wisdom.

October 7

Bring Us Back

Nehemiah was governor of Jerusalem in 444 B.C., about a century after the first Babylonian exiles returned to Jerusalem. He tells of God's ways with earlier Jews returning to the Land and stresses the importance of faithful worship. He gives a summary of a few important things God did for them.

"Lord God, You created and sustain the heavens and earth. You called Abraham from a far land. Because he was faithful to You, You made an everlasting covenant with him. You kept Your promises. When his descendants were enslaved in Egypt, You heard their cry and led them to freedom. Night and day the Light of Your Presence guided them. By speaking through Moses, You not only gave just laws but You sent sustenance for the desert journey.

The Land of Canaan was promised to them if they would go in and conquer it, but they were afraid and refused to obey You. In Your mercy and forgiveness You didn't forsake them. Even when they made a golden idol to replace You, You led them. You provided for their needs so they lacked no essentials. When disobedience brought them trouble, they cried to You for help and You delivered them. Century after century they presumed upon Your mercy and then turned from You. Through their many defeats and exiles You didn't completely destroy them. You saved a remnant, for "You are our God, the great, the mighty, awesome God who keeps covenant with His people and shows mercy." (Nehemiah 1:5) You are still faithful to us today but many of us have played the harlot with You. It's an old human trick. We plead when desperate, then slide into unfaithfulness when life is pleasant. How long, O Lord, will You tolerate unfaithfulness in today's professing Christians? Must we too be conquered and driven from this land?

Help, Lord! Bring us back to faith and obedience.

October 8

Pick Me Up Lord, Psalm 143

This psalm may have been written during David's son's military rebellion against him. His words seem to picture a little child, holding up his arms to be picked up and comforted.

Almighty God, hear my prayer! Listen to my words,
    and in Your faithfulness and mercy, answer me.
Don't judge me harshly, Lord, for no one is truly just.

You know how I feel, Lord. The enemy has knocked me
    down and pounded me into the ground.
I'm in total darkness as to what to do. I feel as though
    I'm already dead -- heavy and listless.
All spirit has been drained from me. I'm desolate.

I remember Your awesome deeds. I contemplate the way
    You work, the earthly wonders You have created.
I study them and am astounded. I hold up my arms to You.
Lord, pick me up! I thirst for You as crops thirst for rain.
Help me quickly or I'm a dead man. I'm dizzy and faint.
Reassure me of Your mercy each morning and that
assurance will go with me throughout the day.

Do it, Lord. I trust You to show me the way. I lift my
wide open soul to You. I'm running to you for protection.
You are my God, so show me the way.

O Lord, resuscitate me for the sake of Your Name, Your
    mercy and justice, bring me out of this crisis.
Overcome those who would destroy me for I belong
    to You.

October 9

Our Lifting Lord

"Lord, You are the One who lifts my head…"
(Psalm 34:3-4)

Sometimes my spirit hangs its head. Maybe I can fool others, but not You, Lord. You and I both know when my soul is disquieted. There can be many physical or psychological causes for this bleak phenomenon. But Lord, when my soul aches, it must be because in exhaustion or dismay, I focus on myself and crowd You out. When I realize what I've done I'm ashamed and lonely for You.

As Your daughter I should come to You at the first sense of a break, but it's hard to see clearly in the midst of a spiritual decline. The Tempter must rub his hands in glee when he sees one of Your redeemed ones do this. David did it. He lived for months with shame and guilt. Finally he turned it over to You in confession and repentance. (Psalm 51) He asked You to forgive him, to make his heart pure and to renew his loyalty to You.

When my children were small they reflected their remorse by downcast heads, flushed cheeks and brimming eyes. I remember gathering the little one close, lifting the chin and kissing away the tears.

You do that with us, Father. You comfort, restore, forgive and encourage us. When we grownups become as a little child, admitting our guilt and weakness, asking for and accepting Your forgiveness and strength we are in a similar way gathered up into Your lap and *hugged.* You lift us from shame and dejection. Your love shines out like light, chasing away the gloom. "They looked to Him and He filled them with Light. Rather than reflecting their shame, their faces glowed with His Light." (Psalm 34:3-5)

All praise to You, merciful Father. You lift us from monochromatic grays to Your Presence of color, light and freshness. You mend our broken places. You restore our souls. Continue to stretch human hearts and minds to take in Your eternal reality.

October 10

Your Bright Touch

Your touch shines bright in ambered fall,
    in early ending days.
Each tree claps hands of differing hue,
    each berry bright with life.

Crimson vine clings to gnarled old oak
    while bluets dance with the breeze.
Goldenrod claims the green hill's slope
    and clouds billow overhead.

Eyes are drawn to surrounding hills
    cutting scallops in the sky.
Distant and cool in purple gauze
    they ring round fall's blaze.

Melodies of sounds and sights blend
    in a hymn of praise,
praise to the One who made all this
    for the children of earth to decode. *

*Decode, to convert into intelligible language, or to fit with the
above usage: to look at God's creation and to ask ourselves, 'How
did all this happen?   Who is behind it?   What is all this beauty
telling me?   What does it mean to me as one person among
billions?'

October 11

Trust in the Lord

Lord, You say, "I will teach you the way to go. I will watch over you and be your Guide. But don't be like the mule or horse. They have no human understanding. They must be harnessed with a bit and bridle in order to guide them to the right destination." (Psalm 32:8-9)

"The Lord will guide you continually. He will satisfy your soul and strengthen you even in times of drought. You will flourish like a watered garden with springs which never fail." (Isaiah 58:11)

"Trust in the Lord with all your heart and don't count on your own understanding. In all you do acknowledge Him and He will direct you." (Proverbs 3:5-6)

The human heart asks, "How? When? How do I know it's You guiding me?"

The Spirit replies, "Trust Me enough to stand on My promises. I will bear your weight. Even though you don't know all there is about My guidance, you do understand certain principles, and there is also My Word. My guidance is never contrary to My Word. Act on what you know. I will lead you in what you don't know. I am building My home in you, so cooperate with Me by working from My Word. Keep temporal needs and activities from pressing familiar principles of My guidance down into your subconscious. Keep them, by My strength and help, in your conscious, working mind.

"Remember, you are Mine and I am in Your mind and heart. Relax in that knowledge, but be vigilant. Set your face 'like a flint' toward Me and rest in faith."

Thank You, Father, for reminding me that if I allow Your Word to leave my conscious mind, doubt is quick to seep in.

Please strengthen my trust.

October 12

Standing on His Promises

What an astonishing gap there is Lord, between Your
faithfulness and ours! We follow ancient Israel's pattern, giving
You our hearts one moment, then running off to follow selfish
desires the next. All the while You are there providing for us and
calling us, bringing situations in which we recognize our need and
ask Your help.

Israelites have lived in the *Promised Land* off and on from
Joshua's time until today -- while we Christians today have been
invited to live in the *Land of Promises.* You led us here by a sure
path through a stormy sea, out of godlessness and into the
Kingdom of Light. You adopted us into Your forever family and
are showing us Your purpose by the light of Your Spirit. Our role
is to follow Your purpose, bless the Light and stay on the path.

Possession of the Land was one of Your promises made
millennia ago in Your covenant with Abraham. It was based on
Israel going into the Land, under the leadership of Joshua, the
Greek name for Jesus, and ridding the Land of its pagan
inhabitants. We today, like ancient Israel, are told to live in Your
Land of Promises under the leadership of *Y'eshua*, Hebrew for
Jesus, and drive out the enemies of our souls so the whole of God's
Land of Promises will be ours. But like them, we are afraid.
Enemies of our souls, doubts, old habits, selfishness, laziness and
moodiness, are strongly entrenched in us and continue to harass us.
It's easier to surrender to them than to trust the only One who is
able to strengthen us even though it's our life's work to trust, obey
and stand on Your promises.

After Moses' death the people were preparing to cross
Jordan River and enter the Promised Land. Lord, Your words of
promise to Joshua were, "I will give you all the land you trust Me
enough to walk on. It's the same promise I gave Moses. I will be
with you, never leaving or forgetting about you. But don't neglect

this Book. Speak its words often, mull it over night and day so you always remember it.

If you do this you will prosper. I'm commanding you, be strong and courageous. No discouragement. No terror, for I am with you wherever you go." (Joshua 1:3-9)

The Israelites had to march into the Land, trusting the whole weight of their lives, their plans and their future on the truth of God's promises.

Ancient Israel's enemies were different from ours. They were mostly physical, external. Today ours are largely spiritual, internal, personal. You, Lord God, have not changed and Your ancient contractual promises are still in operation. You offer Your contract to those who trust You enough to let go of the fence, set aside crutches and put their whole weight on You.

Lord, do I trust enough to stand with You?

October 13

Choose Life

God uses certain people to tell others what He wants them to hear. The Lord God chooses Moses to tell the people he is leading them to the Promised Land. Moses relates God's message to the people, "What I'm commanding you is not beyond your reach. It's not in Heaven, so you don't need to go up and bring it down. It's not across the ocean. You won't have to bring it back to study it. No, the Word is close. It's in your mouth and heart so you may obey it.

"I've set before you life and prosperity, or death and destruction. God's command is to love the Lord God, go His way. Obey His commands and laws. *Then* you will live and prosper and He will bless you in the Land you are going in to possess.

"But if your love and obedience wanes, if you disobey and worship 'gods' of your own making, You won't last long in the Promised Land which you want to claim as your own.

"Today heaven and earth are my witnesses. I have set two options before you, life and death or blessings and curses. Choose life so you and your children may live in the Land. Love Him. Listen to Him and stay close to Him. For He IS your life and He will give you life in the Land He promised Your fathers, Abraham, Isaac and Jacob." (Deuteronomy30:11-20, Genesis 12:3)

God told Joshua, who followed Moses as leader, "This is My command: Be strong and undismayed, for the Lord is with you everywhere you go." (Joshua 1:8-9)

This command from the changeless God is still in force today. It is as pertinent today as it was in the days of Moses and Joshua. If we hope to live in God's *Land of Promises Fulfilled,* we must believe His promises are strong enough, and true enough, to bear the weight of our lives, hopes and actions. This takes strength and courage. Lord, breathe this into Your people everywhere.

October 14

ALL Scripture

"All Scripture is given to us by inspiration from God and is meant to teach us what is true. It helps us realize the wrong in our lives; it corrects our understanding and keeps us on the right path. Through it God prepares us so we know how to do His work in a way which pleases Him." (II Timothy 3:16-17)

A French king had parts of Scripture he didn't like deleted, particularly verses referring to the sin of adultery, for adultery was one of his favorite hobbies.

Today many Christians would gladly leave out or loosen all verses demanding obedience. Obedience to anyone is thought to be demeaning. Biblical commands are warring with current images of freedom. Some simply exclude Scripture from quiet time reading. They substitute tolerant, little poems of God's love and forgiveness. Nothing is read about obedience or God's hatred of sin.

Society is pushing us toward accepting evil. And the foundation of this push toward evil is the success of those who trivialize, revise, or ignore Scripture. The media, TV, movies, books, even certain laws, deluge us in tidal waves of smut and evil. We're drowning in it, brainwashed by it. And it's working. Morality, truth and respect are rapidly eroding, and society as a whole has lost its way. Lord, You don't mince words. If we are truly uneasy with Your commandment to love God first, then perhaps we'll be uncomfortable enough to abandon the route of disobedience and follow You. You gave us Scripture, Lord, to heal our near sightedness, to cause us to see beyond our own wants and instincts and godless culture. All this takes the courage of loving obedience.

Father, help all who bear the name of *Christian* to understand the necessity of loving You enough to *obey* You.

October 15

Finding God's Will

The following is advice from a book in my mother's library by George Muller, pastor and writer from another generation. Years ago I took notes on it for I found it helpful. I still do. It deals with his process in seeking God's will regarding decisions he needed to make. I have paraphrased and condensed it.

It's important to stay neutral in regard to the matter in question. Most of our trouble is right here for our minds are often made up before we seek. Nine tenths of the difficulties are overcome when we are ready to do the Lord's will whatever it may be. When we are in this state it's not long before we know what His will is. Having surrendered the will, we don't leave the results to feelings or impressions. If we do, we make ourselves liable to delusions.

We seek the will of God through or in connection with His Word. If the Holy Spirit guides us He will do it in accordance to Scriptures and never contrary to them.

Next we take into account providential circumstances. These often indicate God's will in connection with His Word and Spirit. We ask God in prayer to reveal His will to us.

It's through prayer, study of His Word and reflection, we come to a deliberate decision and if we are at peace and continue to be after two or three more petitions, we proceed accordingly. In trivial as well as most important issues, Dr. Muller says he has "found this method always effective."

The Apostle quotes Jesus saying, "The watchman, the Father, opens the gate for His Son, the Shepherd, and the sheep hear His voice. He calls His own sheep by name and leads them out. After He brings out all that are His, He leads them. They follow Him because they recognize His voice. They won't follow a stranger. They run from him for they don't know his voice." (John 10:3-5)

October 16

The Lifting of Hands

Amy Carmichael, a missionary to India, is among my favorite authors. In my library I still have a few of her books. Hers was a long and fruitful life, lived for God's glory. As her strength and vigor waned, she continued to write of His faithfulness and mercy.

I find myself in that same position now. Strength is diminished and I must pace myself or trouble results. Last week was too busy. I set too many goals. Along with that, outside circumstances were unusually difficult. As the week drew to a close I was tottery and exhausted. But I had five guests coming for dinner that night. We were ready to sit down for dinner when the room began to spin. Light faded to deep purple. With my remaining strength I dashed for my room, collapsed half on half off my chair. I couldn't think, couldn't pray. As I lay there in a fog of dizziness one of Amy Carmichael's poems rose in my mind. When she was too sick to pray, she often relied on lifting her hands to God as prayer. I couldn't remember the words but I grasped her thought and lifted limp, shaky hands to God as prayer. The quietness of the loving Presence tucked itself around me overcoming anxiety, leaving me limp but at peace. Our awesome God heard my unspoken S.O.S.

After regaining strength and equilibrium I went to the bookcase, asking Him to let me find the small 4x6 book in the over filled shelves. There it was next to the first book I touched.

"When vision fadeth, and the sense of things,
And powers dissolve like colors in the air,
And no more can I bring Thee offerings
Nor any ordered prayer,

October 16

"Then like a wind blowing from Paradise
Falleth a healing word upon mine ear,

Let the lifting up of my hands
Be as the evening sacrifice, the Lord doth hear." *

This isn't a story to cause anyone to marvel, but it touched me deeply for it illustrates the tender, deep love of the Father for His child. He wasn't trying to prove any great thing. He just saw someone He loves, someone who tries to love Him back, reaching out to Him for help. I think He took delight in comforting me.

* From *Toward Jerusalem*, page 61, by Amy Carmichael in 1936, reprinted in England six times. My copy was printed in 1957. The last two lines of the poem are a quote from Psalm 141:2.

October 17

Perseverance

You told a group of people this story, Lord Jesus, about their need to pray and not lose heart, about perseverance in prayer.

There was a hard-hearted judge who cared nothing for God or man. A widow lived in the same city. She constantly went to the judge asking for justice for someone who had cheated her. The judge refused, time after time, to help her. Each time he refused, she returned with the same request. Finally, he said to himself, "This woman drives me crazy! Even though I don't care what happens to her and I certainly don't fear God, I'll grant her request just to get her off my back!"

Jesus asked, "Do you get the point? God is not like this judge. Will He refuse to give His people justice and keep putting them off? I tell you no, He will quickly grant justice to them." (Luke 18:1-8a)

This was not a Jewish judge. Jewish courts had three judges, one for the plaintiff, one for the defendant and an independent. This judge was obviously appointed by the Romans. Roman judges in occupied regions were called robber judges for they acquired their wealth from bribes.

The woman had no money or power. Her defense weapon is her perseverance. The bribe-seeking judge cared nothing for her troubles but he finally gave her justice because he was irritated by her persistence.

Our Judge and Father is ready to supply justice. He doesn't always give us what we ask for, anymore than wise earthly parents grant their children's requests if they know it isn't good for them. We can't see the future, but God does. This must be why You tell us, Lord, not to be discouraged in prayer. Our faith won't fail us and we will not be disappointed if after we have prayed for a certain thing we pray the prayer which You always answer, "*Thy* will be done."

October 18

Follow the Shepherd

Lord, You *are* my Shepherd. I *am* Your sheep. For many years I have been one of Your flock, plodding along slowly after You. You have always been there to lead me, although I've not always been there to follow.

Sheep are simple creatures, concerned with simple things. And such *followers* they are! If a sheep is startled, it runs, with no thought of destination, and its companions follow.

How like sheep we humans are, so seriously concerned with trivia. We copy the latest fashions, acquire the latest cars. We strive for power and prestige. We must know the "in" people, must BE the "in" people. We are a world of sheep.
> "We are little lost sheep, who have gone astray.
> Ba-a, ba-a, ba-a."

Scripture agrees, "All we like sheep have gone astray, we have turned everyone to his own way." (Isaiah 53:6)

Without You to guide and rescue us, Good Shepherd, we fit another line of the melancholy Whiffenpoof song:
> "Gentlemen songsters off on a spree, doomed from here to eternity.
> God have mercy on such as we.
> Ba-a, ba-a, ba-a."

In looking back over the years Lord, I praise You for Your rich mercy in making Yourself known to me, and for Your everlasting love, wrapping me in comforting assurance. Being truly loved is an almost irresistible force. You loved me long before I began to love You. Your faithfulness is another magnetic force. You said You would always be faithful to Your own, faithful in leading, rescuing, protecting, correcting, and You are. You provide

October 18

lush meadows and Living Water to satisfy my hungry soul. You have anointed this oft-battered head with the healing oil of Your restorative Presence.

Although You are faithful to me, I am often unfaithful to You, in thought, word and deed, in coldness of heart, in preoccupation with unimportant things, telling the Creator of Earth and Heaven to wait. But Your mercy waits for my repentance. You will lead me to that fresh green pasture where I will know You as You are and where I may stay with You forever.

Lord, forgive and have mercy on this wandering sheep.
A-a-men

October 19

Criticism

"Why do you look at the speck of sawdust in your brother's eye, when you have a *plank* in your own? You're a hypocrite! Take the plank from your own eye, then you will see clearly enough to remove the speck from your brother's eye." (Matthew 7:3-5)

Criticism of others is a human plague of world-wide proportions. But after we've been in our Father's family with You, Lord Jesus, day in and day out, Your Spirit begins to show us we're not the Great Judges of Time and Eternity after all. You are.

Thanks Lord, for Catherine Marshall's book, *A Closer Walk,* which was a big help to me concerning this human trait which displeases You. She too, had wrestled with it. She tells of how You gave her an assignment. For one week she was to "fast" from criticizing anyone or anything. She argued with You over the assignment, told You that You Yourself had spoken of "righteous judgment." She asked how society could function without godly standards and limits. You replied to her, "Just *obey* Me. Keep an absolute fast from any critical statements."

Catherine remembers that she didn't talk much that day, and no one even noticed! For several years she had been praying for a young man whose life was a tangle of wrong choices. She wondered if her prayers for him had been too negative. That afternoon in prayer, God put a new vision of his life into her mind. She said she knew it was from God, for His "finger prints of joy" were all over it.

She says fresh ideas began to fill her mind. She believed she was seeing what You wanted her to see. Her criticisms of the past had not corrected a single thing. It had only stifled her creativity, in prayer, in relationships, even in writing, and in ideas that You wanted to give her.

October 20

What Can We Do?

"With the criteria you use in judging others, you will be judged." (Matthew 7:1)

Lord, we love our family members. You gave them to us for that very purpose, to love, care for and rear. Even with Your help it's hard. Our difficulties seem to center in our own flawed wisdom and their youthful stretch toward independence. *What can we do?*

We can plead, advise and argue:

"Please try to ..."
"You could ...
"You shouldn't ..."
"If only you would
do this or that…"
"You act like we
are the children
and you the parent…"

We can criticize:

"He won't..."
"He doesn't..."
"I don't want to
be critical but…"
"He knows it all."
"He's thoughtless"
"…doesn't listen"

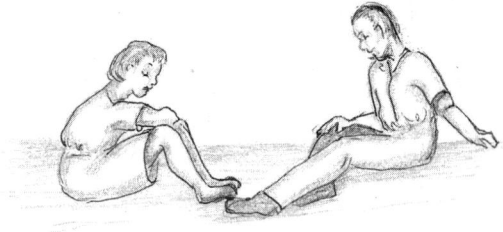

October 20

Or we can pray…

The Lord shows us how to replace negative or critical thoughts into positive prayer.

"Thank You, Lord,
for our precious son.
He's in Your hands
With our trust."
"Forgive us. Protect him…"
"Guide the three of us."
 "Change our hearts."

With trusting prayer and praise we cover him with the protection of our faith in God, like a shield. It releases the Holy Spirit's power to encourage or convict, and keeps love flowing between us.

We are helpless and foolish in solving many problems. You, Lord, are neither. You are eager to help, but we must be open to Your teaching. Like the father of the epileptic son I cry, "Lord, I believe, help my unbelief!" (Mark 9:24)

October 21

We Give Thee Praise

Celtic prayers are filled with simple, basic things, the marvels of Creation, expectations, the joys of seed time and harvest. They ring with praise to God for His protection and blessing. After a mini course in Celtic Christianity, it was requested that each student write a prayer in the Celtic tradition. I found joy in this homework.

We give Thee praise, our Father, for this world of beauty,
    for the hours of our lives to worship Thee.
We praise Thee for Thy gift of forests and hills,
    for shimmering lakes and breeze blown trees,
    for wildflowers dotting the woods with color,
    for Thy marvel of birds on the wing,
    for sunshine and shadow and fragrant days.
We praise Thee, Lord God, for Thy saving grace,
    for being the Water of Life within dry souls,
    for daily nourishment of Bread that is always fresh.
Praise to Thee, Jehovah-Jesus, for the joy of companions,
    the blessings of contemplation,
    the guidance of Thy Word,
    for lifting songs and dance, for merry laughter.
We praise Thee, Spirit of God, for seeking what was lost
    and drawing it back to its eternal home.
We rejoice in Thee for the quietness of peace,
    for the indwelling of Thy Holy Presence.
Praise to Thee, Holy Three, Holy One,
    or Thy all encompassing Self within us,
    surrounding us, above us and among us.   F.N.

October 22

New Hope

Jesus said, "If you ask Me you will receive. If you seek Me you will find Me. Knock on my door and I will open it to you." (Matthew 7:7)

Hope is Beth's * sister who lives out of town. Although she had not opened her life to Jesus, Hope asked our prayer group to pray for her. Her doctor was to remove a large ovarian tumor on Friday and she was afraid. Beth, and the rest of us in the prayer group, soaked her in prayer, asking for physical and spiritual healing. We prayed for an altogether *new Hope*. We wanted Hope's hope to be in God and we asked the *God of All Hope* to take up residence in her life.

Saturday morning Bill and I were driving home from Pennsylvania. I put my head back and fell asleep. As I awoke my eyes fell on a sign on the highway: NEW HOPE, PA. Suddenly I *knew*, without possibly being able to know, the Lord had answered our prayers! I was so convinced I wrote Beth a note and mailed it to her home although I knew she had gone to Washington, DC to be with Hope during the operation. As the note dropped into the mailbox, doubt grabbed me in its powerful grip. I told myself I had done a preposterous thing, presuming on God!

Near 2:00 PM on Tuesday the phone rang. It was Beth alive with joy! She had just arrived at home. My note was waiting. But better yet, it was true! In a final check, to the doctor's surprise and chagrin, he found no growth. The operation was unnecessary.

No, Hope had not opened her life to the Lord. Only part of our prayers had been answered, the one second in importance. But we were all encouraged by what God had done. Faith rushed in and chased out the lurking doubt. We all agreed to hold to God in the belief that in His time the rest of our prayer would be accomplished. We asked that what He had already done would

October 22

give Hope belief in Him as her Savior and give us the expectant faith that He would also heal her soul. After all, the name of our prayer group was *Great Expectations.*

Several weeks later Beth burst into the prayer group, eyes shining and face aglow, a letter from Hope in her hand. She squealed, "It's happened! She asked the Lord into her life and her living! Now she's new inside and out, a truly new Hope!"

Lord God, thank You! You have said "without faith it is impossible to please God." We didn't have much faith, some of us may have had none, but praise Your Name, You were building on our "little bit," preparing us to trust You more.

* names changed

October 23

God Never Dozes Off, Psalm 121

Psalms were often sung by more than one singer or by several choirs. One singer asks a question, using the first person. The answer is sung by another singer or choir.

I look to the hills, watching for help,
    but where does true help come from?
My help comes from the Maker of heaven
    and earth.

He will not let your feet slip.
He who protects you doesn't go to sleep
    on guard duty.
You may be assured, He who watches
    over His own never dozes off,
        never takes a nap.

He only is your Keeper and Protector.
He shields you from the burning sun by day
    and covers you from moon-madness *
    by night.

Jehovah keeps you through all evil.
He holds your eternal soul safe in His hand.

Have no fear, the Almighty will preserve you
    as you go out and as you come in, now
    and forever.

* Our word *lunatic* comes from the early belief that sanity oscillates with phases of the moon.

October 24

Rivers of Living Water

Rivers are beautiful, necessary and a vital benefit. "My" river bends and sparkles as it flows past my balconies. Its life giving substance influences areas far from its source. It's always there, dancing with the sun, mirroring the moon. It never stops. It is meant to flow, carrying life and nourishment to its banks.

Lord, when You touch a life, You put a river of Living Water within that life. The water flows and splashes over its banks to others. You bring moisture and growth to dried up lives. (John 7:36) If we aren't sharing the water You gave us with others, our lives become like the Dead Sea, always taking in but never giving out. You, Lord, are the Source of fresh, flowing water.

A river is persistent. It's meant to flow. When it meets an obstacle, it builds up enough pressure to either move around it or make a new pathway, but it *flows*.

When an obstacle appears in our lives it may be hard to see beyond it. At such times we watch the Source, not the obstacle. The inner River finds a way around it or washes the obstacle away.

Lord, help us keep our eyes only on You. Don't let anything come between us. Again we remember Peter on the stormy sea. He asked that he might come to You across the water. You told him to come. He climbed out of the boat, but when he heard the wind and saw the angry waves, he looked at what he feared rather than to whom he trusted and he began to sink.

You continue to fill us with Your Water of Life. We bring You joy when we give others what You have so graciously poured into us. As we are faithful to You, You use us in causing barren lives to begin to flourish with New Life. That is something only You, Almighty Creator, can do.

October 25

Force of Mass Attraction

The three of us were having a leisurely breakfast one morning, talking of both current and long past events. One in our threesome was Dr. Roy Riviere, physicist, minister and friend from college.

Of course our days at Wheaton came up, reminding Roy of his early but ever continuing romance with the laws of physics. Dr. Hawley O. Taylor, his physics professor, had greatly influenced him. Dr. Taylor was written up in *Who's Who of America*. He was the only one out of seven mathematicians in the U. S. who, without notes, could reproduce Einstein's theory of relativity.

Roy's story went something like this. Early in the course Dr. Taylor asked a rhetorical question, "What is the strongest force in our universe?" The students assumed it to be gravity. Dr. Taylor said, "It's the force of mass attraction, which means that everything in the universe has an attraction, or a pull toward everything else. Gravity is merely one aspect of the force of mass attraction.

Then he said, "Everything in God's creation reveals a facet of His character. An echo of this may be seen in the work of the artist whose 'self' is partly revealed in his painting, music, or the contents of his books. What is God telling us about Himself in creating this force and letting us 'discover' and use it?" Answering his own question, he said, "Yes, He is telling us about Himself. He's telling us that He is attracted to us, wants to be with us, that He loves us."

Taylor went on to tell his idea of what it would be like for him, as a physicist, to be in heaven. In heaven he could stand behind the scenes and watch God create universe after universe, each with its unique force, or primary structure, each expressing another trait of His character.

October 25

He believes, as do most Christians, all Creation is a directional sign post pointing to the Creator, revealing true facets of who He is, His work and His plans for us. Jesus taught in parables. "Eyes that see" recognize that He also *creates* in parables.

October 26

Wordless Message, Psalm 19

The high blue heavens plainly demonstrate
    God's Almighty power,
    as earth displays His craftsmanship.
Each new dawn tells, in pantomime, of His glory
    and each night verifies His wisdom.
No one hears their speech but their message is clear.
Their wordless story is everywhere, pointing clearly
    to Creator God.

God made the sun like an undefeated athlete
        running his daily course, bursting from
        his eastern starting line and sprinting
        westward to pour out life giving light
        and healthy heat.
No place on earth escapes its life sustaining
        properties.

In the same way, the Truth of God circles earth,
        millennia after millennia.
His instructions are without flaw;
        they transform the soul.
They are perfect, bringing wisdom and flooding
        the listening soul with joy.
It's in His Word that our understanding is born
        and through His powerful forgiveness
        we are washed of our sins.
The Lord's directions are not 'virtual reality,'
        they are *eternal* and *actual* reality
        enduring forever.

October 26

God's Word is of more value than bonds or gold
bullion for it nourishes the soul.
This nourishment, the Bread of Heaven, is always
available, new every morning
and fresh every evening. And its taste?
It's better than ripe peaches and cream.

But there's more. His Word is trustworthy,
a warning system, better than
the finest of burglar alarms.
It illuminates dangers ahead and by listening
we avoid both pain and danger.
For who among us can foresee the scope of his
own sin and disobedience?

So Lord, wash me clean and forgive
my secret faults.
Hold me back from willful sins
or they will begin to rule over me.
I want to start each day clean and fresh,
so my words and imagination
will bring You joy,
my Strength and my Redeemer.

October 27

Our Comforting Lord

Jesus said, "I will not leave you without comfort. I will come to you." (John 14:18)

Lord God, You give us many gifts for this life. Among them are four special ones, unsinkable hope, and Your love to light our path. Your peace surrounds us and the truth of Your Word enriches us. I never want to lose sight of these.

But Lord, life can be a minefield of failure, misunderstanding, death, waste and pain. When these explode beneath us we bleed, losing strength and joy. Questions plague us. "Lord, have You abandoned us to battle the twin giants, Doubt and Discouragement, alone? Have You forgotten us?"

Your Word and Spirit rescue us with these words "Can a mother forget the baby at her breast and have no compassion for the little one to whom she gave birth? Even if she could forget," says the Lord, "How could I forget you? Look at My hands. See, I have engraved you on My palms." (Isaiah 49:14-16)

Lord! -- *that engraving is from the crucifixion!* Thank You for being especially close to those whose hearts are broken. You came to mend them, to comfort those who grieve. You bring us beauty in place of ashes and the healing oil of gladness in place of mourning. Your garment of praise replaces our rags of despair. (Psalm 34:18; Isaiah 61:2-3)

In Psalm 34 we see You as the Refuge of all who will come to You, so we wait with patience, knowing You hear our prayers, lighten our pain and lift us from confusion. You, our amazing Lord, will renew our song.

Why should You do such things for us? Because You, "God of All Comfort, comfort us so we may comfort others with the same comfort You have given us." (I Corinthians 1:3-4)

October 28

A Mighty Fortress, Psalm 46

Our God is a mighty fortress, the sure refuge
    of His people.
With Him we need not fear life's earthquakes or
    tidal waves which crash and roar
    or as our mountains of hope crumble
    and fall into the sea.

Water of Life flows from the City of God for the
    Most High is in her midst.
She shall not be torn apart because God is with her.
When this darkness is over the Lord will rescue her.

Nature rampages; human storms come.
Kingdoms rise and fall. Nations boil over or subside,
    but God is Sovereign over nature,
    over time and eternity.
He stands beside us as our Omnipotent stronghold.

Remember the works of the Lord? He speaks
    and terror descends. He says, "Enough!"
    and wars cease across the earth.
He obliterates fearsome weapons
    and man-schemed protections
    are demolished according to His will.

He says to the terrified people running about,
    "Be still and know that I am God.
    All nations will come to Me!"
The Commander of the hosts of Heaven, God of Jacob,
    is among us, and He is here to save!

October 29

Invisible God in Visible Flesh

"'In seeing Jesus, God the Son, we see God the Father, who is invisible. We see Him and come to know God's plan and purpose in creation, for it was by the Son that all things, visible and invisible were created, angels, forces, worlds, and humans. He is before absolutely everything and He holds all things together. He made them in order to complete His purposes.' (Colossians 1:16-18) 'Jesus, was with God at the beginning. Nothing was made that He didn't make.' (John 1:1-3)

"God became Man in the person of Jesus Christ. This is a basic tenant of Christianity. We call this the Incarnation, meaning that God, who is Spirit, entered our material world, entered into flesh, so that the Man, Jesus, is both truly and fully God and truly and fully Man. This means that God really cared deeply about the material world He created. He did not pluck us from the material world to redeem us. He entered the world to become part of it.

"This is why He gave the sacraments. Material things can point the way to spiritual realities because God, by entering our world, sanctified it and lifted it to a new level. Some say, the whole of creation is a sacrament of the whole reality of God. 'The heavens declare the glory of God.' (Psalm 19:1) St. Paul says, 'His invisible attributes are clearly seen, being understood by the things that are made.' (Romans 1:20)

"We don't say, 'I'm on my way to heaven, so the world no longer matters!' We are to preserve its resources, improve its conditions, and bring the Gospel of Christ into every corner of it! As we do so we understand better God's purposes for each of us.'"*

* Anglican Digest, Transfiguration AD 2003, with permission

October 30

Life's In-betweens,
from a letter to my daughter in college

"It often takes perseverance to complete the task at hand. To finish the job builds maturity, character and patience. So go ahead and let patient endurance do its work in you so you will be a competent workman, not lacking tools you need." (James 1:4-6)

That's good advice for everyone. It's given by Jesus' brother. When a project is nearly completed, when the results become clear, we're inclined to short cut it and move on to the challenge of a fresh, unexplored task. These segments of time between one project and another, could be called life's in-betweens. The mind is boiling with eager ideas for project number two. But it's necessary in life's training program to finishing the task we've started. After we take it far enough to see the results it can seem stale, but it brings satisfaction and gives us a leg up in character building to set aside only a *completed* project. Character is something we can't beg, borrow or steal. We must build it within ourselves. It will become a lifetime companion and good friend.

When God finished His creation, He "saw that it was good." (Genesis 1) Paul "finished the race." (II Timothy 4:7) Jesus finished the work He came to Earth to do. When it was completed, He shouted from the cross for all to hear, "It is finished!" (John 19:30)

James continues by saying, "If anyone lacks wisdom, let him ask God, and God, who gives abundantly and mercifully, without criticism, will help you. Ask in faith, not doubt, for those who doubt are like the turbulent sea, never stable, always shifting."

Unfinished tasks and unkempt promises, like unforgiveness, leave raw edges or dangling strings in the fabric of our days. It's not at all unusual for us to trip over them, fall and hurt ourselves and others.

October 31

Ever Present Spirit

We can't see the Holy Spirit. But like invisible wind, sound waves, gravity or other unseen forces, we see the resulting power. That's how it is with the Spirit of God. Scripture tells us He is Truth, Life, Power, our Comforter, Indweller and Advocate. It is He who comes along side to help us. What a joy!

But Holy Spirit of God, not all church members know of Your part in Christian's lives. Some churches have no Trinitarian beliefs. Others teach only Jesus. To have the full joy, peace and guidance promised in Scripture we must know and welcome You, Spirit of God, into our living. Give us eyes to see and hearts to understand that You must participate actively in our plans. Some like to say, half in jest, "Christians are so heavenly minded they are of no earthly good." But honestly, isn't that backwards? Aren't most of us so earthly minded we are of no heavenly use?

Spirit of Holiness, You are totally sufficient for today's needs. It's under Your guidance that we see how important changeless truths are for twenty-first century living. You nudge us with something we need to do or to change. That *something* can be anything from an wrong attitude, a misconception, or needed repentance, to a telephone call we need to make or a check we should send. Perhaps we're fighting doubt or have strayed from a close relationship with You. Whatever it is, You bring it to our attention somehow, through Scripture or perhaps through another person or by Your still, small voice, saying to our spirit, "Listen to this. It's for You."

What You require is that we ask Your help, wait and listen for Your answer, then obey. Waiting and obeying are the hardest because all sorts of 'common sense solutions' may pop into our restless, often frantic, minds.

November 1

Thanksgiving

Lord, accept my thanks for Your Presence
around future's hidden corners.
Thanks for friends and family, near or scattered
across this large land.
Thanks for difficult tests and pleasant joys.
Thanks for time to grieve and laugh.
Thanks for walking today's path with me,
for keeping Your angels close.
Thanks for being my strength right now,
my Bread that's always fresh.
Thanks for loving me today, for shining
bright hope on tomorrow.
I praise with joy every day of the year. Amen

F.N.

November 2

I Trust You, Lord, Psalm 16

Take care of me, Lord. I trust You. I've said to You,
"You are my God. You are the only one
whose help is constant and totally wise."

I honor faith of those who believe in the One True God,
not those who run to gods of their
own design. All others are false.
I can't offer them allegiance or even say their names.

Lord, You have assigned my position and path.
You are joy and security to me. I bless Your Name
and Your wise counsel. You teach me
in the night seasons, directing my soul.

Yes, the patterns of my life are pleasant under
Your guidance.
You have granted me a good heritage.

Lord, You are always near, even at my shoulder.
My heart is glad to be singing Your praise.
Even my perishable, earthly body rests in hope.
You, Jehovah-God, will not leave me in death.
My soul will not decay in a coffin, for You
will not let Your Holy One * see corruption.
You have shown me the Path of eternal life and
victorious living which leads me to Your
side in everlasting joy and eternal praise.

* God's *Holy One* is His only begotten Son.

November 3

Planting Bulbs

It's time to plant tulip bulbs in order to have blooms in spring. There they lie in the basket, small green sprouts pushing through the crisp, brown covering, indicating new life. Then I remember, "Unless a seed falls to the ground and dies it is only a single seed. But if it dies it produces many seeds." (John 12: 24)

While pushing the fat, brown bulbs into the earth, I talked to them, "Die to sight, little bulb, so at the right time you may burst into bloom, proclaiming Him as Creator-Renewer, with the silent boldness of your color and beauty. Be a tiny symbol in a vast world telling briefly of His glory."

Cold penetrated the seat of my jeans, but still I sat, thinking of the Eternal Gardner who plants us separately and uniquely in His Garden. He knows the right place and time, the proper set of events.

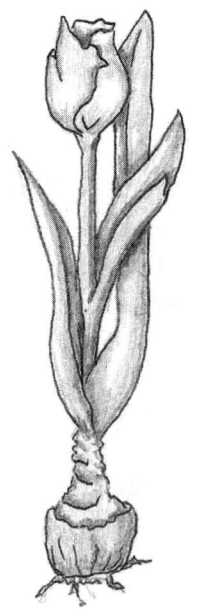

He warms and waters us, enabling us to become the kind of "plant" we are. We grow and develop only as we respond to His growth requirements.

I thought of my parents, whose worn and fragile bodies are returning to dust at West View Cemetery. Their souls are in eternity with the Lord now, awaiting the perfect bloom of bodily resurrection, which throbs with eternal life because the place *of Many Mansions* has a perpetual growing season.

November 4

Prepare a Place

What an opportunity it is to teach Young Life high school girls God's truth -- even if it *is* at 7:00 a.m. on Wednesdays!

In this group we discuss a book called *My Heart, Christ's Home* in which Robert Munger likens the Christian's heart to a residence. The book is based on the fact that if we earnestly invite You, Lord Jesus, You will actually move into our life and make it Your home. You tell us, "If a person loves Me, he will keep My Word. My Father and I will love him and take up residence with him." (John 14:23)

Before Your death You told Your disciples You were going away to make a place for them, but just as truly, You would come back to take them with You to that place. (John 14:1-3) But it's up to us to be *willing* for You to make space in our hearts, minds and lives for You to live and move about freely. The disciples didn't understand this until Pentecost when God poured His Spirit into human hearts.

Lord, You said, "I am knocking at the door. If anyone opens the door of his life to Me, I'll come in ..." (Revelation 3:20) Your "coming in" is the first step. One cannot live in a house until he enters it. Home is a place we always come back to, a gathering place for family and friends. Homes don't just happen. They take work, love, sacrifice, forgiveness and the setting of standards. You want to be there with us so You knock.

If we hear and open the door You step into the foyer of our living, but You want access to our entire living quarters. The foyer is where we greet people formally and casually. Friends and family members are soon taken to the family room, where we sit by the fire and talk. We discuss problems, joys and personal things. You want to communicate with us on every level, Lord. You like to sit across the dining table from us to nourish us with the Living Bread. You want to go into the library where we fill our

November 4

minds and souls with information and inspiration, where we plan our days and future.

When You come into our workshop, You teach us to make beautiful, lasting things. You even want to see our junk closet and basement in order to show us what is trash and what is not. Useful items, which are broken, like relationships, trusts and hearts, are moved to the workshop where You show us the best way to mend them.

So, Lord, after we've asked You into the foyer, the big question here is, are we willing to let You into the rest of the house to remodel as You see fit? You have wonderful plans for our relationships with others. Do You want to change some things we take into ourselves which form our character, or lack of it? Will we invite You into the library of our minds and let You read what we read, watch and hear? Will we open our musty, dark closets to Your fresh air and truth-revealing light? Or do we still say to You, "Wait here in the foyer while I discuss it with my friends and myself?"

November 5

Be Honest in Prayer

David calls out, "O God, hear and answer my prayer. Don't ignore my plea for my own thoughts as well as the threats of my enemies trouble me deeply. I am tied down by anguish, and fear has paralyzed me." (Psalm 55:1-2,4)

How often we *pretend* with others. We act carefree before others when in reality we are wrestling with a burden of worries. We chuckle over comments and events which hurt us, never letting our masks slip.

But Lord, we never need to pretend with You. You just want us to trust You enough to share our real selves with You, our fears, failures, our attitudes, emotions -- even our shame. David is always honest with You. He tells You his doubts and anger, pain, joy and delight.

Jesus was honest with You, Father. He didn't try to hide his fear and dread of the cross. He asked You, "Father, if it's possible, let this cup pass from Me." The horror of the cross brought Him agony even though He was determined to carry out Your will perfectly.

Paul was honest too. He said he was "nervous and trembling with fear" when he first went to preach in Corinth. Because of his frankness, his words and actions proved the reality of his beliefs. (I Corinthians 2:3)

Father, You want honesty from us, not because You don't know but because we need to recognize the truth about *ourselves* so we ask You for help. We need never fear You will be surprised or shocked by what we do, say or think. You already know our dark secrets. In confessing we take off our masks, express and strengthen our trust in You. Only then will You begin to work in our lives.

November 6

Trust God in All Things

David was taken as a young man into King Saul's court as a musician but the king grew insanely jealous of him because the people thought of David, rather than Saul, as their national hero. Saul vowed to kill him. He pursued David and his men relentlessly. (I Samuel 21:10-14, 22:1-5) As the cat-and-mouse game went on and on, David's faith in God's promise that he would be Israel's king began to wither. He took things into his own hands and sought refuge with Saul's enemy, King Achish of Gath. When Achish caught David lying to him, he threw him in prison. Fearing for his life, David put on a convincing act of raving insanity. Rather than killing the "mad man," Achish decided to let the harsh wilderness be his executioner. The king had him dumped in the great wilderness without food, water, weapons or protection.

But God had plans for Israel's future king. He protected him in the wilderness and led him to the deep, twisting Cave of Adullam where he hid out from Saul. His scattered men gathered supplies and joined him there. It is thought that while in the cave David composed the song we know today as Psalm 34. It's based on his experiences in Gath and the wilderness, and on *God's faithfulness.* Acoustics within the sandstone walls must have been perfect, wrapping the men in the clear music of harp and voice.

The first part of the song tells of God's mercy and David's decision to trust and praise Him at all times. "I will bless the Lord at all times. His praise will continually be in my mouth." That decision proved to be a strong shield against despair at being hopelessly out numbered by Saul's warriors. Next he remembers his fear and his shameful act of insanity. He remembers the dangers of the wilderness, the bitter nights and hungry animals, the dehydrating heat at noon, the thirst and hunger. He tells, in song, how the Lord protected him at every turn. "The angel of the Lord encamps, as in a military situation, about those who fear Him."

David gathered his soldiers about him. His leadership, his music and the fire's warm blaze against the chilling night drew them. Most of them had deserted Saul's army to follow David. He loved the rough, rowdy young soldiers as sons and wanted to share his faith with them. Knowing that music tends to lift weary souls, he decided to sing them the story of his adventure and Jehovah's faithfulness and mercy to him. He contrasts the lion's hungry prowling and fierce roaring to the contentment of those who trust the Lord in all things. He sang, "Even powerful lions suffer from hunger but those who trust the Lord shall not want for any necessary thing." He trusts the total trustworthiness of the Lord at every turn.

November 7

Taste and See, Psalm 34:1-10

I will bless the Name of the Lord at all times,
    regardless of circumstances.
My soul is buoyant, weightless with joy.
Consider praising the Lord when trouble surrounds you.
Praise plants seeds of courage and hope within us.
So come, let's join together in exalting Him,
    in telling of His greatness.

When I went to the Lord, He heard my fear filled
    prayer and took the fear away.
I know others who rejoice in His salvation;
    they are radiant with praise,
    not cringing in fear and humiliation.
I can testify to the truth of this for I cried out to Him
    in terror and shame, and He saved me,
    sending warrior angels to surround me.

O my friends, open your eyes and see Him.
Open your mouths and taste Him. Just try Him out.
You will see Him to be good in every sense.
Give Him reverence and trust.
Whoever does this will not be in need
    of any necessary thing.

Do you hear the lions roaring in the hills? As strong
    as they are they often suffer from hunger
    but those who trust and obey shall be nourished.

November 8

Come, Gather Round, Psalm 34:11-22

Come close, my sons, gather round me. I want to tell
you something important. I want to tell you
what the "fear of the Lord" means.
But first let me ask you a question, do any of you here
love being alive, waking up to the freshness
of a new day dawning, watching
Almighty God unfold it through the hours?

If you do, then watch what you say.
Don't be a deceiver, stirring up trouble
with your words.
A lying mouth is a treacherous trap.

Turn away from evil quickly, before it hypnotizes you.
Be fair and do the right thing. Hunt for a peaceful solution
in relationships and when you see it,
catch it and don't let go.
To "fear the Lord" means to hold Him
in reverential trust.

God sees what His friends do. He hears their prayers
but rebels are on their own, alone.
He's reliable. If our hearts are broken, He knows
how to mend them.

Life is rarely easy and godly people have trouble
and pain as surely as all others
but the Lord brings them through.
"God protects all his bones, not one of them is broken." *
Evil will get the best of those who are evil
and enemies of the godly

will be sentenced.
Calamity rolls over them.
Disillusionment drowns them in a tidal wave.
But those who reverence the Lord will be
    redeemed for He is our salvation
    and our refuge in trouble.

* Note: This is prophetic of Jesus' sacrifice. (Exodus 12:46) No bone of the sacrificial lamb was to be broken. (Numbers 9:12) It must be a perfect lamb without blemish. No bone of the True Lamb of God was broken. (John 14:36)

November 9

In God's Hands, Psalm 34:11-22

After David's decision to trust and praise God for everything, he looks at his men. Samuel tells something of David's ragtag army. Some are family members and old friends driven out by Saul's fury, but most are young soldiers who defected from Saul's army because of his cruel insanity. David's soldiers are considered outlaws because of their disloyalty to King Saul.

David wants to share some of his newly learned lessons. He remembers how he took things out of God's hands and into his own. He remembers his lies while trying to undo the mess he had made. He recalls his shame and the cold sweat fear, his tears of repentance and his desperate prayers. Most of all, he remembers the Lord's gracious forgiveness and rescue.

Isn't it the same today? When we repent, remembering our own perfidious nature, our disloyalty and disobedience, and juxtapose it against God's grace and forgiveness, don't we want to rejoice and share with others what He does to mend us?

David said, "Watch what you say. Words slip out before we know it. And watch what you do. Evil is the wrong choice. And evil gains strength on wrong choices. Aim at what's right and move toward it. Lies usually start trouble. One calls for another. My words nearly got me killed. So I urge you, think and choose the right path. Seek the way of peace. When you find it act on it.

"I still don't know how God rescued me. I only know He did. From now on I'm going His way. God can be trusted to look after His own. Let's not fret so much about the evil you see others doing. At the right time Evil will take care of its own.

What is important for us to remember is that the Lord God is our Redeemer and when we come to Him He will not turn us away."

November 10

Our Repeating Lord

Lord, I'm sad, and yet I have to laugh at myself for being so devoid of understanding. Over a period of several years I have asked You the same question over and over, with great earnestness, concerning those I love most. Thank You for so patiently repeating Yourself.

First I asked, "Lord, what must I do so my husband may know the solid, everyday, down to earth joy You bring, even in the midst of tears?"

Your answer: "Inner joy manifests itself. Don't obscure it with dissatisfaction. Trust Me and understand what I'm teaching you. Love him with strength and tenderness, with consideration and pleasure. Stop fretting."

Some two years later I brought You the same question concerning a different situation: "Lord, what may I do so my teenager will love You, and me? She doesn't even seem to like me. I think both You and I bore her."

Your reply: "Love her with persistence and understanding, not in a multitude of endless words. Remember your own youthful rebellions? She's not interested in being changed at this time. You are. A changed mother often leads to a changed child. Be thankful for her, *as she is*."

Another year: "Lord, what else may I do or say so my son will -- ?"

Your answer was basically the same: "My dear daughter, you have said *quite enough*! He needs time to wrestle with himself in some degree of peace. Love him. Pray for him. Laugh with him. Let yourself be full of thanks and quiet expectation. Then faith can shine out.

"You see, the first one in a family to begin unceasing prayer for other members is the first one who wants Me to make changes. So I begin there. In this case, it's you. You are

November 10

becoming a pioneer in a new land, the spiritual land of Nash. You
want to leave your old territory and venture out with Me. You are
blazing the trail for the others.

"Let us work on removing that log from your eye before we
fret about the speck of sawdust in theirs."

Okay, Lord, I see what You mean. But please, I must have
Your help to love with wisdom, not an avalanche of words. Help
me remember to be more wife and mother than lecturer.

Thank You! What a blessing these lessons have been! It's
a joyful adventure to walk life's paths with You!

November 11

Clues to Heaven

Heaven is beyond the reach of our imaginations. The image of heaven dwellers in white bathrobes, sitting on clouds, passing Eternity plunking away on golden harps is pathetic. Let's try scripture. It gives a few clues.

We will be with Him. Jesus' prayer to His Father just prior to His arrest was, "Father, I want those You've given Me to be with Me where I am. I want them to see the glory You have given Me because You have loved Me from before creation." (John 17:24)

St. John's vision: "I saw the new Heaven and Earth. The old ones were gone. So was the Sea. I saw the Holy City, the New Jerusalem, as beautiful as a Bride for her Husband. A voice, like thunder, came from the Throne, 'Now God Himself is living with you. You will be His people and He will be your God. He will dry every tear from your face. *Death, tears, suffering and pain are gone.* The first order of things is gone. Look! I'm making all things new!'" (Revelation 21:1-4)

We will be like Him. "Friends, now we are children of God, and while we don't know just what we will be like, we do know when Christ is revealed, we'll be like Him for we will see Him as He is." (I John 3:2)

We will have glory. This is told with imagery, using gold, jewels, brilliance, glowing luminosity and music in trying to describe it. "New Jerusalem shone with the glory of God; its brilliance like that of precious jewels. Its walls were jasper and the city itself was like transparent gold. The foundation was built of precious stones. The twelve gates were pearl and streets were crystal clear gold.

"There was no Temple because the Almighty Father and

the Lamb are its Temple. The city needs no sun or moon, for the glory of God illuminates it. Its light is the Lamb. Nations will walk in that light. No polluted person will be there, nor will anyone who defiles or deceives." (Revelation 21:18-27)

We will, in some sense, be nourished and entertained. "Blessed are those invited to the Wedding Supper of the Lamb." (Revelation 19:9)

"Then I heard the massed choirs of Heaven, like a great waterfall, like the strong roar of thunder, shouting:

"HALLEUJAH! The Master reigns! Our Sovereign King!

Let us celebrate, rejoice and give Him glory!

The Marriage of the Lamb has come;

His Bride has made herself ready. She was given a bridal gown of shining linen. The linen is the righteousness of the saints." (Revelation 19:6-8)

We will have an official position in the universe. "There will be a day coming when the world will stand before a jury of Believers. We will even judge angels." (I Corinthians 6:2)

Additional references: I Peter 1:3-5, Corinthians 2:9, Ephesians 1:13b-14, I Peter 1: 3-5

November 12

Hope Keeps Popping Up

"It is good that a person should both hope and wait quietly for the Lord's help." (Lamentations 3:26)

Lord, sometimes it seems hearts were made only to be broken. Pain comes from many directions: wars, tragedies, disagreements turned bitter, thoughtlessness, misunderstanding, disease and death.

So the heart breaks, and breaks, and breaks.
What do we do, Lord? We may weep and rage.
We plead and hope. We cry against what we see.
We grumble against You, Lord.

When tears and fury are past we realize we must neither rage nor sulk -- even though we just have. *You* are the Almighty, maker of heaven and earth, Creator of life, God of the Covenant.

So Lord, we move from rage to prayer, not necessarily because we want to, but because there's nothing else to do. We plead with You to heal, to help, to bless. It is not always love which drives us to pray. It's necessity. There's simply no one else to go to. You are always here as I AM, eternal and changeless. We return to You, perhaps grudgingly, but return we do, hoping, asking for help.

Finally we begin to hope again as our trust regains consciousness, and we await the result of Your power and love. The prophet Zechariah tells us "we are prisoners of hope," so we hope. Hope grows into faith. Your Book says faith is the *reality* of things hoped for, the *substance* of things not seen. (Hebrews 11) And so, Lord, we hope. We cannot do otherwise.

November 13

No Chance After Death

Lord, You answered the question of whether or not we are given a second chance for salvation after death. The parable of Lazarus and the rich man is crystal clear. (Luke 16:19-31)

Lazarus, a poverty stricken sick man, sat outside the rich man's gate every day with the neighborhood dogs waiting for scraps from the rich man's table to be thrown out.

Both men died. Lazarus who had honored God went to be with Him in heaven. The rich man found himself in hell. He looked up and saw Lazarus sitting by Abraham and asked for water. Abraham told him there was no passage between heaven and hell. The man asked for Lazarus to be sent to warn his five brothers of their danger. Abraham said, "Your brothers have Moses and the prophets. Let them read and be warned." Again the man argued, "But if someone who died were to return to earth to tell them, surely they would repent."

Abraham replied, "If they do not repent because of what Scripture says, neither will they repent even if someone were to return from the dead."

After all, Someone did return from death with a very specific message. That Someone was You, Lord Jesus. Your Word tells Your truth to the world. But most people don't want the truth – they only want to crown themselves as god.

Isaiah writes, "The people say to pastors and teachers, 'Give us *no more sermons on what is right*! Tell us pleasant things! Give us happy illusions. Leave us as we are and get off your soap box. Stop confronting us with a Holy God!'" (Isaiah 30:10)

"From the time your forefathers left Egypt until now...I have sent My servants and prophets, but you people won't listen." (Jeremiah 7:25)

November 13

Nature proclaims God's existence, His glory, power and wisdom. Reason provides innate realization of the difference between good and evil. But our society, under the leadership of the Evil One, has set out on a successful campaign to desensitize our consciences. Only Scripture tells the whole truth and nothing but the truth.

Bibles and Christian books are still available to us but as a whole we're consumed with *Myself*, the god of this world. Here on earth we are given multiple opportunities to take the right path. But when death claims us, our options are gone. Some will hear Your chilling words, "You didn't want me in life and now it's too late. There's no second chance after death.

November 14

A Golden Moment

Morning's clouds tumble open. Suddenly there's a golden moment as a burst of sunlight spills across the room. Lord, it's beautiful! I wish I hadn't noticed, but the windows are dirty. However, streaky, spotty windows can't hide the glory of today's beauty. They only mute it a bit. Perhaps it's like Your glory bursting in upon a human mind of clay.

Lord, our flash conversation reassures me.

Daughter: Father, what will it be when I see You face to face, when the smudged window of my soul is thrown wide open with nothing between us? Purify this clay, Lord, until it is as fine as human clay can be. But please, walk beside me in the kiln.

Father: I am always with you, My daughter, whether you are in the kiln or on the mountain top. See those trees you love so well? Changes come in them, growth, a broken branch, a turning season. In a similar way you are changing, growing, being pruned, moving into another of life's seasons. Look at the birds you watch with endless delight. They are numerous, yet not one sparrow falls without My knowledge. Aren't You of more worth than they? Let your trust rise like that sparrow in flight.

Daughter: Yes, Father. My trust rises. Your trustworthiness gives it wing.

"I sing because I'm happy. I sing because I'm free.
His eye is on the sparrow and I know He watches me." *

* From the song *His Eye is on the Sparrow*

November 15

The New Covenant of Joy

"Those who know the joy of praise are happy people. They rejoice in You and live in the light of understanding. With Your own strength You lift us up." (Psalm 89:15-16)

Advent angels told shepherds they had "glad tidings of great joy" for them. It was news of Your incarnation, Lord Christ. The pre-existing Christ, who was present with God the Father and God the Spirit, had been born, as a human baby, and would live among His creation so we could come to know Him.

In happy families parents and children enjoy being together. It's the same gladness our heavenly Father has promised to work into His earthly children. Our blessings increase as we learn to live in His Presence.

Father, as Your children, part of our heritage is joy. Jesus gave us His promise on it. "I have told you these things so My joy may be in you and your joy may be complete." (John 15:1-11) "I'll see you again and you will rejoice. Nothing will be able to take away that joy." (John 16:22) Your promised joy, however, only grows in us as the Holy Spirit fills us with Your love.

It's the power of the indwelling Holy Spirit which maintains this life of joy in us, making us content with nothing less. You long for us to love You and have confidence in You, Lord. And the more we seek to follow Your will for us, the stronger our belief becomes that You are content only when Your children live in Your Presence, rejoicing in You. Our assurance grows that what You want for us will be worked into us by Your Spirit.

November 16

New Covenant of Prayer

The Lord says, "Call Me and I will answer you and show you great things of which you have no knowledge." (Jeremiah 33:3)

The fulfillment of the promises of God's New Covenant are dependent on prayer. A covenant is, after all, a contract -- *you do this and I will do that.* A proviso in the new contract reads: "I will put reverence of Me in their hearts, so that they won't depart from Me." (Jeremiah 32:40) To Ezekiel God said, "I will enable them to follow My ways and keep My laws." (36:27)

We lose expectation of actual fulfillment of these promises because of our unbelief and our constant wrangling over the *meaning* of Scripture. We lack faith in God's mighty power. Without the faith to believe His Word means what it says, our Christian experiences will be very limited. But He doesn't leave us floundering. He tells us the way to find such faith. It's through much prayer. "Call Me and I will answer you and show you great things you never considered." It's when individuals turn to God with their whole heart, asking for fulfillment of these promises in their lives that He will accomplish it. It's in *persevering prayer* that our faith is strengthened to take hold of God's promises.

We Believers can help each other in faith. We can ask for and expect, that His promises will be fulfilled in other's lives. We need to pray for our church, ministers and members, for ourselves and families with persevering prayer so the Holy Spirit's power will be recognized and faith will grow in hearts of many.

God says: "I, the Lord have said it; therefore I will do it."

I say: "Spirit of God, I have some faith, but I want more."

November 17

New Covenant in Hebrews

"When God speaks of a *new* covenant, He is making the old Mosaic Covenant obsolete and is ready to put it aside forever." By its obsolescence *Jesus* becomes the Mediator between God and man rather than Levitical priests, who offered animal sacrifices. Of the new contract He says, "I will be merciful to them, forgive and not remember their sin." (Hebrews 8:12-13)

St. Paul tells Timothy, "There is only one Mediator between God and man. He is the Man, Christ Jesus." Jesus, by giving Him-self totally to God's plan of taking our punishment on Himself, became "the Mediator of the new covenant so those who are called may receive the promised eternal inheritance." (I Timothy 2:5, Hebrews 9:15)

Jesus' promise has two parts and is based on a *more perfect* promise. (8:6b) He promises be our Mediator who offers the only sufficient sacrifice for us, and is Himself that sacrifice. Both parts of the covenant are completed in Him. In the first promise, He made restitution for our sin so its power over us is broken giving us access to God's Presence. With this came the fuller promise of the second part: the new heart, freed from sin's power and the Holy Spirit "breathing" into the soul joy in God's Word as well as the power to obey it.

These two parts can't be separated. But many people trust in Christ for forgiveness but fail to claim the whole promise -- the new heart made clean from sin's power with the Holy Spirit pouring in love and joy in His Word and the power to obey bringing access to the whole blessing of the new covenant.

November 17

If we believe this as surely as we believe God forgives those who repent and ask forgiveness, He will put prayerful obedience in our hearts "so we will not wander off from Him."

God asked Abraham, "I AM God Almighty -- is anything too hard for Me?" He gave the same word to Jeremiah regarding the new covenant. Our response to God's question is to give our whole life and self to Him. This means setting aside "new ideas" from revisionism galloping into many churches today. It is incompatible with God's mighty power is as He says, *"I, the Lord have said it, and I will do it."*

Note: the pages in this book referring to the New Covenant are not separate "new covenants." They are promises of empowerments and blessings proceeding and resulting from the Great New Covenant – the coming of God the Son, living among us, teaching, dying, rising again and sending God the Holy Spirit to dwell in those who welcome Him. The promises are being carried out in individuals today.

I have drawn rich blessings from Andrew Murray's writings on the New Covenant. Here I've condensed and partly paraphrased some of his words from *The Secret of The Faith Life* printed by Christian Literature Crusade, USA

November 18

Unclaimed Inheritance

"Let's praise the God and Father of our Lord Jesus, who has blessed us in Christ with every blessing of heaven." (Ephesians 1:3)

"...*has blessed* us with every blessing of heaven" indicates all spiritual blessings are *already* ours. How often we want more wisdom, love, forgiveness, strength or faith. How do we get more? If Christ is living in us, Paul says we *already have* "every blessing of heaven."

Ephesians gives us a bird's eye view of what God has provided for Believers. He shows how spouses and children are to respond to the family in life's struggles. God's strength, insight and loving forgiveness are there for our use. Scripture calls this our *inheritance* from Jesus. When He died and rose again, our inheritance both on earth and in heaven, was activated.

At times we see unclaimed luggage at the airport. It belongs to a traveler. It's the traveler's. But for some reason, unknown to us, he hasn't claimed it. Christians can be like that. We haven't claimed what God has given us, even though it is ours through Christ.

When Christ is in us we have all we need to be changed and to make a difference in the lives around us. We accept His gift with thanks and let it soak through our whole being. We can do this with expectation and the prayer of faith that God will finish the good work He has begun in us. (Philippians 1:6)

Paul writes: "Out of His unlimited resources Christ will strengthen your inner self with the Holy Spirit's power. He will, *through your faith*, actually take up residence in your character, heart and personality. Therefore send your roots deep in Him, in order to be well grounded in God. Then you will begin to understand the length and breadth, the height and depth, the great expanse of His unending love for you.

November 18

"You will know and experience the extent of His love which is so far beyond human knowledge that we will never see the end of it. You will be filled to overflowing with God Himself." (Ephesians 3:16-21)

November 19

Praise Be to God, Psalm 147

Praise be to God, the Lord of glory! To praise Him
        with an open heart is beautiful; it pleases God
        and causes us to realize His Presence with us.
It is a joyful necessity for all who would follow Him,
        for He is the Master Builder of the Holy City.
He gathers His scattered people, mending broken hearts
        and healing sorrow's deep wounds.

God knows the number of the numberless stars.
He knows their names for in His infinite wisdom
        He made each for His own purposes.
His power has no boundaries. He can do all things,
        according to, or apart from, His natural law.
The human mind has no inkling of the infinitude
        of His wisdom or the scope of His might.

He will see to it that the wicked are defeated
        and the righteous upheld.
So Believers, praise Him with voice and harp,
        with trumpet, horn and cymbal
        to extol our God who provides!
He causes clouds to build towers in the sky
        to water the Earth.
Grains and grasses respond with a burst of growth,
        feeding birds and animals.

It is God who gives the horse its strength
        and the runner his endurance,
        yet He takes no particular pleasure
        in the horse's strength
        or in the power of the runner's muscles.

November 19

What brings our Lord joy is His peoples' obedience
as they wait expectantly for His loving mercy.

Let your music rise, O Jerusalem, in a crescendo
of joyful praise!
Sing aloud to your God, O Zion! For it is He
who reinforces your gates and secures the City.
He blesses your children and brings peace to your borders.
It is He who satisfies you with wholesome bread.
His commands travel faster than the speed of light.
They are surer than dawn. He scatters frost and snow,
white and clean, upon the Earth.
Ice forms and hail falls like stones. Who can stop it,
who can withstand His cold?

In the fullness of time His order goes out, warm winds
blow;
the winter freeze gives way to spring.
In the same way His Word goes out, illustrating His laws,
manifesting His character
and Israel is shaped by them.
God's people are unique. The Lord's hand is upon us.
Praise be to God! Alleluia!

Note: The writer of this psalm is not known. Haggai or Zechariah
may have written it for it was sung at the dedication of the second
Temple.

November 20

A Trinity of Virtues

"These things remain: faith, hope, and love, but the most far reaching and important of these is love." (I Corinthians 13:13)

Thank You, Lord, for telling us these three graces are not transient; they make a very big difference in this life and the next. Paul regards love as the greatest. Love does the most to mend relationships and give a new start in this broken world. But truly, Lord, aren't the three inseparable? Without faith in Your death and resurrection we could have no hope in what You say and demonstrate, we could not love You or Your eternal purposes.

Perhaps Paul arranged these three as progressive steps in growing up in You. Faith telescopes out into hope, the joyful expectation and confidence in Your trustworthiness. It's because of these two, faith and hope, that we come to love You and let Your love fill us until that love spills out to others.

Perhaps we could liken the three virtues to conception, birth and growth. When faith is conceived in us by the Holy Spirit, in time it gives birth to hope. Faith and hope together grow in us to be love. Love learns, understands, experiences. Love, as well as the other two becomes bigger and stronger just as the newborn grows into the child and the child into the adult.

These virtues remind us of the Trinity, God the Father, God the Son, and God the Holy Spirit, three Persons, one God, indivisible. Faith, hope and love are the three inseparable links in one chain of Christian maturity. Each link connects and leads us to the others.

November 21

Keep Knocking

We ask what is God like? We want to know. But it's a question which can't be answered completely in this life. We see Him as Creator. We see His power, knowledge, wisdom and glory reflected in sky and earth. We see His provision for His people. We have His Book, but what's He like as a Person as compared to other persons?

Our best understanding of what He's like comes from the life of Jesus as He is fleshed out for us in Scripture, "All of who God is lives in Jesus in bodily form." (Colossians 2:9)

In the story of the Prodigal Son, He is seen as a father eagerly awaiting the return of his rebellious son. He is shown as merciful, as one who hears and answers His children with wisdom and love. (Luke 15:11-31)

We parents try to answer our children's requests wisely, with love. Isn't it interesting to learn that God has the same answers for His children's requests as we have for ours? *Yes. No. Not now. Maybe later.*

Children may have only one parent; some have abusive or uninterested fathers. *God is not like that.* He's always interested.

We may grumble about our needs but needs are part of the Father's provision for us. If we had no wants or needs, would we ever go to God with our requests? Jesus says the Father wants us to come to Him seeking His solution to our need, to knock on doors and He'll open the *right* door for us. Jesus asks rhetorical questions with a smile: "If your child asks for bread you wouldn't give him a rock, would you? Don't you think your Father in Heaven, who loves you eternally, will provide what you need?"

Perseverance is necessary. We must keep knocking, keep seeking. God wants us to bring Him a continual life of prayer. That's the most reliable way we can come to know what He is truly like. (Matthew 7:7-9)

November 22

Moonrise

I watch the river late at night,
   a black abyss beneath me.
I wait and breathe, see and sense
   the quiet of aloneness.
Your swift moon races the clouds,
   outlining them in silver,

      spreading a highway of light
      across the waters
      from its lunar face to my icy feet.
Cold air pierces my summer robe,
   teeth chatter from the chill.
Yet the scene is mesmerizing –
   blackness and brilliance,
   midnight and gold.

The light cobbled roadway beckons me
   where human feet cannot follow.
Only mind and spirit are free to answer
   its summons.
Its beauty is God's call, reminding me
   of His power and glory.
It's in the joy of remembering
   that my soul kneels in worship.

F.N.

November 23

Good Gifts

"Whatever is good comes from God, who never changes or turns away from us." (James 1:17)

Lord, You shower people with gifts, huge ones and tiny ones, eternal ones and temporal ones. Today I am especially thankful for the treasure of my son and daughter. Today we're halfway between their birthdays.

It's hard to imagine what life would have been like without them. I feel so blessed in them for we were uncertain of my ability to have children. Doctors said don't attempt it. After much prayer, Bill and I were led to disagree. Thank You, Lord, for changing our minds.

Those years of growing up together were wonderful, fun, busy, lazy, painful, joyous, happy, sad, prayerful, frustrating, hilarious, sweet years. How I battled with and for them! How I wrestled with You, Lord, as I agonized and prayed over their lacks and hurts and praised over their every good effort and victory. You used the mix of talents and defects of the four of us, our victories and defeats, for our common good, just as You promised You would. You never fail us Lord, even though we fail You in many ways.

I praise You for their strengths, inner beauty, hope, virtue, love, for their growing wisdom and faith. I love the mates You sent our children. I consider them my "in loves," rather than in laws, for I love them as though they were born to me. And the grandchildren, Lord! Five first prizes of humanity. Each unique. Each precious.

Lord, I thank You for their guardian angels and for letting me see mine when I was a child. He was a great, shining power of purpose and purity, clothed in light. Father, keep Your angels close to each one. Protect them from evil and harm and nudge them toward Yourself. My praise comes from a deeply grateful heart.

November 24

Fire in the Mouth

The tongue is a fire in the mouth. It's the broadcast system of the mind, for evil or good. If for evil, it corrupts setting the course of a life on fire ignited by hell. (James 3:6)

Without fuel fires go out, without a tale bearer trouble dies down. (Proverbs 26:20)

A foolish man's words catch him in many traps. They twist his soul. (Proverbs 18:7)

Gossip causes inner wounds deep in heart and mind, it eats like cancer. (Proverbs 18:8)

Those who answer before listening to the whole story come to shame because of their discourteous foolishness. (Proverbs 18:13)

A fool spews out his anger but the wise man holds his tongue and thinks through the situation carefully. (Proverbs 29:11)

Beware of those who talk first and think later. There's more hope for a simpleton than for them. (Proverbs 29:20)

A quiet reply takes the sting out of anger but a harsh one pours kerosene on smoldering coals. (Proverbs 15:1)

A wise person's words are a spring of refreshing water but a fool's words are a debris filled tidal wave. (Proverbs15:1-2)

A helpful word at the right time is welcomed and the kind rebuke of a friend is like a gold ring to keep forever. (Proverbs 25:20)

A summary: Watch your words. Purge out angry criticisms. Say less. Pray and think more. "Let the words and meditations of my mind and heart be pleasing to You, my Lord and Redeemer." (Psalm19:14)

November 25

Love Poured Out

Several days after Jesus called Lazarus from the tomb, He was having dinner at the home of Lazarus and his two sisters, Mary and Martha. Martha served the meal and Mary opened an expensive perfume, poured it over Jesus' feet and wiped them with her hair. Scripture says, "… the fragrance filled the house." (John 12:1-11)

Judas Iscariot grumbled when Mary did this. He claimed it should have been sold "to help the poor." But, Lord, You commended her, recognizing she was doing for You what You had done in her life by Your loving generosity.

"… fragrance filled the house." Was it the fragrance of the perfume or was it the beauty of her love flowing over those present? Neither the fragrance of perfume nor of her loving act would have happened if the alabaster container had not been broken open. Today, Lord, You want us to break open the blessings You've given us, so we may share them with others as the fragrance of Your love.

You didn't promise that those who believe in You will never have trouble. You said true Believers will have Your Spirit living in them and Your Spirit will flow out to others. Your teaching is not so much to realize "who we are" as it is to share who You are. You remake individuals to reflect You, Lord Jesus, and what You pour into us is to be poured out for others.

We can actually bring *You* joy by doing what Mary did. She forgot about economy and self interest. She honored You with the best she had, and the fragrance was beautiful!

November 26

Valley of Everyday

Lord, as I move along, satisfied under Your care and teaching, a break in my cloudy thinking occurs which gives me a deeper understanding of You. When this occurs, foolish, clamoring thoughts are banished. An awed stillness fills my mind and heart. I seem to be on some mountain height, renewed and more conscious of Your power and glory.

Peter wanted to stay on the Mount of Transfiguration. He asked You, Jesus if he, James and John could build shelters and stay there with You. He wanted to live in peace, above the heat and problems of the valley, away from the grind of daily living. Mostly, he wanted the nearness of Your presence. But You led them down, where the people were. (Matthew 17:1-4)

Lord, it must be that You give these flashes of insight occasionally in order to provide strength for valley living, to raise our sights. They can instill light and hope in us which we can take down into the Valley of Every Day, bringing encouragement, patience and hope to others.

Mountain top living is not meant to be a permanent arrangement, not yet anyway. You put us here along with others for whom Your Son died. We must learn to walk, with feet of clay, in earth's valleys manifesting salt and light, fresh bread and living water, reflecting the Savior.

This is not easy, but it *is* an adventure. The good news is that You are with us, beside us, before us and in us. And Lord, help all who have been to the mountain top keep the awe, surprise and praise of Your new insights. Amen

November 27

Love Bounces

My friend Dorothy and I often speak of how God uses everyday things to teach us of Himself, as He does in Scriptural parables. She told me this story of how her dog illustrated a truth. This, in essence, is the story:

I'm always blessed when the Lord shows me how everyday activities can demonstrate a spiritual truth. In this instance He used a dirty, abandoned, little dog as an illustration of His care and what our response should be.

Since we had recently lost our dog, my daughter and I went to the pound to 'shop' for another. Several were available, but one little fellow held special appeal. Hope was written all over him, from his pleading eyes up front to the furiously busy tail in back, making it quite clear that the *whole dog* wanted us to adopt him.

He was matted, bedraggled, and his paw, lifted for a pawshake, was mud-covered. We *chose* him as ours because we knew his heart.

Scripture tells us that God *chose* us, and because He loves us through Christ, He *adopts* us as His children. (Ephesians 1:3-5)

After choosing the dog, we immediately took him to the vet for a good grooming. He was dirty when we got him but if he was going to be our dog he could not remain dirty.

Throughout the Bible God speaks of *washing* us from our sin. "We have been *cleansed,* made holy, through the bodily sacrifice of Jesus Christ." (Hebrews 10:10)

As the vet worked on Rocky, the small tatterdemalion began taking on a new look – and smell.

God *prunes* us. He cuts off the unacceptable. Jesus says, "I am the Vine and My Father is the Gardener. He cuts off branches which don't bear fruit." (John 15:1-2) When we are adopted into God's Family we begin to look and act differently. God plans for Believers to be conformed, shaped like, or molded into the likeness of His Son. (Romans 8:29) We are to be made new after God's pattern, made clean, with new attitudes to reflect Jesus' character.

All the scrubbing, tugging and soapy water had been a scary ordeal for Rocky but it was worth it! The itch was gone. He was clean and sweet, he was beautiful and he knew it! He pranced and danced. He wagged and smiled. That bad smell which he had never been able to outrun was gone! He knew he was loved, although he could never quite figure out why, but because he was loved he returned our love.

So it is with You and me, Lord. You see human need. If we are willing, You take us up, clean us, and nourish us because of the astonishing fact that You love us.

"We love Him because He first loved us." (I John 4:19)

November 29

An Aching Heart

Lord, revisions of the Holy Word
    cause my heart to ache.
It's a foreign land, I can no longer
    find nourishment for my soul.

Where the strong, joyous fellowship
    of hearts one in Truth?
Where the wonder and glory of remembering
    Your cross, the power
    of Your resurrection?

This polluted atmosphere hurts as I breathe it,
    like sand, gritty and cutting.
I miss the transparent air of Your
    unspoiled Word.

I need encouragement of affirming You,
    hearing You as You are,
    O gracious Lord.
Bless and deliver us, Father, as we walk
    from past to future.

F.N.

November 30

Our Persistent Lord

Lord, You are persistent in calling Your children. By being persistent You not only get our attention but set us a clear example. You know prayer isn't easy for us. We're careless and lazy in our prayers. Often we think about and talk about it more than we actually PRAY. Others of us rattle off some familiar phrases while the mind wanders off in the direction of our next project.

Persistence is important, but so is truthfulness. At times I tell a friend in difficulty, "I'll keep you in my prayers" and then, Lord, I *forget*! Surely, by forgetting, I turn my comment into a lie. That must hurt You. Forgive and help me do what I say I'll do. Lately I've begun to ask the person if I can pray with him on the spot, or over the phone whenever it's appropriate.

We can't thank You enough, Lord, You persistently work in our lives by Your grace and not exclusively by how strong or how wobbly-weak our faith may be. Our needs and weaknesses are gifts in disguise, given to us so we will bring them to You.

After Your Ascension the disciples realized they MUST HAVE Your help in living the Christian life, so they followed Your example. They persistently joined together in prayer.

It's no different with us, Your current disciples. We must have Your help in recognizing the difference between the rich, persistent prayer life You want us to have and our many "gimme" prayers, gimme-this and gimme-that. Help us, Lord, to be persistent in prayer and careful to wait for, and listen to the Spirit.

December 1

Don't Forget Us, Lord

Lord, Christmas is drawing near. Soon we celebrate the time Jesus, the Lord of glory, broke through the wall of separation and into the realm of earth. He purposefully took off His robe of power, honor and dominion, and put on the vulnerable robe of flesh.

December is always over full of materialism, and worldly pleasure. It's easy to become distracted and forget You, as the pace whirls faster with each passing day until we become grouchy with fatigue and breathe a sigh of relief when Your birthday is over. Please, Lord, don't forget us. You know we are fragile flesh with forgetful minds. Help us in this holy season to be tender toward You. Bless us, open us, correct us, illuminate and enlarge our spirits and minds. Use us to reflect Your likeness so the Advent Season shines with Your Presence. Amen

Think again of what Jesus said: "Aren't five sparrows sold for a few pennies at the market and not one of them falls to the ground without your Father's knowledge? He knows you down to the exact number of hairs on your head. Don't be afraid, you are of more worth to Him than flocks of sparrows." (Matthew 10: 29-31)

December 2

God is Eternal, Humanity is Transitory
Psalm 90, a Song of Moses

Lord, through the centuries You have been our Home and Refuge.
Before the mountains pushed up, before earth took form,
    even before Time began, You are God.

We mortals return to dust, but You remain.
Thousands of years pass as an hour to You,
    while we slip by as on a swiftly moving
    river, then vanish leaving only whispered memories.
In life's morning we flourish and bloom but when evening comes
    our color fades. We wither and drop.

In Your Presence we see our sins plainly.
They are secrets no longer.
Our days diminish too quickly, as a breath exhaled.
You allot us seventy years of earth life. If because of strength
    we are given more, trouble doggedly pursues us.
Even those extra years vanish as morning mist.

Which of us honors You as we should, Lord? None of us do!
Teach us. Teach us, Lord, to count our days
    and spend each one carefully with wisdom.

Lord, we await Your return. When will You come for us?
Have mercy on us and bless us with Your loving kindness
    so we may praise You all our brief days.
Be our joy, Lord, in spite of the troubles about us.

May we recognize Your works and majesty. Set Your seal
    of approval on us Lord, and confirm the work we have
done. Yes, Lord, confirm it.

December 3

A Stream of Living Blessings

Time has swept my children into adulthood, bringing them children of their own. My prayers accompanied them day after day, year after year. One child confessed Jesus as her Savior. One did not. As he grew, Scripture seemed to interest him – but only as a means of disproving its claims. While this was not the ultimate hope of my prayers, I rejoiced in it for I believe when God's Word goes out it does not come back empty handed. It accomplishes the purpose for which God sent it. (Isaiah 55:11)

We took our son and daughter and their spouses to C. S. Lewis conferences in England led by people with hearts for God, such as Earl Palmer and John Stott. I began to sense a small crack in the tightly closed door of my son's spirit. Nothing was said. It was a tiny spark of light in my heart, of growing anticipation, gladness, increased prayer and praise. He and Laurie read several of Lewis' books. Occasionally they went to church. Their two children requested baptism. Laurie joined a Bible study group. The study included questions to be answered at home. She conferred with her husband, Bill III, on the answers, for as a child Scripture was much of our home life.

Time kept moving on. As my husband and I were leaving their house one evening Bill III stopped me in the foyer, saying, "Mother, I read the Gospel of John through today and I have come to a decision." He began to quote what Jesus said, "I am the Way..." As I recognized the verse I joined him in the quote ... "the Truth and the Life, no one comes to the Father except through Me." (John14:6)

Realization of what had happened to my son swept through me like a flame. Yes, I always believed it would happen when God's time was right for He had assured me of it on two separate occasions. That assurance was my strong comfort during the fifty

December 3

years of prayerful waiting. But when it happened my joy knew no bounds. His head knowledge had become heart knowledge assured. I remembered parts of verses in Isaiah 35 ... *Living water will gush forth in the wilderness and streams will flow in the desert. The burning sand will become a pool and the thirsty ground bubbling springs."*

Yes, Lord, You answered my prayer and sent a stream of living blessings flowing through our family bringing us together for eternity.

December 4

The Other Half

The highest, deepest and widest prayer I prayed for my children was that they and their spouses put their faith in Jesus Christ.

Kakie's faith grew as she did, deepening with maturity. Her husband, Don, came to faith through her. Bill III and Laurie's were slower in coming but when belief came, it came to both at once. I wanted to hear their story.

As the four of us were having dinner I asked how it happened that they accepted Christ at the same time. Bill said, "I give Laurie the credit for that. She took the course at church without me. It involved home study, reading and answering questions. She asked me the questions and my own answers knocked down my defensive walls."

Laurie's reply was, "Yes, and Bill's answers were the key for me. I'd say it was the combination of my questions and Bill's answers which stirred our joint interest and amazement at what God had done."

Their replies moved me deeply. And isn't this how marriage is supposed to work – two entirely different halves coming together in love, trust and commitment to make a whole, each recognizing the value of the other in making their lives complete in Christ?

My husband and I are quite different in many ways, just as Kakie and Don, and Bill and Laurie are. Yet when the two halves join individual incompleteness is modified and we move together by drawing wholeness from our 'other half.'

December 5

The Best Christmas Gift

Lord, the best gift humanity has ever received came to us on Christmas. The Gift appeared on earth's doorstep dressed in tender baby flesh, wrapped, as many gifts are, not in tinsel and bows, but rather in rough homespun. That gift was You, Lord Jesus, Son of God and Son of Man. If You had not come to us by the Spirit of God through the virgin Mary we would be without hope. There would be no "exact likeness of the invisible God" on this earth. The "True Lamb of God who takes away the sins of the world" would never have been offered up in ransom for us. There would be no Jesus, the "Captain of our Salvation," to lead us from the living dead to real and eternal life.

But You *did* come and You brought with You unnumbered blessings to those who love You. This month we celebrate Your birth and who You are.

So how is it, Lord, in the midst of all the singing, remembering and anticipation, the joy, the excitement of giving and receiving that we feel a sort of murkiness of spirit when December closes? We seem to lose the intimate sense of Your Spirit. Somewhere amid the shopping, planning, cooking, wrapping and entertaining, we lose You in the crowds. But even if that happens this year, Lord, I'm amazed and grateful that You never lose any of Your children in the swarming multitudes of earth.

December 5

Especially in December we should listen to Brother Lawrence's advice in his book, *Practicing the Presence of God.* In our first wakeful moment we put ourselves in Your Presence with praise and earnestly request Your guidance in our actions, reactions and plans. If the phone rings at an inconvenient time, rather than letting irritation claim us, we remember God can use telephones for His purposes. After all He created the laws which govern the making and using of the telephone.

When You are my Companion and Guide, when I'm "holding Your hand" as I go through the day, I notice Your Presence cuts out much wheel spinning. It changes my attitude too. Shoving crowds become individual people whom I know You love. You let me look into their eyes, with Your love in my heart and with the prayer that they sense Your love. At times their response is remarkable. But Lord, what happens in me is nothing short of a full blown miracle.

Help me and all of Your sons and daughters to keep our spirits linked with Yours. If we forget You and pick up the hurried, harried, impatient attitude so prevalent this time of year, cause the powerful magnet of Your love to pull us back to You. Amen

"Oh, come and magnify the Lord with me and let us exalt His Name together." (Psalm 34)

December 6

The Child with Many Names

"His Name shall be called Wonderful Counselor, Mighty God, Everlasting Father, Prince of Peace." (Isaiah 9:6)

"The Associated Press carried a story from England about a couple who gave their daughter a hundred and thirty nine names. They call her Tracy, but officially she has a hundred and thirty eight more. Why? They said they wanted to do something unusual.

"This month we celebrate the birth of Jesus, who also had many names. But in His case, all His names and titles are significant. In Bible times a name was more than 'a handle.' It said something about the character of the person who bore it. That's especially important when we realize Jesus is referred to in the Bible by many different titles, each reflecting something about His person and work.

"As Christians we must make sure we know and experience Him in a manner consistent with His names. If we call Him *Jesus* which means *Savior* we must trust Him to deliver us from the power and penalty of sin. If we call Him *Lord* we must allow Him to be just that. And what about names such as *"Wonderful Counselor, Mighty God, Everlasting Father and Prince of Peace?"* Do I act as if that's who He really is?

> "Jesus! Jesus! Jesus! Sing aloud the Name
> till it softly, slowly, sets the heart aflame.

"Jesus is God spelling Himself out in language man can understand."

Note: from *The Anglican Digest,* used with permission

December 7

God of Creation, Psalm 104

Creator God, no tongue can ever tell of Your greatness!
Your splendor covers earth with beauty,
     drenching her in light.
You've pulled the glittering heavens about her as a veil
     and dropped rivers and shining seas
     like jewels upon her breast.
Clouds race as chariots across the skies on windy wings.
You created angels as Your spirit messengers,
     bright and swift as flames.

This planet is secure in space by Your unfailing laws.
Dark waters flooded it, covering the mountains.
At Your command it took shape. Waters receded
     into their assigned places.   Mountains pushed up and
     valleys sank low. You established boundaries so waters
     would never again cover the earth.
You added springs in the valleys and wove streams
     through the land to maintain life.

Birds live among the trees, filling branches with music.
To high mountains You have given water sources and earth
     is sustained by Your provision.
You give life to grass and grain to feed Your creatures.
Grapes yield their wine to lighten man's heart
     from his burden of work.
His face glows with vigor and gladness.

The moon is earth's glowing calendar and sun
     establishes each new day.

December 7

Night falls, and beasts come out to partake of Your
    provender.
As dawn marks another day they return to dens to sleep.
When they go in, people come out to do their work
    until fading light drives them homeward.

What a variety of creatures You have made, Lord,
    and in wisdom provided for each differing need.
Earth is a storehouse, overflowing with provisions.
The sea is there, swarming with creatures, enormous and
    minuscule. Great whales frolic and blow
    geysers of air and water.
Ships sail across its surface as clouds of fish
    sweep beneath them.

All creatures eat from Your hand. If You stop providing
    they return to dust. One look from You
    and earthquakes split the earth.
One touch and mountains melt. Such is Your power!

As long as I have breath I will praise You, Lord.
It gives me deep joy to meditate on Your works.
I pray You are pleased by my thoughts.
Clear away evil and free Your creation from sin.
        Praise the Lord, my soul!
        Bless the Lord, my soul!

December 8

The Real Thing

On Christmas morning all who are parents have probably watched with tender hearted amusement as a baby son or daughter plays delightedly with colorful wrappings and bright ribbons while ignoring the gift itself, rattling the crisp paper and tasting the ribbon while mother is *oohing* and *ahhing* over what daddy gave her.

With an inner smile we acknowledge the fact that our tiny child is missing the point, happy with second best. The baby's response to Christmas gifts is not unlike that of some Believers today. We put great effort into the traditional trivia of the season, trees, wreathes, multiple parties, scores of cards featuring Santa, smiling mice in red hats, boozie celebrants toasting to good cheer.

All these trimmings and feasts may be beautiful and pleasant, but they aren't *The Gift*. Who took Christ out of *Christ*mas? How did He, God's Gift to a hungry, naked, wounded world, get winnowed out of His own birthday celebration? Our "Christian" nation is progressively blotting God out of our consciousness, eradicating His words from schools, His Name from coins, and so on.

C. S. Lewis tells of a conversation his brother overheard while riding the double decker bus to town. As the bus passed a church displaying the manger scene, he heard the woman in front of him say, "Oh, Lor'! They bring religion into everything. Look, now they're even dragging it into Christmas!"

Lord Jesus, amid all our flurry and hurry, may we Believers remember You, God the Son, are the true and eternal Gift of our loving God, the Father. And Father, wrapped with Your Gift of the Savior come the multiple gifts of love, forgiveness, joy, guidance, strength, new life and peace. May we never forget.

December 9

Our Quieting Lord

"Almighty God says, 'It is only in returning to Me that you will be saved. In that quiet confidence You shall have strength.' " (Isaiah 30:15)

Father, this morning as I read the Psalms, I asked You to light up my mind with Your Presence and Truth but time was short and what little I had was riddled with interruptions. Time pressure plus interruptions added up to trouble as I sought companionship with You. Unrelated thoughts strayed through my mind like a flock of wandering sheep, distracting me. I pulled up short and asked You to be Shepherd of my thoughts and gather me together so I might hear You through Your Word.

My eyes fell on the next verse: "Be still and know that I am God; I will be exalted in the earth." (Psalm 46:10) My mind paraphrased Your words to say, "Rest easy, Small One. Don't fret. Be quiet, Sh-h-h! I am here with You right now." Flurry softened into gentle quietness. Your peace "that passes human description" seeped in, gradually filling me. "Lord, You hide me, tuck me away in the Secret Place of Your Presence, away from intrigue and worry. In Your sheltered pavilion You shelter me from discord and panic." (Psalm 31:2)

Father, because of Your ways and Your Words, this day which began in a tangled knot of temporal concerns has become a day of praise -- AGAIN! You've done this before, but I can never take Your astonishing mercy for granted. Your mercy is like You, "new every morning and fresh every evening." Thank You! You *are* my quietness and confidence. You have turned me from dwelling on my weakness to *reveling* in Your strength for today.

December 10

Sign Posts Along The Way

Lord, there are more reasons to praise You than I can grasp. I can't even list all those of which I'm conscious. But it's a joyful thing to consider a few.

I praise You, Father, for Your Great Eternal Plan made before creation. You sent Your Son to earth to implement Your Plan – *to be* Your Plan, *to be* Your Word to us, *to fulfil* the promise of the Father in the person of the Son.

I praise You, God the Son, for Your participation in creation, for the godly parables You have worked into "nature" to be sign posts along the road of life pointing to You. I praise You for Your human courage, obedience and loyalty, for Your precious death and resurrection, for presenting the blood of Your sacrifice before the Father's Presence in order to finalize the salvation of whoever will come to You in repentance and faith, for substituting Your death for mine. I praise You for Your "mercy beyond measure, Your love beyond question, forgiveness without boundary, and truth without fault."

I praise You, God the Holy Spirit, for Your indwelling Presence, for guiding, nudging, restraining, for being God in me, the hope of glory. You teach truth, wisdom and insight when I ask – if I listen. You bring joy, comfort in sorrow, strength in weakness, correction when I stray. You continually show me glimpses of who You are in Your sign posts along the way.

December 11

Our Omnipotent Prayer Partner

"Realizing that Jesus, the very Son of God, our great and eternal High Priest, is at the Father's right hand, let's be sure we hold true to our confession *of* Him as Lord and *to* Him as High Priest. Even though He experienced the fierce power of temptation, He never fell before it. It is because of this that we may confidently approach His throne of grace. We may ask for and receive the merciful help He has for us." (Hebrews 4:14-16)

Lord, You know how it is with us because You have been where we are, confronted on all sides, wrestling with temptations. Your battle against temptation was more fierce than ours could ever be. We fall long before Satan has turned his full power against us. So while we may say truthfully that You were tempted like we are, we must realize that no one has ever been tempted as brutally as You were.

Difficulties are part of our lives. Pain pinches, tears flow, fears and doubts pursue. We come to You for help, Lord, for You know from experience what it's like to be human. You are the perfect High Priest because You are totally Man and totally God. You alone have the power to forgive us and be our Substitute. Your invitation is always open. You invite us to come to You confidently in prayer, not timidly or fearfully, but with hope.

According to I Peter 2:9, You have called us into Your priesthood so that we may minister to and pray for others as well as ourselves. John tells us that You pray for Your people. Lord, if You pray for them and we are to pray for them too, doesn't that mean we may consider You as our Omnipotent Prayer Partner since we are working on the same project!

Be our strength, Lord, in our earthly priesthood so that we may be constant in joining You and others in prayer for Your people.

December 12

From Peter's Letter,
condensation and paraphrase of I Peter 1:1-20

Dear new citizens of the Kingdom of God,

Even though you have lost your previous citizenship in the Kingdom of This World, rejoice, for God has chosen you to be His seed scattered across pagan fields. He has chosen you because of His foreknowledge of your response to Him. His recognizable Spirit lives in you so you may stay obedient because of Jesus' sacrifice.

Be glad and full of praise, not only because of our totally new life, but because Jesus' resurrection has planted living hope within us. Because of it we have an astonishing inheritance which can't be eroded by taxes or stolen by scam artists. Even our own deaths cannot dilute our inheritance because it's waiting for us in heaven where our salvation is to be completed. Don't worry. It's safe there, guarded by the Almighty's power and shielded by our faith. The realization of this truth brings joy and enduring peace, even in the midst of these human trials and sufferings.

God doesn't waste our pain. When it comes He uses it to toughen and refine our faith, much as gold is refined by fire. Our faith is precious to us. It's worth more than gold could ever be. Gold isn't eternal. Faith is. But faith can be proven to be either false or genuine. (Matthew 7:16) These current troubles will purify and prove it. It's your purified faith which yields eternal reward when Christ closes down our earth life. Gold can neither purchase faith nor the reward which faith brings.

Even though we can't see Jesus now, we can know and trust Him because we have His Spirit. With His indwelling Spirit comes the indescribable joy of knowing the goal of our eternal salvation is being worked out in us *now*.

December 12

In the past prophets have written of this salvation and of the grace given to us, but they didn't understand it. They searched carefully through all the ancient Scriptures trying to discover when and under what circumstances this would happen. But the Holy Spirit who pressed them into writing about the suffering and the following glory, revealed that these things were for generations far ahead of them in time. They were for you and me! Even the angels are standing on tiptoe with anticipation of understanding these things. The Holy Spirit and Christ's apostles are explaining them to you now.

Because of all this, get ready for action. Learn self control and fix your faith totally on the grace of God. It will be fully understood only when Jesus is revealed in all His glory and power. Be like obedient children, thriving under parental care. Don't let the world shape your thinking by its evil ways, as you did before you knew the Master. God, who called us, is holy. He wants us to learn holiness and be shaped like Him, not like the world.

He is the impartial Judge of everyone's work -- so live your life here as a visitor or pilgrim, trusting God in reverence. You already know you have been bought back from the law of sin and death, which your forefathers and their society taught them. Your redemption was not paid by the slippery substance we call money. Jesus paid our sin debt. He is the true Pascal Lamb of God, whose death and resurrection is the Father's plan and purpose, made before creation, for our redemption, which has only been revealed to us in these latter days.

December 13

Old Prophecy Fulfilled

God speaks to Evil in the first prophecy of the Redeemer:
"...I will put enmity between you and the woman, between her offspring and yours; He will crush your head and you will bruise His heel." (Genesis 3:15)

God chooses Messiah's line through Abraham:	Genesis 12:1-3
Blessing would come through Isaac:	Genesis 17:19
Of Isaac's two sons He chooses Jacob:	Genesis 49:10
Of Jesse's eight sons He chooses David:	I Samuel 16:11-13
Messiah shall reign on the throne of David:	Isaiah 9:6-7

Born of a virgin: Isaiah 7:14   fulfilled: Luke 1:31-35
Born in Bethlehem: Micah 5:2,   fulfilled: Matthew 2:1
Sojourn in Egypt: Hosea 11:1,   fulfilled: Matthew 2:13
Teach by parables: Psalm 78:2,   fulfilled: Matthew 13:34-35
Hated. Rejected: Psalm 69:4,   Psalm 22:6-8,
                     fulfilled: Matthew 37:39-40
Triumphal entry in Jerusalem: Zechariah 9:9,
                     fulfilled: Matthew 21:9
Betrayed: Zechariah 11:12-13, Psalm 41:9,
                     fulfilled: Matthew 26:14-16
Put to death: Isaiah 53:8b-9,   fulfilled: Matthew 27:50
Died with criminals: Isaiah 53:12,   fulfilled: Matthew 27:38
Hands and feet pierced: Psalm 22:16, Zechariah 12:10
                     fulfilled: John 19:23
Beaten and spat upon: Isaiah 50:6,   fulfilled: Matthew 27:30
Offered gall and vinegar to drink: Psalm 69:21
                     fulfilled: Matthew 27:48
Side pierced: Zechariah 12:10, Psalm 22:18,
                     fulfilled: John 19:34

December 13

Gambled for His clothing: Psalm 22:18
                              fulfilled   Matthew 27:37
Dying words: Psalm 22:1, Psalm 31:5,
                              fulfilled   Luke 23:46
Not a bone broken: Exodus 12:46, Numbers 9:12,
                              fulfilled   John 19:33-37
Would rise the third day: Hosea 6:2, Jonah 1:17,
                              fulfilled   Luke 11:29-31
Buried in grave of a rich man: Isaiah 53:9,
                              fulfilled   Luke 23:50-53
Quality and purpose of His life: Isaiah 53,
                              fulfilled   John 10:10b

The Old Testament Jews were given word pictures of who Messiah would be, what He would be like, what would happen to Him and why. They were told to expect Him and be watchful. He came as God's New Covenant in Isaiah in the center of history. When He came, some believed as they saw Scripture fulfilled in Him. Most did not.

Today we read the Old Testament prophecies and see their fulfillment in the New Testament in Jesus. We realize that up to now He has kept His promises concerning His coming as the Son of Man / Son of God. What reason do we have to doubt Him now? He's told us when the time is right He will come back to take us with Him. In the meantime He tells those who are in Christ, "I have come so you may have Life and have it *more abundantly*."

If the heart, mind and soul are empty rather than more abundantly filled shouldn't we wonder why? Have we, like foolish sheep, wandered off to feed in the world's seductive meadows? When this happens don't we recognize our emptiness and long to turn back to Him to fill our hollow souls?

December 14

Superior to Angels,
Hebrews I

Ever since Creation God communicated Himself to humanity in many different ways to our forefathers through the prophets. But since the birth of Jesus He speaks to us through the person of His Son. The Son is His heir and the lawful owner of all things. It is through Him that God created the worlds and the endless space in which they move.

God's Son is the three dimensional, free standing, flesh and blood image of the invisible God, the exact enactment of His glory. He is the perfect representative of God's power to hold the universe together and keep it moving.

The Son is the one who, after He laid down His life as ransom for our guilty lives, sat down at His Father's right hand. In providing the sacrifice for our sins He is far above angels, who are created beings, while He is God who created them.

Has the Father ever said to an angel, "You are My Son, today I have begotten You?" (Psalm 2:7)

Again He says of Messiah, "I will be His Father and He will be My Son." (II Chronicles 17:13)

When He brings His only begotten Son to earth He says, "Let all God's angels worship Him." (Hebrews 1:6b)

To His servants, the angels, He says, "You are bright as flames and swift as the wind." (Psalm 104:4)

But to His Son He says, "Your kingdom, O Lord, endures forever. You delight in truth and hate injustice.

December 14

Therefore Your Father has commissioned You and given You more joy than Your companions."

God the Father calls His Son, *Lord* when He says, "Lord, You laid earth's foundation in the first place and the shining heavens are Your workmanship. Wondrous as they are, someday the worlds will perish, but You remain. They will wear out like an old coat. You will fold them up and replace them.

"But You, My Son, will never wear out or change or be replaced. The number of Your years will neither end nor fail in their purpose."

To which angel did the Father ever say, "Come sit at My right until I make a footstool of Your enemies?"

No, angels are not sons but spirit servants of God sent to assist those who are to receive salvation.

Note: This and the next two entries are paraphrases of the first three chapters of Hebrews.

December 15

Angels Don't Control Earth
Hebrews II

God's message of the Old Covenant sent by angels has been proven true, therefore we must hold firmly to God's truth so we don't drift away. If this Old Covenant word sent by angels is binding, and if broken carries its own penalties, how foolhardy it is to disregard the message of the New Covenant carried personally by the Messiah Himself! Do we really think we can escape God's judgment if we ignore His merciful salvation? Our Lord first made His salvation known. Then His followers accurately repeated His words to us. As we begin to open ourselves to salvation, God underscores the truth of His purpose with blessings and the gift of the Holy Spirit.

The coming new world of which we are speaking will not be governed by angels but by man, with the Man Christ Jesus as the Head. In observing the earth the writer of Psalm 8 marvels at God's involvement with mankind:

> "It all causes me to wonder, Lord, why You bother with us earthlings. We're just minuscule dots in this throbbing cosmos. Yet You created us only a bit lower than the angels. You honor us with Your love. You crown us with Your mercy. You visit us with Your forgiveness. You placed all creation under our feet."

In Jesus' earth life, He carried the human position as Servant. But now God has given Him His new position and put Him in total control of all creation. This is not completed yet, but we see Jesus who was made lower than the angels, now crowned with honor and glory because He willingly suffered death for all humanity.

December 15

It was by the merciful and divine character of God that He who made all things for His glory should allow Jesus to suffer for us.

Jesus is the captain of our salvation leading vast billions of imperfect people to holiness through His perfect sacrifice. His holy death stamped our debt *paid in full*. It made us holy. It made His Father our Father. We are members of God's Forever Family and He doesn't hesitate to call us His brothers and sisters. He said, "I will declare the Father's Name to My brothers in worship service and we will praise Him together." (Psalm 22:22) And, "Here I am with the children the Father has given Me." (Isaiah 8:17b-18a)

God didn't become incarnate as an angel but as a human being. Since we are human flesh and blood, it was necessary for Jesus our Savior to be human in every way for His sacrifice to be efficacious for us. By dying in the place of fallen mankind, Jesus the Man, broke Satan's power of sin and death over us.

Jesus did all this for us in order to be our merciful, understanding High Priest, faithful to God in dealing with the sins of His people. Because He put on the complete robe of humanity, going through our same temptation and suffering, He knows the powerful pull of temptation. He also knows exactly how to help us when we come to Him, our Eternal Priest, with our doubts, sorrows and temptations.

Lord Jesus, thank you for being faithful to God's eternal plan. Where would we be without You? Thank You that You didn't come *from* the human race, You came *into* it from heaven. You are God becoming Man, not man becoming God.

December 16

Superior to Earth's Heroes
Hebrews III

Since it is God who called us and set us aside for Himself let's look seriously at Jesus, our Priest, for He is the very hub of what we believe. Moses was a faithful servant in preparing the house God designed for future use. He was considered a hero of God's people, but it is Christ, the faithful Son of God, who is the true and eternal Hero, worthy of all honor and praise.

We Believers are God's House, the temple in which He lives, if we hold to the confidence and hope to which we testify. (II Corinthians 6:16)

Listen to what the Holy Spirit is telling us:
"Whenever you hear God's voice, or realize He is nudging you,
     don't close your ears the way your ancestors
     did when they rebelled against Me.
They saw how I cared for them during those forty trying years
     in the wilderness, yet they constantly provoked Me
     with their stony hearts, doubting Me. Disobeying Me.
I realized they would not listen. It was almost as though they had never known Me. In My provocation I promised that they would never come into My rest." (Psalm 95:8-11)

"Therefore, dear friends, be careful that your hearts and minds stay true to the living God. For it is through unbelief and ignoring Him that we lose touch with Him. We must all encourage each other in the faith TODAY, while the Lord grants us time. Set a watch over your heart, keeping it ever tender toward God.
"Don't be like the rebellious ones of old who turned deaf ears to God. After all His guidance, care and protection in bringing Moses to lead them out of slavery in Egypt, they were the very ones who provoked God for forty long years, and died in the

wilderness. It was to them God made the promise that they would never rest from wandering nor would they reach the Land of Promise."

Lord God, You have done great things for me. Things I thought were impossible were made possible by Your generous mercy and unlimited power. You found me as I was wandering on the sinner's path. To rescue me from danger You interposed Your most precious blood. And yet, Lord, even while loving You, at times I wander from You. I often pray lines from the hymn, *Come Thou Fount of Every Blessing:* "Prone to wander, Lord, I feel it. Prone to leave the God I love. Here's my heart, O take and seal it. Seal it for Thy courts above." Amen

December 17

A Unique Genealogy

"This is the record of the genealogy of Jesus Christ, the Son of David, the Son of Abraham . . ." (Matthew 1:1)

God's plans for Christ's birth began before creation. Peter tells us, "God didn't pay our ransom with shares of stock or diamonds but with the death of God's True Lamb, who had no defect of sin. God chose Him as our Redeemer before He laid down earth's foundation stones." (I Peter 1:19-20)

In Genesis God tells the serpent, "Because you lied to Eve, you and the woman will be enemies. Your progeny will be against hers. Messiah will crush your head a mortal blow, and you will strike His heel, painful but curable by God's mighty power. (Genesis 3:15)

Centuries passed between Adam and Abraham. God made another promise to Abraham and his old, barren wife. It was the preposterous promise that through one of Abraham's descendants all nations of the world would be blessed. And the "foolish old man" believed and God counted his belief as righteousness.

Matthew begins Jesus' earthly genealogy with Abraham. His record may be tedious reading but it's important, for it's the first New Testament clue concerning Messiah. It starts in the first verse of the first chapter of the first book in the New Testament. It underscores the fact that Jesus came through a *specific* line of ancestors foretold by the prophets. No other ancestral line could bring forth the Messiah. This genealogical record illustrates God's building of His earthly kingdom, generation by generation, century by century until all was in readiness.

Lord Jesus, Your famous human ancestors, Abraham, David and others, were honored heroes of Israel, rich and powerful in their time. Each received God's promise of an even more illustrious Son who would save "whosoever will," but when You came into Your human life, the Jews, "sons of Abraham," were a scorned people.

After centuries under the rule of pagan conquerors, Jews were a despised race, under still another world power, Rome.

Isaiah describes Israel as a chopped down tree root in bone dry soil, gasping for life. He describes You, Lord, as a tender green shoot pushing up from depleted ground.

Your Plan looked impossible, as if earth's fierce armies had crushed it. But God had told Moses His Name: *Jehovah, I AM, I WAS, I WILL ALWAYS BE.* Your Purposes are like Your Name. They always were, always are and always will be. Neither millennia, cultural changes, power shifts nor public opinion can alter Your eternal purposes or promises.

Therefore, "in the fullness of time," when everything was ready, You came, the long Promised One, Son of Abraham, Son of David, Son of Man (by Mary), and Son of God (by the Holy Spirit), in fulfillment of the ancient promise.

December 18

The Forerunner

The Advent of the Ages, as told in the Gospel of Luke, is so familiar we can practically quote it. But Lord, when we are quiet and listening with the heart, the familiar Words never seem tiresome. They come to us as fresh, fragrant and satisfying as newly baked bread.

Zechariah, a priest of Israel, was a descendant of Aaron, the brother of Moses. By Zechariah's time there were about twenty thousand priests. For all priests to have opportunity to serve, they were divided into twenty-four divisions of approximately one thousand each. Mornings and evenings of holy days a perfect lamb in its prime was sacrificed for the sins of the nation. Before the morning and after the evening sacrifice incense was burned. As the scented smoke rose it was to carry the sacrifice and prayers of the priest to God as a "sweet smelling savor."

The priests were chosen by lot to burn the incense. On this day the lot fell on Zechariah. Both Zechariah and Elizabeth were old. Their childlessness distressed them for it was considered by society to be God's judgment on them. All their married life they prayed for a child but now in old age they had lost hope. But with this opportunity to lift prayer to God rising in the aroma of incense, Zechariah could not resist lifting his own longing prayer to God once again.

Luke tells the story this way. Zechariah was on duty in the Temple. An arrow of fear shot through him when Gabriel, the messenger angel, was suddenly THERE, standing by the altar of incense. Gabriel said, "Don't be afraid, Zechariah. God has heard your prayer. You and Elizabeth will have a son named John. He will be filled with the Holy Spirit from birth. The Spirit of power which filled Elijah will be in him. Your son John will be the herald of the long promised Messiah."

December 18

As John grew into manhood he recognized his calling. Zechariah and Elizabeth had surely told him of Gabriel's message.

John saw himself as the one prophesied by Isaiah the prophet. (40:3) "A loud voice calls in the wilderness! 'Get ready for the Lord. Mend the broken highway through the desert for our God. Fill in the valleys, smooth out the rough places, so that God's glory will be revealed for all to see!" (Matthew 3:1-3)

John's purpose was to alert people of the arrival of God's "new thing," the New Covenant in the person of Messiah Jesus. Both Isaiah and Jeremiah speak plainly of it. (Isaiah 43:19 and Jeremiah 31:31) John told the people, "Do some serious work on the path you walk, on the way you live. Take a look at your life. Turn from your evil ways. Repent, and be baptized as a sign of your repentance!"

Just as surely as ancient Israel was called to repent when Jesus, God's Son, came to earth as the Father's Suffering Servant, so we are being called to repent, for God the Son will once again cross the threshold of Time. This time He will come, not as the sacrificial Lamb of God, but as King of the Universe, Ruler of Time and Eternity, both as Judge and as merciful Savior.

December 19

A Heavenly Messenger

Mary's parents had arranged for her to marry Joseph, a descendant of King David, but in truth it was God the Father who was the matchmaker.

Mary was alone, weaving, or working on her wedding garment. Suddenly, an icy shiver of fear shot up her back. Gabriel, the messenger angel, stood before her! He said, "Good morning, Mary. Don't be afraid. God is pleased with you. You will have a baby Son, named Jesus. He will be the Son of God and His Father will give Him the throne of David, His ancestor. He will reign over the house of Jacob, and His Kingdom will never end."

Richard Wumbrand, a political prisoner in Romania, shared what a fellow prisoner wrote concerning Gabriel's announcement to Mary. It went something like this. A young virgin was sitting alone, working quietly when an angel stood before her. The angel told her that she, a creature, would hold in her arms the Creator who would be her Baby. She, a creature, would bathe her Creator. He would later cleanse millions from their sins. She, a creature, would hold the tiny hands of her Creator as He learned to walk. From her He, the Word of God, would learn to talk. He would be the brightness and joy of her house and all humanity.

But she would also weep at the foot of His cross, where God's Son, her Son, would die for her, and our, salvation. Her joy would return with the assurance of His resurrection and ascension. She would join Him there in eternal joy when her life here was over.

Lord, we thank you for Mary and for her willingness to be Your obedient servant. You used her as the agent of bringing Jesus from heaven to earth to be our Savior. Jesus came into humanity from Heaven. He was God becoming Man, not man becoming God.

December 20

The Willing Heart of Mary

Even though the prophet Isaiah foretold that "a virgin shall conceive and bear a son" it was a most unusual announcement which Gabriel made to Mary. Her reply was, "Let it be with me as you have said." In effect, she said what Jesus, her Son, would later say to God in the Garden as He contemplated His crucifixion: "... Thy will be done." Mary's willingness to comply with God's plans shows her complete trust in the purposes of God.

When she heard of her cousin Elizabeth's pregnancy, Mary couldn't wait to see her. At Zechariah's house Mary called out to announce her arrival. When Elizabeth heard her voice, baby John gave a sudden leap in her womb and Elizabeth was filled with the Holy Spirit. In a great surge of joyful understanding she almost shouted,
> "O Mary! You are the most blessed of all women,
> and the Baby in your womb is blessed!
> Why am I so honored that the mother of my Lord
> should come to be with me?
> When I heard your greeting the baby within me
> leaped for joy! Most blessed woman,
> you believed God would do what He promised!
> You trusted Him to do what He said
> would happen."

Mary replied:
> "My soul is fairly bursting with the joy of God my Savior!
> He chose ME, ordinary me, to be honored for ages to come!
> Almighty God has done astonishing things for me,
> things I will never forget.
> The holy Name of God is to be praised, and magnified
> for His great mercy!

December 20

His mercy washes over us like waves of the sea,

moving from generation to generation
covering those who trust Him.

He lifts the humble and allows the arrogant to fall.
He short circuits the power of the contemptuous and
gives understanding to the penitent.
He satisfies the hungry soul even as the glutted ones lust
for fulfillment.
He assists Israel as a father helps his son.
He never forgets His eternal covenant with Abraham
and his descendants."

Lord, Mary's willingness to be the vessel to expedite Your plans brings untold blessings for all eternity. Can my sometimes grudging willingness make any eternal difference with anyone? Change me so I am joyfully willing.

December 21

John is Born

When Elizabeth's baby was eight days old, relatives and friends came to the circumcision and the naming ceremony. They rejoiced and marveled at what God had done for their neighbors.

Zechariah had been without speech since the day the angel told him that he and his wife would, after all these years, become parents of a boy. When asked if the child would be named after his father, Elizabeth said, "No. His name is John." Zechariah had to confirm the choice of the name in writing, and when he did his speech returned and he began to praise God. Neighbors were astonished and news spread across the hill country. There was much speculation as to what the child would be, for they knew the hand of God was on him.

Zechariah prophesied :
"Praise to Jehovah, the covenant-keeping God of Israel!
He has come to free His people, to bring the power
    of salvation to the House of David,
    just as He promised through His prophets.
He promised our father Abraham that salvation would
    come.
And you, my little son, will be the Prophet of the Most
    High,
    going before the Promised One to prepare people
    for His coming, to show them His salvation.
This is all because of the gracious mercy of our Lord.
God's light of mercy will dawn upon us from Heaven
    shining on those who live in the shadows of death.
His light will illuminate our path, leading us to peace."

And the boy grew, as boys will do, and became strong and courageous. He lived in the desert until the time was right for him to preach his message of the need for repentance.   (Luke 1:80)

December 22

The Believing Heart of Joseph

"Mary stayed with Elizabeth about three months and then returned home." (Luke 1:56)

Mary returned from her visit with Elizabeth but before the wedding took place Mary knew she was pregnant. Poor Joseph, he knew he was not the father of the Child. What a multitude of emotions must have tangled in his mind! Mary told an amazing story about an angel, David's throne and God's Covenant with Abraham. Joseph wrestled with doubt, hurt, anger, disappointment and his love for Mary. He wanted to believe her but, *things like that just don't happen!* Nevertheless, he didn't want her to be disgraced or possibly stoned for adultery, so he decided to "put her away quietly." After twisting and turning restlessly on his bed, at last he fell asleep. God sent a dream in which the angel said, "Joseph, son of David, don't be anxious about this. Go ahead with the marriage for this Baby was conceived through the Holy Spirit. You will name Him *Jesus,* for He will save His people from their sins." It happened this way to fulfill the prophet's words: "The virgin will conceive a child. He will be called *Emmanuel,* which means *God is with us."*

The angel not only told Joseph how Mary conceived the child, he told him the Baby would be the promised Messiah, Son of God and Son of Man from Mary's body, housed in her womb, nourished by her blood, breath and life.

Conceptions have not been known to occur in this manner but it is well within the power of the One who created the laws of nature. He, as Creator, may overrule His own laws as suits His purposes.

Joseph believed God and dedicated himself to be the servant of God, just as Mary had when she told the angel Gabriel, "I am God's servant. Let it be to me as you have said." (Luke 1:38)

December 23

The First Christmas Tree

With Christmas only a few days away, the mind sweeps out its corners, checking to see that all has been done, cards mailed, packages wrapped, fix ahead dishes prepared. The house sparkles. Warm cookies advertise themselves. The tree is especially beautiful, evoking memories of years gone by. Sipping a cup of tea, I find my mind drifting way past our current millennium. Verses from Isaiah paint word pictures of Christ represented by a fresh branch springing from a chopped down tree stump. But Isaiah's Branch is not from a tree at all. It is the Man of whom the prophet uses words like *root, sprout, ground* and *branch* to describe. "In that day the Lord's *Branch*, the Messiah, will spring up, green and flourishing." And again, "He grew up like a tender *shoot*, like a *root* from arid soil. (4:2 and 53:2)

"A thriving green sprout will spring from the chopped down stump of Jesse, and that *Branch* will bear abundant fruit. God's Spirit will live in Him, the Spirit of wisdom and understanding, the Spirit of guidance and power, the Spirit of knowledge and reverence for the Lord. He won't judge by appearances or by hearsay. No, it is only with truth and righteousness that He will judge the needy people of earth.

The above prophesies have been fulfilled. The following await the Lord's timing.

"Evil people will be crushed simply by the words of His mouth. One breath from Him and they will fall. Righteousness and faithfulness will surround Him with pure justice as He rebuilds the Land.

"Carnivorous and domesticated animals will live together so peaceably small children may play safely amongst them. There will be neither killing nor injury on My Holy Mountain, for all earth will be covered with and permeated by the Living God just as totally as waters cover the ocean floor.

"In God's love a new government will be established, and in faithfulness to God the Father, a Man of the lineage of David will be its King. He is a Man who demands justice and brings it about quickly." (16:5)

"In that day the *Root* of Jesse, our Redeemer, will be the rallying point for the people. The nations from all the earth will come to Him and His peace will be glorious." (11:1-10)

"On this mountain God will tear away the thick blanket of darkness which covers the minds of all the nations. He will destroy death and wipe tears from all faces. Every sign of disgrace He will remove from His people." (25:7-8)

"Look at what I will create, new heavens and a new earth. The old ways will be no more, in fact they will not even be remembered. Be glad! Rejoice! The people's expectation of My plans will bring them joy. I will have great delight in the exuberant pleasure of My people. There will be no tears, for sorrow will not touch them." (65:17-19)

December 24

In the Stable

The night is dark. Starlight traces edges of the Judean hills with silver. Christmas hymns tell us the night is silent, the night is holy. It's as if earth holds her breath, waiting.

Mary and Joseph are in a cave, which is often called a stable for it is used as a shelter for animals. They are exhausted from their long trip from Nazareth followed by their fruitless search for lodgings. Looking about them at the dirty cave where sheep have trodden their droppings into the sand and straw, they try to decide how to make do with what's available to them. They know the Baby could be born at any time now, and He must have a bed. How may they improvise?

"Look at this, Mary! Why wouldn't this feed trough do for a crib? We could clean it up, fill it with clean hay and wrap Him in the cloth you wove for just such a purpose."

Mary agrees. "That should work. Let's clean out an area next to the wall, or perhaps a niche or corner, out of the path of the animals."

After handling all foreseeable needs to the best of their ability, they sit down to their meager meal of bread, olives, a bit of cheese and a few dates. But Mary is too tired to eat. She only wants to rest! Her back aches sharply, her feet and ankles are hot and swollen. Small, cramp like twinges cause her to wonder, could this be the time? Yes, it's the time. The birth process has begun, wrapping her in a blanket of pain.

The Baby arrives, with the newborn's usual cry of dismay at the physical shock of coming from the warmth of the womb into a strange, cold place.

Mary had just one thought before sleep claimed her, "God has given Him the same name as Joshua, our hero of old, who led our people into the Promised Land. He rescued them from slavery. The angel told us this Child would save His people from their sins

December 24

and inherit the throne of His ancestor, David. I wonder just what that will entail." (Luke 1:26-38)

The Epic of the Ages, the earth life of Y'eshua, Son of Man, Son of God, had begun.

Note: Joshua, Y'eshua and Jesus are the same name. One is Greek, the next is Hebrew and the last is English, but all mean *the Lord saves*.

December 25

Let Earth Receive Her King!

It's no ordinary citizen whose birthday we celebrate in December. His coming to earth is the event of the ages. He wants us to receive Him, to know Him personally as Redeemer, Friend and Master. We may know *about* Him through Scripture as the Alpha and the Omega, the first and the last. For He is the One who stands at the beginning and the ending of Time, bordering, enclosing, ordering, and owning human and natural history from start to finish. We've come to know Him personally through the indwelling Holy Spirit. He is our peace and hope, the One who encourages, teaches, corrects, comforts and saves.

He is no stranger, this One who came as the Baby of Bethlehem. He was there when we were born and He will be no stranger when He greets us at the end of life's journey. Nor will we be strangers to Him for He knows us through and through. (Psalm 139) The reality of His purpose becomes our joy, assurance and love throughout our years. It's no wonder we sing,

"JOY TO THE WORLD, THE LORD IS COME!

LET EARTH RECEIVE HER KING!"

December 26

Stunned But Curious Shepherds

Caesar Augustus, the Roman Emperor, ordered a census to be taken of his Empire. It happened around 4-6 BC. Joseph, a descendant of David, took Mary, his betrothed and traveled to Bethlehem, David's city to be registered. No lodgings were available due to the glut of travelers carrying out Caesar's command, so they took refuge in one of the caves used to shelter animals. While they were there Mary's Baby was born. Shepherds, on their way to Jerusalem, had stopped in a nearby field for the night with their flocks. Their sheep would be needed as sacrifices in the Temple. Suddenly the night sky blazed with light and an angel stood before them. They were terrified, disoriented! The angel told them not to be afraid. He said, "I have good news for you. Today in Bethlehem the Savior was born for you. He is the Promised One, the Lord. You will find Him wrapped in homespun sleeping in a feeding trough."

The sky was crowded with shining hosts of Heaven singing:

"All glory to God Most High!
Peace has come to earth to
those blessed with His favor!"

The angel left them stunned but curious and excited. Regaining their composure, they readily agreed on what they should do. "*Let's go see* this special Baby the angel told us about." Wasting no time, they set off and found Mary and Joseph. The Baby was snuggled down in hay, wrapped in homespun and asleep in the feeding trough.

The shepherds didn't keep the events secret. With great excitement shining in their eyes, they told what they had seen and heard about the Baby. Those who heard were amazed and told others but Mary kept all these things in her heart. Expectancy was born in many a faithful heart that day.

December 27

The Satisfied Heart

When the Baby was eight days old Mary and Joseph took Him to the Temple in Jerusalem to be circumcised, dedicated to the Lord and named *Jesus,* as Gabriel had instructed. According to Moses' law, "Every firstborn male shall be consecrated to the Lord." The law also required the parents to offer "two doves or two young pigeons as sacrifice."

The day the family went in for dedication an old man named Simeon was led by the Holy Spirit to go to the Temple. He was a godly man and went there often to pray expectantly for Israel. The Spirit had shown him that before he died he would see the long promised Messiah. Simeon saw the parents and the Baby as they were fulfilling the law's requirements. He was filled with joyful awe.

"Almighty God, You have fulfilled
Your promise to me and now I am satisfied
to leave this life in peace, for these old eyes
have beheld Your Salvation.
He is here for all the world to see.
He will bring God's light of recognition to
the Gentiles and great glory to Your people
Israel." (Luke 2:29-32)

Mary and Joseph were startled and didn't say a word, but old Simeon blessed them and addressed Mary with his prophecy.

"This little Boy is God's instrument.
He will cause the regeneration of many in
Israel and the fall of others. He will be mis-
understood and rejected by the majority.
Their rejection of Him will reveal the

falsity of their hearts. Because of Him,
pain like the thrust of a sword will pierce
your soul." (Luke 2:34-35)

Anna was there in the Temple. She was a very old widow, over a hundred, a prophet and the daughter of a prophet. Night and day she worshipped in the Temple. As Simeon spoke to the family, she came close to them and radiantly praised God. She talked about the Baby to those nearby who were also waiting for Israel's redemption.

When Mary and Joseph had fulfilled the law's demands they went back to Bethlehem where, according to tradition, they lived for two years.

December 28

Is There Still No Room?

Lord, it's just past Your birthday. Christians round the world are speaking of You and singing Christmas hymns. We try to stretch our imaginations back through time to Bethlehem.

You and Your parents were turned away from the inn. That seems totally inappropriate, Lord, that You, God's Son, should be refused shelter. But on the other hand, it is a telling preview of how the True Lamb of God would be received by the world He came to save.

In this respect the world does not seem to have changed much in two millennia. As a whole, You are still not welcome. Many of us give the festival of Your birthday more attention than the Honoree.

> Help us, Lord! December is cluttered
> with trivia, shopping,
> planning, entertaining.

> We look to find room for You,
> but tides of the Season
> sweep us into the Sea
> of Forgetfulness.

> When night falls, so do we,
> in exhaustion, uncomfortable
> with the realization we, like they,
> have pushed You out.

> Send Your Spirit, Lord of Holiness,
> like a cooling breeze to earth
> as she simmers contentedly
> in a frenzy of frivolity.

December 28

> Let Your angels flood the world,
>   speaking again the message of heaven.
> Help us see clearly to make room
>   for Christ the King.
>   F.N.

The days of celebration are past. We are tired. We would just like to eat cold cereal for dinner and fall into bed. We have reviewed the events of Your advent. We've prayed, praised, sung hymns, given gifts, shared love for one another and marveled at Your mercy and forgiveness. But Lord, are our minds and hearts still so crowded with all of this that there is no room left for You?

Have mercy on us, Lord, and revive us again.

December 29

The Seeking Heart

"Seek and you will find . . ." Matthew 7:7

As the large number of travelers returned to their home towns after the census was completed, Mary and Joseph were able to leave the cave and find lodging in Bethlehem. Since the Baby was too young to travel the distance back to Nazareth, Joseph resumed his carpentry work in Bethlehem and the Baby resumed His growing.

Herod the Great was King of Judea at the time. He was surprised one day when a group of learned scholars arrived saying they had seen the star of the one born to be King of the Jews. They were seeking Him in order to give Him gifts and honor.

This news disturbed Herod deeply. Iron willed resolve rose within him: *"I, Herod, am King of the Jews -- and there will be no other!"* Rumors of a 'new king' spread like wildfire. Herod called an emergency meeting of all chief priests and teachers of Scripture to ask them where Messiah would be born. They replied, "In Bethlehem of Judea, for Micah has written, 'Bethlehem, even though you are a small village, you are not unimportant because a ruler will rise from you who will lead and rule My people.'" (Micah 5:2)

Herod secretly called the men from the East and said, "Go find the Child and when you find Him bring me word so I may also worship Him."

After leaving Herod the travelers were delighted to see that the star had moved on ahead and stopped over the place where Jesus and His parents were staying. They entered the house and saw Mary and the Child. Kneeling before Him, they opened their cases and gave Him gifts of gold, frankincense and myrrh. The gifts themselves were prophetic of His purpose. Myrrh was a painkiller, which the soldiers offered Him on the *cross*, and He refused. Frankincense was a spice used in preparing bodies for *burial.* Gold was symbolic of His eternal power and glory after the *resurrection.* Gifts fit for a king.

Once again an angel participated in God's plan. In a dream he warned the magi not to return to Herod but to take a different route to their own country. The Almighty foiled Herod's evil scheme of killing his imagined rival in two ways: He sent the right message to the right people, and those right people were obedient to the message.

Upon arriving back in their own country, the scholars of astronomy were sure to have shared their discoveries with their peers. The Good News was spreading.

December 30

It Ends With a Beginning

Wake up! Wake up! An old year's passing on tired feet,
    with cares untold.
So much occurred which can't be righted, people neglected.
    Unfinished projects – learn from them!

Look up, be quick! A new year's speeding on shining wheels,
    transporting hope.
A brand new beginning, so fresh, unencumbered by worries,
    unspoiled by deeds. May it come!

We enter its swift vehicle of necessity and speed on.
    Regardless of new year's turbulence,
        One stands with me – steady.
He is no stranger. We've walked and talked, I've fought and run.
    We've laughed before. Let's move on.

My trust is this: He is my Light. No dark can quench Him.
        He is beside me. Why should I fear?
Through all years He has been my Helper. His help is never
    too early, never too late. It's right on time
        for He never changes. F.N.

December 31

A New Frontier: Old Age

Lord, I'm writing this to try to make things clear to myself, things I've hardly thought of till now.

You have the cosmic responsibility of human redemption, so You never grow old. But Lord, I'm feeling very old today. Many things ache. My friends keep dying. Memory is becoming iffy. It's not always pleasant, but I'm glad to be this old – most of the time. It's as though a new frontier has opened for me and I'm a pioneer woman in a strange land, making my way. Rough mountain ranges and deep valleys lie ahead. Can I cross them with joy?

Everything isn't different in age. You are the one omnipotent SAME in my life, always here: merciful, creative, generous, forgiving. You know that while I'm growing down toward the last gate, my heart and soul are still maturing, growing up toward You.

Like the sailors on Columbus' ships I'm discovering with great joy that earth is not flat. Neither is life with You, Lord. I'll never sail off the edge of Your mercy. There's beauty in this adventure younger people cannot grasp. "There are islands of peace, shores of certainty, tides of mercy and ripples of joy in my sea of weakness," * put there by Your loving care.

Lord, I realize the deeper I move into this territory, the rougher the terrain becomes. But I have Your promise that You are Emmanuel, God who is here with me.

* This is in my diary. I don't know if I wrote it or read it somewhere.

Conclusion

River Dreaming

A multitude of thoughts flow through my mind as I *river dream* here on the balcony in late afternoon's golden light. Eighty years of living is a lot of living -- yet I'm surprised at how swiftly they have passed. The psalmist says, "Man's days are like grass, he flourishes like flowers of the field; the wind blows over it and it's gone and his place is remembered no more." (Psalm 103:15)

Writing has always been a pleasure for me. I remember my first "book." I was almost eight. When school was out our extended family spent summers in the North Carolina mountains. I was the youngest child and at times the bigger boys and girls wanted to play without me. I didn't mind because I could go to the 'movies in the sky.' I liked to lie on my back on the fragrant, sun warmed pine needles and watch the wonderful things clouds could do. Animals of all kinds played tag. Threatening armadas of gray bellied ships sailed the skies. Cloud people changed shape and size, before my wondering eyes.

When school began our teacher had us write of our summer activities. *Goody Cloud Man*, written in my best handwriting and illustrated with a brand new box of crayons, was the result of my effort. This current book is close to being finished. After writing it I feel as the hard working farmer must feel as he brings in the harvest, joy, relief and a sense of accomplishment, even some loneliness for it. As with the farmer, it was not all fun. Discouragement, weariness, emptiness and dead ends all visited me. But the overall pleasure outweighed the difficulties. Rereading my old journals, some of which are in this book, often inspired and lifted my spirit when it stumbled or wanted to quit.

Cancer, disintegrating bones, and restricted arteries hindered my speed but it increased my reliance on God. The joy I have in Him gives me strength. (Nehemiah 8:10) The Lord Himself, in His mercy, stood beside me year after year, in pain and joy, firm, steady and accessible. I have come to appreciate what

Conclusion

King Solomon says, "The path of trusting the Lord is like the first gleam of dawn, shining ever brighter until the full light of day." (Proverbs 4:18) It's only as we obey and love Him that we prove the truth of this verse.

To sum up my eighty years of living, learning, stumbling, climbing, falling and getting up, I borrow a line from myself used in an earlier book. "I've come to the conclusion that spiritual transformation is a lifetime pursuit. The Lord is not through with me yet. He is making changes in me to this very day, thanks to His unending mercy!"

OF GOD'S HIGH CALLING

A NOTE ABOUT THE AUTHOR

Frances Johnston Nash was born into an old established Atlanta family in 1925. She is a graduate of North Avenue Presbyterian School for girls (now Westminister High School) and Wheaton College, Wheaton, Illinois with a BA in art. She has taught in both public and private schools and is a life long student of the Bible and teacher in various churches. Fran married E. William Nash, Jr. in 1949. They have a son, Bill III, and a daughter, Katherine Nash Roberts plus five grandchildren. They are retired and live in Jacksonville, Florida.